GERMAN FOR MUSICIANS

JOSEPHINE BARBER

German for Musicians

WITH A FOREWORD BY
Dietrich Fischer-Dieskau

FABER MUSIC
in association with Faber & Faber · London

First published in 1985 by Faber Music Ltd
in association with Faber & Faber Ltd
3 Queen Square London WC1N 3AU
Typography by M & S Tucker
Printed in England by The Thetford Press

© 1985 by Josephine Barber

British Library Cataloguing in Publication Data

Barber, Josephine
   German for musicians.
    1. German language   2. Music – Terminology
   I. Title
   438'.002478   PF3120.M8
   ISBN 0-571-10053-8

Contents

1 GUIDE TO THE PRONUNCIATION OF GERMAN

2 FUNDAMENTALS OF THE GERMAN LANGUAGE

1

2

8

Ferien *p.58*

The present tense of the irregular verb **wissen** *to know* · **Man** *one* ·
Prepositions that govern either the accusative or the dative case ·
Personal pronouns in the nominative, accusative and dative cases ·
The prefix **da-**

Exercises *p.61*

Waldesgespräch, Joseph von Eichendorff *p.62*

9

Ein Ausflug ins Grüne *p.63*

The genitive case · Genitive endings · Prepositions that govern the
genitive case · Mixed declension nouns · **Wer?** · **Was?** · The prefix
wo-

Exercises *p.66*

Die Lorelei, Heinrich Heine *p.67*

10

Fröhliche Weihnachten und ein glückliches Neues
Jahr! *p.69*

Reflexive verbs · Possessive adjectives

Exercises *p.71*

Erlkönig, Johann Wolfgang Goethe *p.72*

11

Über *Wozzeck*, Konrad Vogelsang *p.74*

Separable verbs · Inseparable verbs · **Hin** and **her**

Exercises *p.76*

Die Nacht, Hermann von Gilm *p.77*

12

Die englischen Lautenisten, N. Lloyd *p.78*

The future tense · Comparative and superlative of adjectives ·
Comparative and superlative of adverbs

Exercises *p.80*

Morgen, John Henry Mackay *p.81*

4 REFERENCE

Acknowledgements

Thanks are due to the publishers for permission to reproduce the following copyright texts:

Note by Konrad Vogelsang on the orchestration of *Wozzeck*, from *Dokumentation zur Oper 'Wozzeck'*, 1977, Laaber-Verlag, Laaber; 'Die englischen Lautenisten' by N. Lloyd from *Grosses Lexikon der Musik*, 1974, Bertelsmann Lexikon-Verlag, Gütersloh; Robert Wolf on 'Stille Nacht', sleeve-note to record AMS 3522, Verlag Schwann-Bagel, Düsseldorf; Extract from *'Über den richtigen Vortrag der sämtlichen Beethoven'schen Klavierwerke'*, in *Erinnerungen an Beethoven*, ed. Paul Badura-Skoda, 1963, Universal Edition A.G., Vienna; Extract from *J.S. Bach, Kompositionen für die Laute*, ed. H.D. Bruger, 1921, Möseler Verlag, Zurich; Extract from *Die Familie Mendelssohn 1729-1847* by S. Hensel, Verlag Karl Alber GmbH, Freiburg; 'Auch kleine Dinge', trans. Paul Heyse, Mundus Verlagsgesellschaft mbH, Stuttgart; Extract from the libretto of *Wozzeck* by Alban Berg, 1923, Universal Edition A.G.; 'Surabaya Johnny' from *Happy End* by Kurt Weill and Bertolt Brecht, 1929, Universal Edition A.G.; Extract from *Gertrud* by Hermann Hesse, Suhrkamp Verlag, Frankfurt am Main; 'Frühling', 'September', and 'Beim Schlafengehen' by Hermann Hesse, Suhrkamp Verlag; Extract from Cosima Wagner's *Tagebücher*, vol.1, 1976, R. Piper & Co Verlag, Munich; Extract from *Leutnant Gustl* by Arthur Schnitzler, S. Fischer Verlag GmbH, Frankfurt am Main; Extract from *Die Welt von Gestern* by Stefan Zweig, S. Fischer Verlag GmbH; Extracts from *Richard Strauss und Hugo von Hofmannsthal: Briefwechsel*, Atlantis Musikbuch-Verlag, Zurich; 'Warm die Lüfte' from *Alfred Mombert, Dichtungen: Gesamtausgabe in drei Bänden*, 1964, Kösel-Verlag, Munich.

For supplying prints and granting permission to reproduce illustrations, thanks are due to the following: Bertolt-Brecht-Erben and Frau Brecht-Schall, p.157; Bildarchiv der Österreichischen Nationalbibliothek, pp.29, 56, 88, 98, 117, 122, 131, 140, 147, 165, 169, 173, 180, 181, 183, 187; Bildstelle Hochbauamt, Stadt Nürnberg, p.160; British Library, p.133; Ing. Norbert Gradisch, p.173; Hulton Picture Library, p.153; Frau Olda Kokoschka, p.180; Nationale Forschungs – und Gedenkstätten, Weimar, p.72; Richard-Wagner-Museum, Bayreuth, pp.194, 197; Städtisches Verkehrsamt, St Goarshausen, p.68; Dr Jaromir Svoboda, p.105; Mr Ian Temple, p.48.

Foreword

The German language, with its many
consonants, is regarded as difficult to sing,
if not inimical to singing. This book is
designed not only to overcome this
prejudice but also to help musicians of
every kind with the practical use of
German. It is in the English-speaking
countries that the most successful efforts
are being made to master the German
language, with remarkable results,
particularly in the performance of Lieder.
Yet there can be no doubt that *German for
Musicians* will prove a real asset to every
young singer and instrumentalist who
needs to become acquainted with the
German language, written or spoken.

Dietrich Fischer-Dieskau

Introduction

German is now recognized as a necessary part of music education. It is not only singers but also accompanists, répétiteurs, conductors, musicologists, research students, teachers and orchestral players who have discovered the need for German in their professional lives. This book, which is the result of teaching experience at the Royal Northern College of Music and the University of Manchester Music Faculty, tries to help by providing a course which is both a practical manual for musicians and an introduction to the language and literature of Germany and Austria.

German for Musicians is designed for music students embarking on a course in basic grammar; singers; those needing to revise a knowledge of German which has become rusty; and those who simply delight in the musical and literary heritage. It may also be useful as a handbook of musical terms for the performing musician. The guide to pronunciation deals with the spoken language and diction for singers. But a v.ritten guide has limitations and ideally singers should work with a language coach too.

German grammar is presented in twenty lessons, which can be covered in one academic year, the time usually allocated to language study in music colleges and university music departments. However, this book has been designed as much for individuals working on their own as for use in class. Lessons 1 to 10 are a survival course for visitors to German-speaking countries; here the texts are fabrications based on everyday vocabulary. Lessons 10 to 20 leave the realm of daily life and introduce texts on musical subjects. Although these have, in some cases, been adapted, they remain challenging and develop the skilful use of the dictionary and intelligent guesswork.

Each lesson concludes with a poem from the Lieder repertoire. These poems may either be read in addition or as an alternative to the prose extracts. Experience has shown that this is an effective way for singers to learn German in the early stages, to acquire meticulous pronunciation and some familiarity with the tradition of German Lieder.

The texts in Part 3 have been chosen from works spanning five centuries. They are arranged roughly according to difficulty, with due regard to variety. This selection may be enjoyed by musicians who already have some knowledge of German and who would like to practise and extend it in the field of music.

Part 4 contains reference material for research students and practical information for performing musicians. Answers to the grammar exercises may also be found here for students working on their own.

That this book exists at all is due to the kindness of all those who have supported the venture by giving generously of their expertise and encouragement. In particular I should like to thank Dr Christopher Hall, Professor R. E. Keller and Dr Hannah Hickman for their most helpful criticism of the manuscript in its various stages; Hilde Beal, John Cameron and Dr Martin Durrell for help with the pronunciation guide; Dr Douglas Jarman, David Ledbetter, Professor Julian Rushton, Dr Peter Skrine and Celia Skrine for advice on the selection of texts; Graham Barber, Alexander Crowe, Neil Morris and Gabriele Reinsch for providing reference material; Eileen Grimes for typing the manuscript; Frau Dr Brigitta Zessner-Spitzenberg of the Bildarchiv der Österreichischen Nationalbibliothek for assistance with picture research; and Patrick Carnegy of Faber Music for his interest in the project from the outset.

J.B.

1 GUIDE TO THE PRONUNCIATION OF GERMAN

This section presents, first of all, the basic rules for the pronunciation of spoken German. The principles of German singing diction, where they differ from those of the spoken language, are dealt with on pp. 16-20.

On the whole German pronunciation follows a regular pattern. Once the basic rules have been assimilated, attention should be paid to the exceptions as some of the commonest German words do not conform to the rules. For any words pronounced in an unusual way a dictionary that indicates word stress, the length of vowels and phonetic symbols is invaluable. The *Collins German Dictionary* can be recommended as it gives all this information in a reference work of manageable size.

Comparisons with standard English can sometimes be helpful, but because of the various ways of pronouncing English in Britain and throughout the world, the International Phonetic Alphabet (IPA) symbols are given here too. It is as well to remember that even where the IPA symbols are identical the similarities between German and English sounds may be no more than approximate.

Spoken German

Stress

The stress usually falls on the first syllable of a word: **Vorstellung**, **Garten**, **Junge**, **Mädchen**, **arbeiten**.

Foreign words often stress another syllable: **Musik**, **Klavier**, **Orchester**, **Symphonie**.

Inseparable prefixes **be-**, **emp-**, **ent-**, **er-**, **ge-**, **ver-**, **zer-** are never stressed: **befinden**, **Empfehlung**, **verstehen**.

Word elements

To understand the basic pronunciation rules — for example, the effect of single or double consonants on the length of vowel, or the devoicing of consonants — it is necessary to recognize where the divisions between word elements occur: **Bot/schaft**, **Bild/nis**, **Mäd/chen**, **Schick/sal**, **ver/einigen**.

To help with this, here is a list of the common prefixes: **be-**, **emp-**, **ent-**, **er-**, **ge-**, **ver-**, **zer-**. Here are a few words in which

3

prefixes occur: **entsagen, erhalten, gefallen**.

Prepositions can also be used as prefixes: **ausgehen, ein-steigen, stattfinden, wegfahren**. So can **hin** and **her**: **hingehen, herkommen**.

The common suffixes are: **-bar, -chen, -haft, -heit, -keit, -lein, -lich, -ling, -los, -nis, -sal, -sam, -schaft, -sel, -tum, -ung, -wärts**. Here are a few words in which suffixes occur: **wunderbar, lieblich, Schicksal, Heiligtum, Hoffnung**.

Consonants

There is no difference between the pronunciation of single and double consonants.

German letters	IPA symbols	English comparisons	Comments on usage	German examples
b	b	*big*	at the beginning of a word or word element and before a vowel	**Brot** **bis** **Ebbe** **verbergen**
	p	*help*	At the end of a word or word element and in a final group of consonants **b** is devoiced and pronounced as a *p*.	**halb** **hübsch** **ob** **abfahren**
c	ts	*bets*	In modern German this letter occurs alone only in words of foreign origin. It has three sounds.	**cis** **Cello** **Cafe**
	tʃ	*check*		
	k	*cake*		
ch	ç		This form of **ch** occurs in the suffix **-chen** and after **ä, e, i, ö, ü, ai, ei, äu, eu, y, l, r, n**. Place the tip of the tongue behind the bottom teeth and gently hiss the *h* in the name *Hugh*. It is a soft sound made at the front of the mouth.	**Mädchen** **Bächlein** **Blech** **ich** **Töchter** **Küche** **reich** **Sträucher** **feucht** **Psyche** **welche** **Storch** **manche**

German letters	IPA symbols	English comparisons	Comments on usage	German examples
	ç		at the beginning of foreign words before **i, e**	**Chemie** **China**
	k	*choir* *Christ*	at the beginning of foreign words before **a, o, r**	**Chor** **Christ**
	x	Scottish *loch*	This occurs after **a, o, u, au**. It is produced in the throat. Place the tongue as for *k* and say *h*. The sound is made further back than for *k*.	**Bach** **Loch** **Buch** **Rauch**
chs	ks	*stacks*	whenever **ch** is followed by **s** in the same word element	**wachsen** **sechs** **Ochse** **Sachs**
ck	k	*luck*		**Glück**
d	d	*dog*	at the beginning of a word or word element and before a vowel	**dann** **Erde** **geduldig**
	t	*hat*	At the end of a word or word element **d** is devoiced and pronounced as *t*.	**Rad** **Wald** **freundlich** **Handwerk** **Stadt**
f	f	*fish*		**frei** **finden** **Griff** **gefunden**
g	g	*goat*	at the beginning of a word or word element, and before a vowel	**gehen** **Gruß** **Königin** **ewige**
	k	*back*	At the end of a word or word element and in a final group of consonants **g** is devoiced and pronounced as a *k*.	**Tag** **liegt** **wegfahren**

5

German letters	IPA symbols	English comparisons	Comments on usage	German examples
	ʒ	*measure*	**g** is pronounced in this way in only a few words of foreign origin.	**Genie** **Regie** **Garage**
-ig	iç		When **g** follows **i** at the end of a word or word element it is pronounced as in the German word **ich.**	**König** **ewig** **selig** **Traurigkeit** **Heiligtum**
	ik	*trick*	When **ig** occurs before the suffix **-lich,** the **g** is pronounced as *k*.	**königlich** **wonniglich**
h	h	*house*	**h** is pronounced at the beginning of a word or word element and before an accented vowel.	**Hund** **haben** **wohin** **Schönheit** **daher**
			At the end of a word or word element and after an accented vowel **h** is silent. In old German spelling where **h** occurs after **t** it is silent.	**wohl** **ihr** **kühl** **Schuh** **gehen** **Goethe**
j	j	*young*		**ja** **jung**
	ʒ	*treasure*	**j** is pronounced in this way in some foreign words.	**Jury** **Jalousie**
k	k	*key*	Both letters are pronounced when **k** is followed by **n.**	**König** **Knabe** **Knie**
l	l	*love*	This is a firm forward **l,** similar to the initial English *l* but never pronounced back in the mouth as in *milk* or *world*.	**Liebe** **Fall** **mild** **Held** **Hälfte**

German letters	IPA symbols	English comparisons	Comments on usage	German examples
m	m	*mother*		**Mann** **Mutter** **immer** **Raum**
n	n	*nun*		**nein** **Wonne** **wenden**
ng	ŋ	*singer*	**ng** is always pronounced as in English *singer* and never with a hard *g* as in English *finger*.	**Sänger** **Ding** **jung** **Finger** **streng**
nk	ŋk	*think*	As in English, **n** is pronounced *ng* when it is followed by *k*.	**denken** **sinken** **Funk**
p	p	*post*		**Paar** **Person** **Mappe**
pf	pf	*camp-fire*	Both letters are sounded when **p** is followed by **f**.	**Pferd** **Pfeife** **Pflanze**
ps	ps	*stamps*	Both letters are sounded when **p** is followed by **s**.	**Psalm** **Psyche**
qu	kv		**q** is always followed by **u** and the two letters together are sounded as *kv*.	**Qual** **Quelle** **bequem**
r	r		In spoken German the **r** is produced in the throat, unlike the English and more like the French. At the beginning of a word or word element, in initial consonant groups and	**reden** **streng** **treu** **starren** **Müllerin**

German letters	IPA symbols	English comparisons	Comments on usage	German examples
			before a vowel the **r** is strong.	
			The **r** is very weak before consonants or in the middle of a word.	**Stern** **Garten** **Herz** sofort
	ɐ	*ear* *poor* *beer* *air*	At the end of a word or word element the **r** is not sounded, but its effect is apparent because it is pronounced as a vowel and so the vowel becomes a diphthong. The final *r* has a similar effect on the preceding vowel in English.	**der** **ihr** **für** **Ohr** **Uhr** **verstehen** **erfinden**
-er	ɐ	*sister* *data*	The **r** in the unstressed ending **-er** at the end of a word or word element is not sounded at all. The **-er** ending is pronounced as a vowel.	**Tochter** **Wasser** **meiner**
s	z	*zoo*	at the beginning of a word or word element and before a vowel	**sehen** **langsam** **Gesang** **Schicksal**
	s	*miss* *ice*	At the end of a word or word element and in a final group of consonants, this sound is devoiced and pronounced *s*.	**das** **Mannes** **Häuschen** **Aussprache**
ss	s	*missile*	**ss** has the same sound as **s** in final position.	**Tasse**
ß	s	*mass*	**ß** has the same sound as **ss**. It is written after a long vowel, at the end of a word or word element and before t.	**Straße** **mußte** **Kuß** **heiß** **Fußreise**

German letters	IPA symbols	English comparisons	Comments on usage	German examples
			ß is replaced by ss when printed in capital letters, and in some English editions of German works.	
sch	ʃ	*shoe*		Schule rauschen
	sç		When s ends one word element and ch begins another each must be pronounced separately.	Häuschen
sp	ʃp	*fishpond*	at the beginning of a word or word element	spielen springen Vorspiel
	sp	*wasp*	at the end of a word or word element	Knospe
sz	sts	*lasts*		Szene
st	ʃt	*fish-tank*	at the beginning of a word or word element	Stadt streiten verstehen
	st	*waist*	at the end of a word or word element	Last festhalten Liebste
t	t	*tea*		Bett treten Tag
th	t	*tea*	th is rare in modern German spelling. The h is silent. In old German spelling where h occurs after t it is silent.	Theater Thema Thron Goethe
ti	ts	*bets*	When t is followed by i and another vowel the t	Nation Patienten

German letters	IPA symbols	English comparisons	Comments on usage	German examples
			is pronounced *ts* and the vowels that follow are sounded separately; **Nation,** for example, is almost a three-syllable word.	**Station**
tsch	tʃ	*check*		**Kutsche** **tschüs**
tz	ts	*nets*		**sitzen** **Netz** **Satz**
v	f	*father*	As an initial letter and as a final letter **v** is pronounced *f*.	**viel** **von** **Vater** **brav** **aktiv**
	v	*vase*	Between vowels and in many words of foreign derivation **v** is pronounced as *v* in English.	**Violine** **Klavier** **Vase** **aktive** **November** **Evangelist**
w	v	*value*		**Wasser** **wer** **verschwinden** **schweben**
x	ks	*fox*		**Hexe** **Xylophon**
z	ts	*mats*		**Zug** **Mozart** **Scherz** **zum**

Vowels

Vowels are either long or short. As a general rule vowels are short when followed by more than one consonant; they are long before one consonant, before **h** and before **ß**.

The list below shows some pairs of related vowels. The long vowel is placed first in each pair.

sagen	Mann	den	Bett	ihn	Sitte
Tod	Sonne	gut	Mutter	Träne	hätte
schön	Götter	Brüder	Küsse	lyrisch	Myrte

However, monosyllabic words often have short vowels in spite of the single consonant: **es, das, was, um, in, ob, ab, mit.**

Verb endings do not make a vowel short if it is long in the infinitive: **leben, er lebt; sagen, er sagt.**

Pure Vowels

*Words marked with an asterisk contain vowels that are sounded in the same way as those in other examples in the column; they are exceptional because, according to their spelling, they should not be pronounced in that way.

German letters	IPA symbols	English comparisons	Comments on usage	German examples
a aa ah	aː	*father*	long vowel	**Vater** **Paar** **Jahr** **Straße** **ja**
a	a	*fun* cf. French *bas*	short vowel, usually followed by a double consonant	**Halle** **Mann** ***hat** ***das** ***ab** ***an** ***was**
ä	ɛ	cf. French *mère* *faire*	Long open vowel. The English *air* is similar but the German vowel is not a diphthong.	**Träne** **Mädel** **Fähre** **Mädchen**
	ɛ	*get*	Short vowel, usually followed by two consonants. This letter has the same sound as the short **e**.	**Nächte** **Männer** **älter**

German letters	IPA symbols	English comparisons	Comments on usage	German examples
e eh ee	e:	cf. French *thé*	long closed vowel, more like the English *ee* than *ay*	**leben** **sehnen** **Seele** **den** ***stets**
er ehr eer	e:ɐ	*ear*	When followed by **r** this pure vowel becomes a diphthong. It is pronounced more like English *ear* than *air*. There are a few important words that have this long closed vowel sound although the vowel is followed by more than one consonant (which would normally make the vowel short). They are listed here as exceptions.	**mehr** **der** **er** **schwer** **Meer** ***Erde** ***erste** ***werden** ***wert** ***Schwert** ***Herde** ***Pferd** ***Beschwerde**
e	ɛ	*get*	short open vowel, usually followed by two consonants	**Bett** **denn** **Herz** ***es** ***des** ***weg**
er-	ɛɐ	*air*	The prefixes **er-**, **ver-**, **zer-** have a short open vowel. The **r** is not rolled and it changes the vowel to a diphthong, rather as in English *air*.	**erhalten** **vergehen** **erscheinen**
-e -el -en	ə	*the* *magnet* *begin* cf. French *le*	This vowel is essentially unstressed. It is like the French *le*. The final **-e** is never mute.	**einen** **geliebt** **Wonne** **befinden** **guten** **Tugend** **Himmel**

German letters	IPA symbols	English comparisons	Comments on usage	German examples
-er	ɐ	*data* *sister*	When the unstressed **e** is followed by **r** at a word ending the sound is slightly more open than a final **e**. The **r** is not pronounced.	**Wunder** **Tochter** **seiner**
i **ih** **ie**	iː	*we* *feed*	long pure vowel	**sie** **Liebe** **Stil** **ihn** **Melodie**
ir	iːɐ		When followed by **r** the pure vowel becomes a diphthong. The **r** is not rolled, it is pronounced as a vowel.	**mir** **vier** **ihr**
i	i	*hit*	short vowel, usually followed by two consonants	**frisch** **immer** **Kind** **tritt** **Wirt** ★**Viertel** ★**in** ★**ich** ★**bis** ★**mit** ★**wohin**
o **oh** **oo**	oː	cf. French *trop*	long pure vowel	**so** **groß** **Tod** **wohl** **Boot** ★**Obst** ★**Mond** ★**Trost** ★**Ostern**
or **ohr**	oːɐ		When followed by **r** the pure vowel becomes a diphthong.	**Ohr**

German letters	IPA symbols	English comparisons	Comments on usage	German examples
o	ɔ	*hot*		**Sonne** **voll** **kommen** **fort** ***ob** ***von** ***Hochzeit**
ö öh oe	ø:	cf. French *deux* *peu*	Long vowel, longer than the similar French sound. With lips loosely rounded, as if whistling, say *turn*.	**Töne** **Vögel** **Höhle** **Goethe** ***trösten** ***höchstens** ***Österreich**
ö	œ	cf. French *cœur*	short open vowel, similar to the sound of English *fern*	**Götter** **möchte** **löschen**
u uh	u:	*mood*	long pure vowel	**Schuh** **nun** **du** **Fuß** ***husten**
ur	u:ɐ		When followed by r the pure vowel becomes a diphthong. The r is not pronounced.	**nur** **uralt**
u	u	*put*	short vowel, usually followed by two consonants	**Pult** **und** **Kummer** **Busch** ***Kuß** ***zum** ***um** ***unangenehm**
ü üh y	y:	cf. French *lune*	With lips forward and loosely rounded say *ee*. In words of Greek derivation this sound is written as **y**.	**kühl** **grün** **Bücher** **typisch** **lyrisch**

14

German letters	IPA symbols	English comparisons	Comments on usage	German examples
ür	y:ɐ		When followed by **r** the pure vowel becomes a diphthong.	**für**
ü **y**	y		short vowel, usually followed by two consonants	**Mütter** **hübsch** **küssen** **Gürtel** **Hymne** **Symphonie** **sympathisch**

Diphthongs

German letters	IPA symbols	English comparisons	Comments on usage	German examples
ai **ay** **ei** **ey**	ai	*life*	The quality of the vowel is more open than in English.	**weit** **reich** **ein** **Mai** **Bayreuth** **Meyer**
au	au	*mouse* *found*	The quality of the vowel is more open than in English.	**Traum** **schauen** **kaum**
eu **äu**	ɔy	*boy*		**Träume** **Häuser** **Freude** **treu**
ie	iə	*familiar*	When the two letters **ie** are unstressed at the end of a word, they are pronounced as a diphthong. They are also pronounced this way in a stressed final syllable ending in **n**.	**Lilie** **Familie** **Melodien** **Symphonien**
	i:	*bee*	**ie** in stressed position is pronounced **ee**.	**Melodie** **Symphonie** **sie** **Partie**

Diction for Singers

Singers need to examine German pronunciation in great detail as even sounds that have the same IPA symbol in English and German may have a different quality in German pronunciation. The most effective way for the ear to become familiar with these sounds is to listen to German singers. Dietrich Fischer-Dieskau is an artist who sings with great clarity and interpretative beauty and he provides a fine model for the distinctive features of sung German. But, of course, performances differ, and singers may vary some aspects of diction to suit the style of music, the acoustics and the relative importance of the words, and for expressive effect.

Here are some features of German that require special attention by English singers:

The long e

This vowel, as in the words **den, Sehnsucht, Seele, der, sehr, Meer,** must be sung closed, i.e. nearer to the English *ee* than *ay*.

There is an important group of words where the **e** is pronounced in this way even though it is followed by more than one consonant: **Beschwerde, Erde, erst, Herde, Pferd, Schwert, stets, werden, wert.**

The unaccented e

This vowel, which is essentially unstressed in speech, is sung as in the English *begin* and *the*. If it is sung on a long note, care must be taken to keep it bright: **Liebe, Wonne, geliebt, besitzt.**

The endings -en, -el, -es, -et

These endings, which are normally unstressed in speech, also have the unaccented **e** vowel described above: **Nachtigallen, Himmel, Alles, gewartet.** The vowel **e** is sometimes sung like the **e** in **Bett** or *get* when the situation demands that it be specially well projected — in a large hall, on a long note, or for dramatic emphasis: **Alles weiß ich.**

The ending -er

This ending is normally sung as a vowel, slightly more open than the unaccented **e** discussed above. So although the **r** is not rolled there is a difference between these endings, the **-er** being closer to the English ending in *sister* and the final **-e** a little brighter:

meiner	**meine**
Lieber	**Liebe**
blauer	**blaue**

The German r

It is a common error for English singers to overemphasize the German **r**. It is not always pronounced in speech, and nor is it in singing. There are three basic **r** sounds: 1 strong; 2 weak; 3 pronounced as a vowel. In speech the **r** is produced at the back of the mouth, rather like the French *r*, but in singing it is always at the front as in Italian.

1 The **r** is strongly rolled at the beginning of a word and in an initial group of consonants: **Ruhe, rauschen, treu, Träume**.

2 The **r** is less strong between two vowels and before an unaccented ending: **geredet, darum, heraus, fahren**. Here the **r** is flicked rather than rolled. The **r** is very weak in spoken German before a consonant, but it is usually flicked in singing and may even be strongly rolled for expressive purposes: **Schmerz, Herz, warten, Morgen**.

3 The **r** is normally pronounced as a vowel at the end of a word or word element, and in the prefixes **er-, ver-, zer-**. This means that the vowel sounds as a diphthong: **der, mir, nur, nieder, vergehen, erkennen**. When the final **r** is flicked, as it often is for verbal or musical emphasis, at a cadence or at the end of a phrase, the preceding vowel is pure: **vergehen** as in **Bett**; **mir** as in **sie**; **nur** as in **gut**.

Here are some examples of all three types of **r**.

1 rolled **r**: **Ich grolle nicht, und wenn das Herz auch bricht**

2 flicked **r**: **Darum, o Herr, entfloh ich dir.**

3 **r** pronounced as a vowel: **Bis zu der Liebsten Haus**

Double consonants

Although there is no difference in the sound of single and double consonants in speech, most German singers accentuate double consonants and in slow music elongate them for expressive effect: **Himmel, Wonne, Stille**.

Separation of syllables

In German there is no natural liaison between words. This means that in singing care must be taken not to carry the final sound from a preceding word over to the vowel of the next word or word element. It is a case of beginning the new vowel sound cleanly, without any run on from preceding sound (cf. English *an / aim, a / name*):

> **Guten / Abend**
> **mit / ihr**
> **die / Erde**
> **schaut sich / um**
> **unsere Liebe muß / ewig bestehen**

This careful beginning of a word with a vowel often requires a light glottal stop, but the correct use of the glottal stop need not spoil the legato line. German singers will sometimes elide words for the sake of legato, especially after **r**.

A neatly flicked **r** may replace a glottal stop: **ist gar ergeben und treu**. The same usage occurs in English: *Behold a Virgin shall conceive and bear a son*.

Adjacent consonants

In German, as in English, adjacent consonants should be pronounced separately at the end and beginning of words if the music allows it (cf. English *that dream, his shoes*).

The German words that follow show the juxtaposition of unfamiliar consonants that should be pronounced separately, and without elision:

> **herrlichste**
> **Schlafenszeit**
> **es schimmert**
> **es singt**
> **Lied der**
> **Jesus sprach**

In quick passages, where there is no time for separate pronunciation, it is desirable to connect the consonants (just as in English *that dream*):

Abenddämmerung
nicht zu

Marking up a text

It is advisable to have a system of marking up a text, which shows the points of pronunciation that need to be taken into consideration when singing. The signs suggested here are simple to remember and easily marked on a copy.

closed **e**	é	Séele, Érde, dén
open **e**	è	Hèrz, vèrgéhen
long vowel	ō	nūn, Tōd, Mōnd
short vowel	ŏ	Kŭß, Sŏnne, Wŏrt
rolled **r**	ⓡ	tr̮eu, r̮auschen
flicked **r**	r̲	Ga<u>r</u>ten, Schme<u>r</u>z
no **r**	r̸	niede<u>r</u>, de<u>r</u>
glottal stop	|	muß | ewig, nur | Eine, ver/einigen
liaison	na͜	hin͜aus
adjacent consonants	s̲ s̲	Jesu<u>s s</u>prach
adjacent consonants connected	t̸z	nich<u>t</u>zu
double consonants	**mm**	Himme<u>l</u>

The song overleaf, from Schubert's 'Schwanengesang', is marked up in a way that should be helpful to a singer in his first attempts at singing in German.

Das Fischermädchen

Du schönes Fischermädchen,
Treibe den Kahn ans Land;
Komm zu mir und setze dich nieder,
Wir kosen Hand in Hand.

Leg an mein Herz dein Köpfchen
Und fürchte dich nicht zu sehr;
Vertraust du dich doch sorglos
Täglich dem wilden Meer!

Mein Herz gleicht ganz dem Meere,
Hat Sturm und Ebb und Flut,
Und manche schöne Perle
In seiner Tiefe ruht.

2 FUNDAMENTALS OF THE GERMAN LANGUAGE

1

Begrüßungen

Guten Morgen!
Guten Morgen!
Wie geht es Ihnen?
Danke, gut. Und Ihnen?
5 Auch gut, danke.

Guten Tag!
Guten Tag!
Wie heißen Sie bitte?
Ich heiße Elisabeth Braun. Wie ist Ihr Name?
10 Mein Name ist Franz Schmidt. Wohnen Sie in Köln?
Ja, ich wohne in der Goethestraße. Und Sie?
Ich wohne nicht in Köln. Ich komme aus Bonn.

Guten Abend Frau Müller.
Guten Abend Herr Doktor.
15 Ein schönes Konzert.
Wunderbar. Das Orchester spielt sehr gut heute.
Gute Nacht!
Gute Nacht!

Hallo Karl!
20 *Grüß dich.*
Wie geht es dir?
Danke, gut. Und dir?
Auch gut. Was machst du hier in Berlin?
Ich studiere an der Musikhochschule.
25 Welches Instrument spielst du?
Ich spiele Klavier. Was machst du?
Ich studiere Musikwissenschaft an der Universität.
Was spielst du?
Ich spiele Geige. Spielen wir zusammen?
30 *Ja, gerne. Aber wo? Wo wohnst du?*

Ich wohne in der Lessingstraße. Und du?
Ich wohne in einem Studentenheim.
Dann spielen wir in der Musikhochschule.
Ja, gut.
35 Viel Spaß beim Studium!
Danke. Auf Wiedersehen.
Tschüs!

Begrüßungen *greetings*; (ß this letter must sometimes be written instead of **ss** and is always pronounced like **ss,** see p.8; ¨ this sign, which can appear on **ä ö ü äu,** is called an Umlaut, see p.11–15); *3* **Wie geht es Ihnen?** *How are you?* (polite form); *21* **Wie geht es dir?** *How are you?* (familiar form); *27* **die Musikwissenschaft** *musicology*; *35* **Viel Spaß!** *Have a good time!*

Personal pronouns in the nominative case

This case is used for the subject of a sentence:

ich *I*
du *you* (familiar singular form)
er *he*
sie *she*
es *it*
wir *we*
ihr *you* (familiar plural form)
Sie *you* (polite form, singular and plural)
sie *they*

The familiar forms of the pronouns are used in addressing friends, relatives, children, animals. They are used increasingly in Germany today, especially among young people.

The pronoun **Sie**, the polite form, is always written with a capital letter.

Regular weak verbs in the present tense

The German infinitive ends in **en**. To form the present tense, endings are added to the stem of the infinitive in the following way:

	spielen	*to play*
ich	**spiele**	*I play*
du	**spielst**	*you play*
er	**spielt**	*he plays*
sie	**spielt**	*she plays*
es	**spielt**	*it plays*
wir	**spielen**	*we play*
ihr	**spielt**	*you play*
Sie	**spielen**	*you play*
sie	**spielen**	*they play*

Similarly: **heißen** *to be called*; **hören** *to hear, listen to*; **kaufen** *to buy*; **lernen** *to learn*; **machen** *to make, do*; **rauchen** *to smoke*; **studieren** *to study*; **üben** *to practise*; **wohnen** *to live*

The **sie** and **es** forms of the verb are always the same as the **er** form; they will not usually be given in tables of conjugations.

Gern

The word **gern** or **gerne** means *gladly* or *with pleasure*. It is also used with a verb and is then usually translated thus:

Ich spiele gern Geige. *I like playing the violin.*
Ich singe gern. *I like singing.*
Wir wohnen nicht gern in der Stadt.
We do not like living in the city.

Notice that **gern** is placed after the verb in positive sentences and after **nicht** in negative ones.

Nouns

All nouns in German are written with a capital letter. There are three genders of nouns: masculine, feminine and neuter. There are therefore three forms of the definite article:

masculine **Der Wagen ist alt.** *The car is old.*
feminine **Die Schule ist groß.** *The school is big.*
neuter **Das Haus ist nicht neu.** *The house is not new.*

and three forms of the indefinite article:

masculine **Ein Mann raucht eine Zigarette.**
A man is smoking a cigarette.
feminine **Eine Frau kauft Kaffee.** *A woman buys coffee.*
neuter **Ein Kind lernt gut.** *A child learns well.*

Agreement with nouns

Pronouns must agree with the noun in gender, but adjectives that do not precede the noun do not agree:

Ist der Wagen alt? *Is the car old?*
Ja, er ist alt. *Yes, it is old.*

Ist die Schule groß? *Is the school big?*
Ja, sie ist groß. *Yes, it is big.*

Ist das Haus neu? *Is the house new?*
Nein, es ist nicht neu. *No, it is not new.*

Some clues for distinguishing gender

Although it is generally not possible to tell the gender of a noun from the appearance of the word or from its meaning, there are a few useful guide-lines:

Words ending in **-er, -ig, -ling, -en** are usually masculine:

der Maler *painter*
der König *king*
der Frühling *spring*
der Hafen *harbour*

Words ending in **-heit, -keit, -ion, -in, -ie, -ik, -schaft, -tät, -ung** are always feminine:

die Schönheit *beauty*
die Schwierigkeit *difficulty*
die Interpretation *interpretation*
die Lehrerin *teacher (female)*

die Familie *family*
die Musik *music*
die Universität *university*
die Hoffnung *hope*

Nouns that come from verbs and gerunds are neuter:

das Versprechen *promise*
das Klingeln *ringing*

The suffixes **-chen** and **-lein** form diminutives; these words are always neuter and the vowel in the noun is modified with an Umlaut:

das Brot *bread*	**das Brötchen** *bread roll*
die Magd *maid*	**das Mädchen** *girl*
der Bach *stream*	**das Bächlein** *little stream*
das Haus *house*	**das Häuschen** *little house*

In dictionaries nouns are usually followed by *m*, *f* or *n* to indicate gender.

EXERCISES

Translate:
1 Der Student wohnt in London und studiert an der Musikhochschule.
2 Der Mann raucht gern Pfeife.
3 Die Frau studiert nicht gern.
4 Was machen Sie?
5 Das Orchester spielt eine Symphonie.
6 Wir lernen Deutsch.
7 Das Kind kauft das Buch.
8 Der Mann ist sehr alt.
9 Du spielst gut.
10 Wir hören die Musik. Sie ist schön.

Answer these questions:
11 Ist der Wagen neu?
12 Ist das Instrument alt?
13 Wie heißen Sie?
14 Wo studiert der Student?
15 Wie geht es Ihnen?

16 Hört ihr gern Musik?
17 Ist das Land groß? Nein, . . .
18 Ist die Stadt klein? Nein, . . .
19 Singen Sie gern?
20 Welches Instrument spielt Karl?

Translate:

21 I like listening to music.
22 The woman does not play well.
23 We live in London.
24 The child is learning German.
25 They like practising.
26 How are you? Very well, thank you.
27 He buys the book.
28 The house is big and old.
29 Do you smoke?
30 Goodbye.

Wanderers Nachtlied I

Über allen Gipfeln
Ist Ruh,
In allen Wipfeln
Spürest du
5   *Kaum einen Hauch;*
Die Vögelein schweigen im Walde.
Warte nur, balde
Ruhest du auch.

Johann Wolfgang Goethe, 1749–1832

Songs for voice and piano by Franz Schubert, 1824; Robert Schumann, 1850; Franz Liszt, c1848

1 **der Gipfel** *mountain top*; *3* **der Wipfel** *treetop*; *4* **spüren** *to feel*; *6* **die Vögelein** *little birds*; *7* **warte nur** *just wait*

Goethe in der Campagna
The German artist Johann Heinrich Wilhelm Tischbein (1751–1829)
painted this oil portrait of Goethe after their meeting in 1786, at the start
of Goethe's two-year Italian journey.

2

Studenten in Köln

Drei Freunde wohnen in Köln. Alle drei studieren an der Musikhochschule. Peter ist zwanzig Jahre alt und wohnt in einem Studentenheim. Er spielt Flöte. Die Flöte ist ein Blasinstrument.

5 Anna kommt aus London und ist Engländerin. Sie wohnt mit zwei Studenten in einer Wohnung. Diese Wohnung ist groß und jeder hat sein eigenes Zimmer. In der Wohnung sind drei Schlafzimmer, ein Wohnzimmer, ein Eßzimmer, eine Küche und ein Badezimmer. Anna
10 spielt Schlagzeug: Pauken, Trommel, Becken, Xylophon. Diese Instrumente sind Schlaginstrumente.

Gabriele wohnt bei ihren Eltern in einem alten Haus. Die ganze Familie ist musikalisch. Gabrieles Vater ist Dirigent und leitet ein Orchester. Ihre Mutter ist Sängerin
15 und auch Lehrerin und unterrichtet an einem Gymnasium. Gabriele hat drei Geschwister: zwei Brüder und eine Schwester. Der älteste Bruder spielt Bratsche und Gabriele spielt Geige. Die Geige und die Bratsche sind Streichinstrumente. Der andere Bruder spielt Klavier. Das Klavier
20 ist ein Tasteninstrument. Die drei Geschwister spielen oft zusammen. Die Schwester heißt Katharina. Sie spielt kein Instrument, sie studiert Gesang. Sie ist Sopran und hat eine sehr schöne Stimme.

4 das **Blasinstrument** *wind instrument*; *10* das **Schlagzeug** *percussion*; *11* das **Schlaginstrument** *percussion instrument*; *14* der **Dirigent** *conductor (musical)*; **leiten** *to conduct*; *15* **unterrichten** *to teach*; das **Gymnasium** *grammar school*; *16* die **Geschwister** *brothers and sisters*; *18* das **Streichinstrument** *string instrument*; *20* das **Tasteninstrument** *keyboard instrument*; *22* **Gesang studieren** *to study singing*

The present tense of the irregular verb **sein**

sein	*to be*
ich bin	*I am*
du bist	*you are*
er ist	*he is*
wir sind	*we are*
ihr seid	*you are*
Sie sind	*you are*
sie sind	*they are*

Es gibt, es sind

The phrases **es gibt** and **es sind** are both used in German to mean *there is* or *there are*:

Es gibt zwei Theater in dieser Stadt.
There are two theatres in this town.
Es sind keine Menschen dort.
There are no people there.

Verbs with stems ending in **t** or **d**

These verbs insert **e** before the ending in the **du**, **er** and **ihr** forms for ease of pronunciation:

arbeiten	*to work*
ich arbeite	*I work*
du arbeitest	*you work*
er arbeitet	*he works*
wir arbeiten	*we work*
ihr arbeitet	*you work*
Sie arbeiten	*you work*
sie arbeiten	*they work*

Similarly: **er wartet** *he waits* **er findet** *he finds*

Numbers

0	**null**	7	**sieben**	14	**vierzehn**
1	**eins**	8	**acht**	15	**fünfzehn**
2	**zwei**	9	**neun**	16	**sechzehn**
3	**drei**	10	**zehn**	17	**siebzehn**
4	**vier**	11	**elf**	18	**achtzehn**
5	**fünf**	12	**zwölf**	19	**neunzehn**
6	**sechs**	13	**dreizehn**	20	**zwanzig**

21 einundzwanzig	60 sechzig	101 hunderteins
22 zweiundzwanzig	70 siebzig	102 hundertzwei
30 dreißig	80 achtzig	1000 tausend
40 vierzig	90 neunzig	1006 tausendsechs
50 fünfzig	100 hundert	1,000,000 eine Million

1984 neunzehnhundertvierundachtzig
1984 eintausendneunhundertvierundachtzig

Plural of nouns

The articles **der**, **die** and **das** all become **die** in the plural. The noun itself usually changes its form and examples of these changes are given below:

das Mädchen	*girl*	-	die Mädchen
der Bruder	*brother*	∴	die Brüder
der Tag	*day*	-e	die Tage
der Sohn	*son*	∴e	die Söhne
der Mann	*man*	∴er	die Männer
das Kind	*child*	-er	die Kinder
die Frau	*woman*	-en	die Frauen
die Tasche	*bag*	-n	die Taschen
das Auto	*car*	-s	die Autos
das Geheimnis	*secret*	-se	die Geheimnisse
die Freundin	*friend*	-nen	die Freundinnen

Plurals are usually given in dictionaries after the noun:

Apfel *m* (∴) *apple*

Sometimes the plural form is given after the genitive form:

Apfel *m* (-s, ∴) *apple*

Compound nouns

If a noun is made up of more than one word, the gender is that of the last word:

der Gast *guest*
das Haus *house*
das Gasthaus *inn*

Feminine noun forms

Nouns denoting people or professions often have a feminine form ending in **-in**:

der Student	die Studentin
der Freund	die Freundin
der Lehrer	die Lehrerin
der Sänger	die Sängerin

Words like **der**

The words below follow the pattern of the definite article:

masculine	feminine	neuter	plural	
der	die	das	die	*the*
dieser	diese	dieses	diese	*this*
welcher	welche	welches	welche	*which*
jener	jene	jenes	jene	*that*
jeder	jede	jedes	jede	*each*

Words like **ein**

The words below and all possessive adjectives follow the pattern of the indefinite article:

masculine	feminine	neuter	plural	
ein	eine	ein		*a*
kein	keine	kein	keine	*no*
mein	meine	mein	meine	*my*

EXERCISES

Write out in full (e.g. Fünf und sieben ist zwölf.):

1 $10 + 17 = 27$
2 $8 + 3 = 11$
3 $2 + 6 = 8$
4 $44 + 9 = 53$
5 $121 + 45 = 166$

Answer these questions:

6 Wieviele Geigen spielen in einem Streichquartett?
7 Wie alt sind Sie?
8 Was für ein Instrument ist eine Oboe?
9 Was für ein Instrument ist eine Orgel?
10 Was für ein Instrument ist eine Trommel?
11 Was für ein Instrument ist eine Bratsche?

33

12 Was ist Herbert von Karajan von Beruf?
13 In welcher Stadt arbeitet er?
14 Woher kommen Sie?
15 Was sind Sie von Beruf?
16 Wohnen Sie in einem Haus oder in einer Wohnung?
17 Wieviele Studenten wohnen mit Anna in der Wohnung?
18 Wieviele Zimmer hat die Wohnung?
19 Wieviele Geschwister hat Gabriele?
20 Welches Instrument spielt Peter?
21 Woher kommt Anna?
22 Wie alt ist Peter?
23 Wo wohnt Gabriele?
24 Was ist Gabrieles Vater von Beruf?
25 Was ist ihre Mutter von Beruf? Wo arbeitet sie?

Translate:
26 I am studying singing.
27 This woman is a singer.
28 This music is beautiful.
29 Anna and Gabriele like playing together.
30 This instrument is very old.

Liebst du um Schönheit

> Liebst du um Schönheit, o nicht mich liebe!
> Liebe die Sonne, sie trägt ein goldenes Haar!
> Liebst du um Jugend, o nicht mich liebe!
> Liebe den Frühling, der jung ist jedes Jahr!
> 5 Liebst du um Schätze, o nicht mich liebe!
> Liebe die Meerfrau, sie hat viel Perlen klar!
> Liebst du um Liebe, o ja mich liebe!
> Liebe mich immer, dich lieb ich immerdar!

Friedrich Rückert, 1788–1866

Songs for voice and piano by Robert Schumann, 1840;
Gustav Mahler, 1905 (*Rückert Lieder*)

1 **liebst du** *if you love* (this inversion of pronoun and verb is frequently used to suggest *if*; it is not a question as there is no question mark); **um** *because of, for the sake of*; *4* **der** *which* (relative pronoun); *5* **der Schatz** *treasure*; *8* **immerdar** *forever, evermore*

3

Die Stadt

Köln liegt am Rhein. Es ist die viertgrößte Stadt der Bundesrepublik Deutschland und hat neunhundert-fünfzigtausend Einwohner. In der Stadtmitte sind viele wichtige Gebäude, das Museum, das Opernhaus, das
5 Schauspielhaus, die Universität, die Musikhochschule, die Kunsthalle, die Konzerthalle, der Hauptbahnhof, viele Kinos, der alte und berühmte Dom und natürlich viele andere Kirchen. Köln hat auch eine U-Bahn. Die Geschäfte und großen Kaufhäuser sind am Neumarkt. Die
10 Straßen vom Hauptbahnhof zum Neumarkt sind nur für Fußgänger. Autos dürfen hier nicht fahren.

Bonn, die Hauptstadt der Bundesrepublik, liegt auch am Rhein, ist aber nicht so groß wie Köln. In der Stadtmitte, die auch hier eine Fußgängerzone ist, sehen
15 Sie das alte Universitätsgebäude und das schöne Rathaus am Markt. In der Bonngasse ist das Beethovenhaus, wo der Komponist geboren wurde, und am Münsterplatz ist das Beethoven-Denkmal. Am Rheinufer ist das Bundeshaus.

20 Entschuldigen Sie bitte! Wie komme ich zum Bahnhof?
Sie gehen hier am Rheinufer entlang. Dann gehen Sie links, und dann rechts und dann geradeaus und dann sind Sie am Bahnhof.
Vielen Dank.
25 *Bitte schön.*

Entschuldigen Sie bitte! Wo ist das Rathaus?
Es tut mir leid, ich weiß es nicht.

1 der **Rhein**; *Rhine*; *1/2* die **Bundesrepublik Deutschland [BRD]** *Federal Republic of Germany*; *4* **wichtig** *important*; *5* das **Schauspielhaus** *theatre*; *6* die **Kunsthalle** *art gallery*; der **Hauptbahnhof** *main railway station*; *7* **berühmt** *famous*; *8* die **Kirche** *church*; die **U-Bahn** *underground train*; *9* das **Kaufhaus** *department store*; der **Neumarkt** *Newmarket* a large shopping square in Cologne; *11* **der Fußgänger** *pedestrian*; **dürfen** *to be allowed, may*; *16* **die Gasse** *lane, narrow street*; *17* **geboren** *born*; **der Münsterplatz** *Cathedral Square*; *18* **das Denkmal** *monument*; **das Ufer** *river bank*; *19* **das Bundeshaus** *parliament building*; *20* **Entschuldigen Sie bitte!** *Excuse me please!*; *22* **geradeaus** *straight on*; *25* **Bitte schön.** *Don't mention it. It's a pleasure.*; *27* **Es tut mir leid** *I am sorry*; **ich weiß es nicht** *I do not know*

The present tense of the irregular verb **haben**

	haben	*to have*
ich	**habe**	*I have*
du	**hast**	*you have*
er	**hat**	*he has*
wir	**haben**	*we have*
ihr	**habt**	*you have*
Sie	**haben**	*you have*
sie	**haben**	*they have*

Gern used with **haben**

This is the way to express a liking or fondness for something, when **lieben** *to love* would be too strong:

Ich habe diese Stadt gern. *I like this town.*
Ich habe diesen Wagen gern. *I like this car.*

Notice that **gern** comes at the end of the sentence, not after **haben**.

Nicht and **kein**

The word **nicht** is used to make a verb negative:

Wir wohnen nicht in Berlin. *We do not live in Berlin.*

The word **kein** must be used to make a noun negative:

Das Haus hat keinen Garten. *The house has no garden.*
Sie kauft kein Brot. *She does not buy any bread.*

You will see from the sentences above that **nicht** is usually translated as *not*, and **kein** as *no* or *not any*.

The accusative case

This case is used for the direct object in a sentence. If the noun that is the object is masculine, then some change must be made to the article or the word preceding the noun to indicate the accusative case:

nominative	accusative
der	**den**
dieser	**diesen**
ein	**einen**
kein	**keinen**

Er kauft den Wagen. *He buys the car.*
Ich liebe diesen Mann. *I love this man.*
Er trinkt keinen Kaffee. *He does not drink coffee.*

No change is made for feminine and neuter nouns and there is no change in the plural:

Die Frau hat keine Kinder. *The woman has no children.*
Die Lehrerin hat jedes Kind gern.
The teacher likes every child.
Er spielt meine Geige. *He is playing my violin.*

Prepositions that govern the accusative case

The accusative case is also required after these prepositions:

bis *until*
durch *through*
entlang *along* (this usually follows the noun)
für *for*
gegen *against, towards*
ohne *without*
um *round*
wider *against, contrary to*

Der Hund läuft um das Haus. *The dog runs round the house.*
Der Brief ist für meinen Mann. *The letter is for my husband.*
Das Mädchen geht langsam durch die Stadt.
The girl walks slowly through the town.
Sie gehen die Straße entlang.
They are walking along the street.
Das Boot segelt gegen den Wind.
The boat sails against the wind.

EXERCISES

Answer these questions:

1 Haben Sie einen Hund? Nein,...
2 Haben Sie eine Schwester? Nein,...
3 Hast due einen Wagen? Nein,...
4 Hörst du das Lied? Ja,...
5 Spielt er ein Instrument? Nein,...
6 Haben Sie diese Stadt gern? Ja,...
7 Hat dieser Mann Kinder? Nein,...
8 Gibt es ein Opernhaus in dieser Stadt? Ja,.../Nein,...
9 Haben Sie einen Bruder? Nein,...
10 Fahren Sie diesen Wagen gern? Nein,...

Complete these sentences:

11 Das Auto fährt langsam durch...Stadt.
12 Der Tourist geht um...Dom.
13 Die Kinder laufen...Bonngasse entlang.
14 Das Buch ist für...Lehrer.
15 Wir haben...Garten.
16 Sie hat...Kirche gern.
17 Der Bus fährt schnell um...Bahnhof.
18 Der Verkäufer kauft...Autos.
19 Haben Sie...Bruder?
20 Nein, ich habe...Geschwister.

Answer these questions:

21 Wieviele Einwohner hat Köln?
22 An welchem Fluß liegt diese Stadt?
23 Wo sind die Geschäfte und Kaufhäuser?
24 Wo ist der Kölner Dom?
25 Wo sind die wichtigen Gebäude?
26 Welche Stadt ist die Hauptstadt der Bundesrepublik?
27 In welcher Straße ist das Beethovenhaus?
28 Wo ist das Beethoven-Denkmal?
29 Wo ist das schöne Rathaus?
30 Wo ist das neue Bundeshaus?

Translate:

31 Excuse me please! How do I get to the town hall?
32 You go left and then right and then straight on.
33 Thank you very much.
34 Excuse me please! Where is the station?
35 I'm sorry, I don't know.

Der Jäger

Mein Lieb ist ein Jäger,
Und grün ist sein Kleid,
Und blau ist sein Auge,
Nur sein Herz ist zu weit.

5 Mein Lieb ist ein Jäger
Trifft immer ins Ziel,
Und Mädchen berückt er,
So viel er nur will.

Mein Lieb ist ein Jäger,
10 Kennt Wege und Spur,
Zu mir aber kommt er
Durch die Kirchtüre nur.

Friedrich Halm, 1806–71

Song for voice and piano by Johannes Brahms, 1884

6 **trifft** *hits* (third person singular of **treffen**); 7 **berücken** *to ensnare*; 8 **so viel er nur will** *as many as he wants*; 10 **der Weg** *path*; **die Spur** *track*

4

Die Mahlzeiten

Frühstück ist um acht Uhr morgens. Wir essen Brötchen mit Butter und Marmelade. Wir trinken Tee oder Kaffee dazu, mit Milch, aber ohne Zucker.

Wir essen um eins zu Mittag. In den meisten Familien
5 gibt es zu dieser Zeit ein gutes, warmes Essen: Fleisch, Gemüse und Salat und dann Nachtisch.

Deutsche Hausfrauen trinken gern eine Tasse Kaffee um vier Uhr nachmittags, und sie essen Kuchen dazu — Käsekuchen, Nußtorte, oder Apfelkuchen mit Schlag-
10 sahne.

Nach der Arbeit ist um sieben Uhr Abendbrot. In Deutschland ißt man Käse und Wurst auf mehreren Sorten Brot — Weißbrot, Graubrot, Schwarzbrot oder Knäckebrot. Vor dem Essen sagt man 'Guten Appetit' und
15 antwortet 'Danke, gleichfalls!'

Die Deutschen trinken abends zu Hause oder in einem Weinhaus gern ein Glas Wein. Aber noch mehr Leute trinken das gute deutsche Bier. Die Gaststätten sind bis spät in die Nacht geöffnet, sie schließen erst um ein
20 oder zwei Uhr morgens.

die **Mahlzeit** *meal*; *1* das **Frühstück** *breakfast*; **morgens** *in the morning*; *4* zu **Mittag essen** *to have lunch*; *5* das **Essen** *food, meal*; das **Fleisch** *meat*; *6* das **Gemüse** *vegetables*; der **Nachtisch** *dessert*; *11* das **Abendbrot** *supper*; *12* der **Käse** *cheese*; die **Wurst** *sausage*; *17* **noch mehr** *even more*; *18* die **Leute** *people*; die **Gaststätte** *public house*; *19* **geöffnet** *open*; **erst** *not until, only*

Strong verbs

These verbs usually change the vowel in the second and third person singular as well as adding the normal present tense endings. However, it is sometimes possible to tell a strong verb only from the past tense. Here are some examples of verbs that show a vowel change:

	fahren	essen	sehen	lesen
	to drive, go	*to eat*	*to see*	*to read*
ich	fahre	esse	sehe	lese
du	*fährst	*ißt	*siehst	*liest
er	*fährt	*ißt	*sieht	*liest
wir	fahren	essen	sehen	lesen
ihr	fahrt	eßt	seht	lest
Sie	fahren	essen	sehen	lesen
sie	fahren	essen	sehen	lesen

	nehmen	geben	sprechen	schlafen
	to take	*to give*	*to speak*	*to sleep*
ich	nehme	gebe	spreche	schlafe
du	*nimmst	*gibst	*sprichst	*schläfst
er	*nimmt	*gibt	*spricht	*schläft
wir	nehmen	geben	sprechen	schlafen
ihr	nehmt	gebt	sprecht	schlaft
Sie	nehmen	geben	sprechen	schlafen
sie	nehmen	geben	sprechen	schlafen

Die Katze schläft den ganzen Tag.
The cat sleeps the whole day.
Sprichst du Deutsch? *Do you speak German?*
Er ißt gern Kuchen. *He likes eating cake.*
Nimmst du Tee mit Zucker? *Do you take sugar in your tea?*

Wie spät ist es? *What is the time?*

01.00	**Es ist ein Uhr nachts.**
14.00	**Es ist zwei Uhr Nachmittags.**
	Est ist vierzehn Uhr.
15.30	**Es ist halb vier.**
	Es ist fünfzehn Uhr dreißig.
13.15	**Es ist Viertel nach eins.**
	Es ist dreizehn Uhr fünfzehn.
06.45	**Es ist Viertel vor sieben morgens.**
	Es ist sechs Uhr fünfundvierzig.
04.05	**Es ist fünf Minuten nach vier.**
	Es ist vier Uhr fünf.
21.50	**Es ist zehn vor zehn abends.**
	Es ist einundzwanzig Uhr fünfzig.

Notice that half past the hour is expressed as halfway to the next hour in German.

The twenty-four-hour clock is used in Europe for timetables, theatre programmes and official documents.

The imperative

This is the form of a verb used for commands. There are four parts of the verb:

gehen	*to go*	
Geh!	*Go!*	familiar singular form
Geht!	*Go!*	familiar plural form
Gehen Sie!	*Go!*	polite form, singular and plural
Gehen wir!	*Let us go!*	first person plural form

Any vowel change in the present tense is still there in the imperative but Umlaut modifications are lost:

Nimm!	*Take!*
Gib!	*Give!*
Schlaf!	*Sleep!*
Fahr!	*Drive!*

The imperative of **sein** *to be* is irregular:

Sei ruhig!	*Be quiet!*
Seid ruhig!	*Be quiet!*
Seien Sie ruhig!	*Be quiet!*
Seien wir ruhig!	*Let us be quiet!*

EXERCISES

Give the correct form of the verb in parentheses:

1 Wir (sein) oft in München.
2 Wer (geben) dem Kind einen Apfel?
3 Das Baby (schlafen) jede Nacht zehn Stunden.
4 (Nehmen) er Zucker?
5 (Sprechen) Sie Deutsch?
6 (Sehen) du das alte Rathaus?
7 Ich (sein) sehr glücklich hier.
8 (Fahren) dieser Bus zum Bahnhof?
9 (Essen) du gern Käse?
10 Mein Vater (lesen) gern Bücher.

Complete with the correct form of the imperative:
11 (Laufen) schnell durch den Park, Kinder!
12 (Trinken) den Wein, meine Damen und Herren!
13 (Nehmen) den Apfel, Klaus!
14 (Gehen) heute abend ins Theater.
15 (Halten)! Da kommt ein Auto.

Answer these questions:
16 Wann beginnt der Film? (19.30)
17 Wann essen Sie zu Mittag? (12.30)
18 Wann fahren Sie ins Büro? (8.00)
19 Wann fährt der Zug nach Wien? (21.50)
20 Wie spät ist es? (10.15)
21 Was trinken Sie morgens?
22 Was essen Sie zum Frühstück?
23 Was essen Sie zu Mittag?
24 Trinken Sie gern Bier?
25 Was sagen die Deutschen, bevor sie essen?

Translate:
26 Do you like eating cake?
27 I like drinking a glass of wine in the evening.
28 Supper is at seven o'clock.
29 Take this cup of coffee.
30 The concert begins at 8.00 p.m.

Der Tod und das Mädchen

[DAS MÄDCHEN:]
Vorüber! Ach, vorüber!
geh, wilder Knochenmann!
Ich bin noch jung, geh, Lieber!
und rühre mich nicht an.

[DER TOD:]
5 *Gib deine Hand, du schön und zart Gebild!*
Bin Freund und komme nicht zu strafen.
Sei gutes Muts! ich bin nicht wild,
sollst sanft in meinen Armen schlafen!

Matthias Claudius, 1740–1815

Song for voice and piano by Franz Schubert, 1817

1 **Vorüber!** *Pass on!*; *2* **der Knochenmann** *man of death* (literally *boneman*); *4* **anrühren** *to touch*; *5* **das Gebild** *creature*; *7* **Sei gutes Muts!** *Be of good courage!* (**gutes** is an archaic form); *8* **sollst** (*you*) *shall*

5

Einkaufen

– Auf dem Markt

Bitte schön?
Ich möchte zwei Kilo Äpfel, bitte.
Ja, das macht DM 3,50 [drei Mark fünfzig]. Noch etwas?
Ein Kilo Trauben zu drei Mark.
5 Noch etwas?
Ein Pfund Tomaten, bitte.
Das macht zusammen DM 8 [acht Mark].
Danke schön.

– Im Supermarkt

Ich hätte gern 500 Gramm Käse und 200 Gramm
10 Leberwurst. Was macht das?
Das macht DM 7,80. Zahlen Sie bitte an der Kasse.
Wo ist der Wein? Ich möchte eine Flasche Weißwein.
Hier links ist der Wein.
Danke schön.
15 *Bitte schön.*

– Im Kaufhaus

Was möchten Sie bitte?
Ich möchte einen Schreibblock. Was kostet dieser?
Der kostet DM 3,40.
Gut, ich nehme diesen Schreibblock, einen Bleistift und einen
20 *blauen Kugelschreiber.*
Haben Sie sonst noch einen Wunsch?
Ja, wo finde ich Schallplatten?
Schallplatten sind auf der zweiten Etage.
Danke schön.

– Bei der Post

25 Was zahle ich für einen Brief nach England?
Eine Mark.

Und für eine Postkarte?
Siebzig Pfennig.
Dann möchte ich sechs Briefmarken zu siebzig und drei
30 zu eine Mark.
Das macht zusammen DM 7,20.

– Im Hotel

Guten Abend!
Guten Abend! Haben Sie ein Zimmer frei?
Ja. Was für ein Zimmer möchten Sie?
35 *Ich möchte ein Einzelzimmer mit Bad oder Dusche.*
Ja. Für wie lange?
Für eine Nacht.
Es tut mir leid, ich habe kein Einzelzimmer frei. Ich habe
ein Doppelzimmer mit Bad auf der ersten Etage.
40 *Was kostet das Zimmer?*
Es kostet DM 80 mit Frühstück und Bedienung und
Mehrwertsteuer.
Ja, gut. Kann ich mit Reiseschecks bezahlen?
Ja, gerne. Ich gebe Ihnen den Schlüssel.

das Einkaufen *shopping*; **2 ich möchte** *I would like*; **3 die Mark** *(German)*
mark; **noch etwas?** *Anything else?* **6 das Pfund** *pound*; **9 ich hätte gern** *I
would like*; **11 die Kasse** *cash desk*; **17 der Schreibblock** *writing pad*;
19 der Bleistift *pencil*; **20 der Kugelschreiber** *ballpoint pen*; **21 Haben
Sie sonst noch einen Wunsch?** *Would you like anything else?*; **23 die
Etage** *floor, storey*; **26 der Pfennig** *(German) penny*; **35 das Einzelzimmer**
single room; **41 die Bedienung** *service*; **42 der Mehrwertsteuer** *VAT*;
43 der Reisescheck *traveller's cheque*; **44 der Schlüssel** *key*

Modal Verbs

The six modal verbs are irregular in the present tense:

	können *to be able to,* *can*	**müssen** *to have to, must*	**sollen** *to be supposed to,* *ought*
ich	kann	muß	soll
du	kannst	mußt	sollst
er	kann	muß	soll
wir	können	müssen	sollen
ihr	könnt	müßt	sollt
Sie	können	müssen	sollen
sie	können	müssen	sollen

45

	dürfen	wollen	mögen
	to be allowed to, may	*to want*	*to like, may*
ich	darf	will	mag
du	darfst	willst	magst
er	darf	will	mag
wir	dürfen	wollen	mögen
ihr	dürft	wollt	mögt
Sie	dürfen	wollen	mögen
sie	dürfen	wollen	mögen

These verbs are sometimes called 'auxiliary' verbs as they usually need to be followed by another verb if the sentence is to be complete. In this they are like their English equivalents:

Ich will heute abend arbeiten. *I want to work tonight.*
Kann er gut spielen? *Can he play well?*
Sie müssen langsam fahren. *You must drive slowly.*

The other verb is an infinitive and comes at the end.

Notice that **mögen** is more often used in the subjunctive to mean *would like*:

Wir möchten Deutschland besuchen.
We should like to visit Germany.
Was möchten Sie? *What would you like?*
Ich möchte eine Tasse Kaffee. *I should like a cup of coffee.*

Uses of the infinitive

After a modal verb, the infinitive comes at the end of the sentence or clause:

Ich will das Buch lesen. *I want to read the book.*
Darf ich heute nach Hause fahren? *May I go home today?*

When the first verb is not modal, the infinitive is preceded by **zu** and comes at the end of the sentence or clause:

Es beginnt zu regnen. *It is beginning to rain.*
Wir hoffen, Sie nächstes Jahr zu sehen.
We hope to see you next year.
Sie versucht, besser zu spielen. *She is trying to play better.*

46

Um...zu with the infinitive.

There is a simple way of expressing purpose using the infinitive with **um...zu**:

Wir fahren in die Stadt, um das Konzert zu hören.
We are driving into town to hear the concert.
Sie geht auf den Markt, um Obst zu kaufen.
She is going to the market to buy fruit.

EXERCISES

Write the correct form of the verb in parentheses:

1 Man (dürfen) im Theater nicht rauchen.
2 Er (sollen) vier Stunden pro Tag üben.
3 (Wollen) du diesen Film sehen?
4 Der Herr (können) das Gepäck hier lassen.
5 Ich (wollen) meine Familie besuchen.
6 (Können) ich mit Reiseschecks bezahlen?
7 Er (müssen) um zehn Uhr am Bahnhof sein.
8 Ihr (sollen) früh ins Bett gehen, Kinder.
9 Sie (dürfen) nicht auf der Autobahn halten.
10 (Können) Sie Deutsch?

Translate:

11 Sie schlafen jetzt, um später nicht müde zu sein.
12 Die Jungen laufen schnell nach Hause, um das Fußballspiel zu sehen.
13 Viele Hausfrauen arbeiten, um Geld zu verdienen.
14 Ich hoffe, um sechs Uhr da zu sein.
15 Die Kinder gehen in das Kinderzimmer, um dort zu spielen.

Answer these questions:

16 Was kosten zwei Kilo Kartoffeln auf dem Markt?
17 Was kostet der Schreibblock?
18 Wo sind die Schallplatten im Kaufhaus?
19 Was kosten die Briefmarken bei der Post?
20 Was kostet ein Doppelzimmer im Hotel für eine Nacht?

Translate:

21 I should like this bottle of wine.
22 I should like one pound of cheese.
23 How much is this book?
24 Have you a double room for one night?
25 Can I pay by traveller's cheques?

Atlas
In Greek mythology Atlas, a Titan, was condemned by Zeus to carry the world on his shoulders. (Sculpture in lead, Kinross House, Scotland.)

Der Atlas

Ich unglückseliger Atlas! Eine Welt,
Die ganze Welt der Schmerzen muß ich tragen.
Ich trage Unerträgliches, und brechen
Will mir das Herz im Leibe.

5 *Du stolzes Herz, du hast es ja gewollt!*
Du wolltest glücklich sein, unendlich glücklich,
Oder unendlich elend, stolzes Herz,
Und jetzo bist du elend.

Heinrich Heine, 1797–1856

Song for voice and piano by Franz Schubert, 1828
('Schwanengesang')

1 **der Atlas** *Atlas* (proper name), in Greek mythology Atlas, a Titan, was condemned to carry the world on his shoulders; *2* **der Schmerzen** *of sorrows* (genitive plural of **der Schmerz**); *3* **Unerträgliches** *the unbearable*; *4* **mir das Herz** *my heart*; **der Leib** *body*; *5* **du hast es ja gewollt** *you wished it* (perfect); *6* **du wolltest** *you wanted* (imperfect); *8* **jetzo** *now* (archaic form of **jetzt**)

6

Das Wetter

Heute ist der erste Mai. Es ist ein schöner Frühlingstag.
Die Sonne scheint, der Himmel ist blau, aber die Luft ist
kühl. Im Frühling werden die Tage länger, und es wird
wärmer. Die Bäume werden grün, die Blumen blühen,
5 und die Vögel zwitschern im Wald.

Im Sommer ist es warm und oft sehr heiß. Im Juli
haben die Kinder Schulferien, und viele Leute verreisen.
Im August regnet es oft, aber dann ist der Sommer bald zu
Ende.

10 Im Herbst wird das Obst an den Bäumen reif. Die
Blätter fallen. In England kann es zu dieser Jahreszeit
neblig sein.

Im Winter ist das Wetter schlecht. Es ist kalt und
windig und es regnet. Manchmal schneit es auch. Schnee
15 liegt auf der Erde. Dann sind die Kinder sehr glücklich,
denn sie lieben den Schnee. Die Tage sind kurz; um vier
Uhr nachmittags ist es schon dunkel. Im Dezember ist
Weihnachten, und dann kommt Silvester, der letzte Tag
vor dem Neuen Jahr.

2 **der Himmel** *sky*; **die Luft** *air*; 7 **die Schulferien** *school holidays*;
verreisen *to go away*; 12 **neblig** *foggy, misty*; 18 **Weihnachten** *Christmas*;
Silvester *New Year's eve*

The present tense of the irregular verb **werden**

werden *to become*
ich werde
du wirst
er wird
wir werden
ihr werdet
Sie werden
sie werden

Weak nouns

There are a number of masculine nouns that take the ending **-n** or **-en** in all cases except the nominative singular. They are called weak nouns:

> **Der Junge läuft schnell.** *The boy runs fast.*
> **Ich mag den Jungen nicht.** *I do not like the boy.*

So if a noun ends in **-en,** it may not be plural, it may be a weak masculine noun in a case other than the nominative singular:

> **Die Uniform ist für den Soldaten.**
> *The uniform is for the soldier.*
> **Die Jungen spielen Fußball.** *The boys are playing football.*

Some common weak nouns are:

> **der Bauer** *peasant, farmer*
> **der Dirigent** *conductor*
> **der Held** *hero*
> **der Herr** *gentleman* (**Herr S.** *Mr S.*)
> **der Jude** *Jew*
> **der Junge** *boy*
> **der Knabe** *lad, boy*
> **der Mensch** *person, human, man*
> **der Polizist** *policeman*
> **der Prinz** *prince*
> **der Soldat** *soldier*
> **der Student** *student*

The words usually appear in dictionaries thus:

> **Junge** *m* (**-n, -n**) *boy*
> **Herr** *m* (**-n, -en**) *gentleman*
> **Mensch** *m* (**-en, -en**) *person, human, man*

Word order

The verb must be the second idea in the sentence, though not necessarily the second word.

> **Meine Schwester und ich gehen heute abend ins Theater.**
> *My sister and I are going to the theatre this evening.*

If the sentence begins with something other than the subject, the verb and its subject must be inverted so that the verb maintains its position as second grammatical unit.

Heute abend gehen meine Schwester und ich ins Theater.
This evening my sister and I are going to the theatre.
Im Winter regnet es oft. *It often rains in winter.*
Am Sonntag lese ich gern die Zeitung.
I like reading the newspaper on Sunday.
In England trinken wir viel Tee.
In England we drink a lot of tea.

Days of the week, months and seasons

Die Wochentage	**Die Monate**	**Die Jahreszeiten**
Montag	**Januar**	**der Frühling**
Dienstag	**Februar**	**der Sommer**
Mittwoch	**März**	**der Herbst**
Donnerstag	**April**	**der Winter**
Freitag	**Mai**	
Samstag/Sonnabend	**Juni**	
Sonntag	**Juli**	
	August	
	September	
	Oktober	
	November	
	Dezember	

EXERCISES

Rewrite these sentences putting the underlined words at the beginning of the sentence and making any necessary changes in the word order:

1 Es regnet oft <u>im August</u>.
2 Das Konzert ist <u>bald</u> zu Ende.
3 Wir fahren <u>jeden Sommer</u> nach Italien.
4 Die Kinder kommen <u>um zwölf Uhr</u> nach Hause.
5 Die Tage sind <u>im Sommer</u> lang.

Answer these questions:

6 Wie ist das Wetter heute?
7 Wie ist das Wetter im Winter?
8 Wie ist das Wetter im März?
9 Wie ist das Wetter im November?
10 Wie ist das Wetter im Juli?
11 Wann blühen die Blumen?

12 Wann fallen die Blätter?
13 Wann wird das Obst an den Bäumen reif?
14 Wann wird es früh dunkel?
15 Wann ist Weihnachten?

Translate:

16 She loves the boy.
17 The money is for this student.
18 The farmers work in winter.
19 I love the spring.
20 It is getting dark.

Schlechtes Wetter

Das ist ein schlechtes Wetter,
Es regnet und stürmt und schneit;
Ich sitze am Fenster und schaue
Hinaus in die Dunkelheit.

5 Da schimmert ein einsames Lichtchen,
Das wandelt langsam fort;
Ein Mütterchen mit dem Laternchen
Wankt über die Straße dort.

Ich glaube, Mehl und Eier
10 Und Butter kaufte sie ein;
Sie will einen Kuchen backen
Fürs große Töchterlein.

Die liegt zu Haus im Lehnstuhl,
Und blinzelt schläfrig ins Licht;
15 Die goldnen Locken wallen
Über das süße Gesicht.

Heinrich Heine, 1797–1856

Song for voice and piano by Richard Strauss, 1918

4 **hinaus** *out*; *5* **das Lichtchen** *little light*, (**-chen** suffix for diminutive);
6 **das** *which* (relative pronoun); **wandeln** *to walk*; *8* **wanken** *to totter*;
10 **kaufte sie ein** *she was buying*; *15* **wallen** *to tumble*

7

Unterwegs!

Herr Schmidt fährt jeden Tag mit dem Auto zur Arbeit.
Die Fahrt dauert eine halbe Stunde, denn er fährt in der
Hauptverkehrszeit. In Deutschland fahren die Autos
rechts. Frau Schmidt fährt jeden Morgen mit der
5 Straßenbahn. Sie kauft eine Fahrkarte im voraus, und
dann entwertet sie sie in einem Automaten beim Ein-
steigen. Der Sohn Richard fährt mit dem Fahrrad zur
Universität. Seine Schwester geht zu Fuß zur Schule.
Wenn Sie ins Ausland fahren, können Sie entweder
10 mit dem Auto oder mit dem Zug fahren, oder Sie können
fliegen. Wenn Sie mit dem Zug fahren, kaufen Sie die
Fahrkarte am Schalter in der Bahnhofshalle: 'Ich möchte
eine Rückfahrkarte nach Wien, bitte.' Aber wenn Sie
fliegen, kaufen Sie den Flugschein nicht am Flughafen,
15 sondern im voraus in einem Reisebüro.
Wenn jemand eine lange Reise macht, sagt man 'Gute
Reise!'

unterwegs *on the way*; *2/3* **die Hauptverkehrszeit** *rush hour*; *4/5* **die
Straßenbahn** *tram*; *5* **im voraus** *in advance*; *6* **entwerten** *to cancel*; **beim
Einsteigen** *on entering*; *9* **das Ausland** *abroad*; *9/10* **entweder...oder**
either...or; *12* **der Schalter** *ticket office*; *14* **der Flughafen** *airport*;
15 **sondern** *but* (this is used instead of **aber** after a negative)

The dative case

This case is used for the indirect object in a sentence. It conveys
the meaning *to* or *for*:

> **Ich gebe meiner Mutter den Bleistift.**
> *I give my mother the pencil.*

In English we understand the word *to* without saying it. In
German the indirect object, *my mother*, is in the dative case and
the direct object, *the pencil*, in the accusative case.

The article changes in all three genders in the dative case;

53

there is also a change in the plural:

nominative singular		dative singular	
der Mann	**ein Mann**	**dem Mann**	**einem Mann**
die Frau	**eine Frau**	**der Frau**	**einer Frau**
das Kind	**ein Kind**	**dem Kind**	**einem Kind**

nominative plural	dative plural
die Kinder	**den Kindern**
keine Menschen	**keinen Menschen**

There are similar changes for **dieser, welcher, jeder, jener** and **kein**.

All nouns end in **-n** in the dative plural; if the nominative plural does not end in **-n** (e.g. **die Kinder**), **-n** is added for the dative plural: **den Kindern**.

Verbs that are followed by the dative case

The indirect object occurs mainly after verbs of giving, showing and communicating, and these verbs also take a direct object:

geben *to give*		**wünschen** *to wish*	
schenken *to present*		**zeigen** *to show*	

Sie gibt dem Kind ein Buch. *She gives the child a book.*
Sie zeigt dem Mann den Ring. *She shows the man the ring.*

Notice that the noun in the dative case precedes the noun in the accusative case.

In addition certain verbs are always followed by the dative case even though they take a direct object in English:

danken *to thank*		**helfen** *to help*	
folgen *to follow*		**versprechen** *to promise*	

Ich danke dir recht herzlich. *Thank you very much.*
Er folgt dem Mann die Straße entlang.
He follows the man along the road.
Sie hilft meiner Mutter in der Küche.
She helps my mother in the kitchen.

Prepositions that govern the dative case

The dative case is also necessary after these prepositions:

aus *out of*
außer *except*

bei *at, the house of* (cf. French *chez*), *with*
entgegen *towards* (this preposition may follow the noun)
gegenüber *opposite* (this preposition may follow the noun)
mit *with*
nach *after, to* (with countries and big towns, and in the phrase
  nach Hause *home*), *according to* (when **nach** means
  according to it sometimes follows the noun)
seit *since* (note that the present tense in German with **seit** is
  translated as the past tense in English)
von *from*
zu *to, at* (**zu Hause** *at home*)

Sie kommen aus der Kirche.
They are coming out of the church.
Er fährt mit dem Auto. *He goes by car.*
Gabriele wohnt bei ihren Eltern.
Gabriele lives with her parents.
Nach dem Konzert gehen wir essen.
After the concert we are going for a meal.
Meiner Meinung nach ist er zu alt. *In my opinion he is too old.*
Ich lerne Deutsch seit einem Jahr.
I have been learning German for a year.
Der Dom ist dem Bahnhof gegenüber.
The cathedral is opposite the station.
Wir fahren nach Frankreich. *We are going to France.*
Die alte Dame bleibt zu Hause. *The old lady stays at home.*
Er läuft nach Hause. *He runs home.*

It has become usual in both spoken and written German to
combine the preposition and article in some instances:
zu dem — zum, zu der — zur, von dem — vom.

Wir fahren zum Bahnhof. *We are driving to the station.*
Sie geht zu Fuß zur Schule. *She goes to school on foot.*
Der Briefträger kommt vom Postamt.
The postman comes from the post office.

EXERCISES

Complete these sentences:
1 Herr Schmidt schickt... Dame schöne Blumen.
2 Hilft sie... Mädchen bei... Arbeit?
3 Der Polizist folgt... Jungen die Straße entlang.

4 Der Verkäufer zeigt . . . Mann die Autos.
5 Sie gibt . . . Freundin die Noten.
6 Das Geschäft ist . . . Bahnhof gegenüber.
7 Der Vater spielt am Wochenende gern mit . . . Kinder-.
8 Nach . . . Konzert wollen wir bei mein- Freund ein Bier trinken.
9 Mein- Meinung nach ist er mit . . . Schüler- zu streng.
10 Fahren Sie mit . . . Bahn oder mit . . . Bus?

Answer these questions:
11 Wie fährt Herr Schmidt zur Arbeit?
12 Wer fährt mit der Straßenbahn?
13 Wie fährt Richard zur Universität?
14 Wie geht seine Schwester zur Schule?
15 Wo kaufen Sie den Flugschein, wenn Sie fliegen?

Translate:
16 Have a good journey!
17 I should like a ticket to Vienna.
18 I should like a return ticket to Cologne.
19 Run home quickly!
20 I am working at home.

Das Fischermädchen

Du schönes Fischermädchen,
Treibe den Kahn ans Land;
Komm zu mir und setze dich nieder,
Wir kosen Hand in Hand.

5   Leg an mein Herz dein Köpfchen
Und fürchte dich nicht zu sehr;
Vertraust du dich doch sorglos
Täglich dem wilden Meer!

Mein Herz gleicht ganz dem Meere,
10 Hat Sturm und Ebb und Flut,
Und manche schöne Perle
In seiner Tiefe ruht.

Heinrich Heine, 1797–1856

Song for voice and piano by Franz Schubert, 1828
('Schwanengesang')

2 **der Kahn** *small boat*; *4* **kosen** *to talk lovingly, chat intimately*; *7* **sich
vertrauen** *to entrust oneself* (with the dative); *9* **gleichen** *to be like* (with the
dative); *11* **manche** *a good many, many a*

Ein Schubert-Abend
The Austrian artist Moritz von Schwind (1804-71) was a close friend of
Schubert, and one of the circle of friends who met regularly for informal
music making. Here he portrays such a gathering at the house of Josef
von Spaun. (Sepia drawing, 1868.)

8

Ferien

HERR SCHMIDT:
Wie lange haben Sie Sommerferien?

FRAU MÜLLER:
Die Kinder haben sechs Wochen Schulferien, und mein Mann hat drei Wochen Urlaub.

HERR S:
Wohin fahren Sie dieses Jahr?

FRAU M:
5 Wir fahren Ende Juli nach Österreich und verbringen zwei Wochen auf einem Bauernhof, richtig auf dem Lande. Wir kennen den Ort schon, denn wir fahren jedes Jahr zu Weihnachten dorthin und laufen Ski. Aber im Sommer soll es auch schön sein, denn wir wandern sehr gern in 10 den Bergen. Wohin fahren Sie?

HERR S:
Wir fahren nach England zu einem Ferienort an der Küste. Die Kinder möchten baden, und sie spielen gern am Strand.

FRAU M:
Aber ist es in England nicht zu kalt?

HERR S:
15 Es kann natürlich sein, daß wir schlechtes Wetter haben, denn wir fahren erst im September. Aber Devon ist auch landschaftlich schön, und wir können ins Grüne fahren, wenn es uns an der Küste zu kalt wird.

die **Ferien** *holidays, vacation*; 3 der **Urlaub** *holiday, annual leave*; 4 **wohin** *where to, whither*; 5 **verbringen** *to spend time*; 6 der **Bauernhof** *farm*; **auf dem Lande** *in the country*; 8 **dorthin** *there, thither*; **Ski laufen** *to ski*; 9 **denn** *for, as*; 10 der **Berg** *mountain*; 16 **erst** *not until*; 17 **ins Grüne** *into the countryside*; 18 **wenn** *if*

The present tense of the irregular verb **wissen**

wissen *to know*

ich	weiß
du	weißt
er	weiß
wir	wissen
ihr	wißt
Sie	wissen
sie	wissen

This verb is used for the meaning *to know a fact*:

Ich weiß, wo er wohnt. *I know where he lives.*
Ich weiß nicht, wann der Film beginnt.
I do not know when the film begins.

Kennen *to know* is used for the meaning *to be familiar with*. This verb is regular in the present tense:

Ich kenne diesen Mann. *I know this man.*

Man *one, you, people*

This word (cf. French *on*) is used frequently in German and is often translated by some other phrase in English:

Man fährt am besten auf der Autobahn nach Düsseldorf.
It is best to drive to Düsseldorf on the motorway.
Man weiß nie, wie das Wetter wird.
One never knows what the weather will be like.

Man is declined: **man** (nominative), **einen** (accusative), **einem** (dative).

Es tut einem leid. *One is sorry.*

Prepositions that govern either the accusative or the dative case

The prepositions below take either case, according to the meaning. The accusative case is used to indicate movement to another place. The dative case is used to indicate location.

an *at, by, to*
auf *on, onto*
hinter *behind*
in *in, into*

neben *next to, beside*
über *over, above*
unter *under, below*
vor *in front of, before, from, ago*
zwischen *between*

Die Flasche ist auf dem Tisch. *The bottle is on the table.*
Er stellt die Flasche auf den Tisch.
He puts the bottle on the table.

It has become usual in both spoken and written German to combine the preposition and article in some instances:
in dem — im   in das — ins   an dem — am   an das — ans.

Der Mann sitzt im Garten. *The man is sitting in the garden.*
Ich gehe gern ins Theater. *I like going to the theatre.*
Die Kinder spielen am Strand.
The children are playing on the beach.

Personal pronouns

nominative	accusative	dative
ich	mich	mir
du	dich	dir
er	ihn	ihm
sie	sie	ihr
es	es	ihm
wir	uns	uns
ihr	euch	euch
Sie	Sie	Ihnen
sie	sie	ihnen

When pronouns are used instead of nouns, they must agree in number, gender and case with the nouns they replace;

Ich höre die Musik. *I hear the music.*
Ich höre sie. *I hear it.*

Der Brief ist für meinen Mann. *The letter is for my husband.*
Er ist für ihn. *It is for him.*

Die Lehrerin gibt den Kindern die Schokolade.
The teacher gives the children chocolate.
Sie gibt sie ihnen. *She gives it to them.*

Komm mit mir. *Come with me.*

Notice that the accusative pronoun precedes the dative pronoun.

The prefix da-

When the pronoun is governed by a preposition and refers to a thing rather than a person, the prefix **da-** is added to the preposition:

damit *with it*
davon *from it*
dadurch *through it*

The prefix **dar-** is added if the preposition begins with a vowel:

darauf *on it*
darunter *under it*
daraus *out of it*

Sie schreibt mit dem Bleistift. *She is writing with the pencil.*
Sie schreibt damit. *She is writing with it.*

Der Hund schläft unter dem Bett.
The dog sleeps under the bed.
Der Hund schläft darunter. *The dog sleeps under it.*

EXERCISES

Complete these sentences:

1 Die Katze springt auf...Bett.
2 Die Hausfrau geht in...Geschäft.
3 Die Großeltern gehen jeden Sonntag in...Kirche.
4 Der Kellner stellt die Flasche auf...Tisch.
5 Sie sitzen in...Kino und lachen.
6 Die alte Dame sitzt an...Fenster und träumt.
7 Er steckt das Geld in...Tasche.
8 Nach...Essen kocht meine Mutter Kaffee für...Gäste.
9 Der Polizist wartet vor...Tür.
10 Wir wander in...Bergen.

Replace the underlined words with pronouns:

11 Der Kellner stellt die Flasche auf den Tisch.
12 Ich gehe oft mit meiner Freundin spazieren.
13 Das Kind spielt mit dem Ball.
14 Der Polizist folgt dem Jungen die Straße entlang.
15 Ich liebe meine Geschwister.

Answer these questions:

16 Wie lange haben die Kinder Schulferien?
17 Wohin fährt Frau Müller?

18 Wohin fährt die Familie Schmidt?
19 Wann fahren sie?
20 Was machen die Kinder?

Translate:
21 Do you know this town?
22 Do you know where I live?
23 We are spending a week in the country.
24 I would like to go to Austria.
25 They like walking in the mountains.

Waldesgespräch

Es ist schon spät, es ist schon kalt,
Was reitst du einsam durch den Wald?
Der Wald ist lang, du bist allein,
Du schöne Braut! ich führ dich heim!

5 *'Groß ist der Männer Trug und List,*
Vor Schmerz mein Herz gebrochen ist,
Wohl irrt das Waldhorn her und hin,
O flieh! Du weißt nicht, wer ich bin.'

So reich geschmückt ist Roß und Weib,
10 *So wunderschön der junge Leib;*
Jetzt kenn ich dich — Gott steh mir bei!
Du bist die Hexe Lorelei.

'Du kennst mich wohl — von hohem Stein
Schaut still mein Schloß tief in den Rhein.
15 *Es ist schon spät, es ist schon kalt,*
Kommst nimmermehr aus diesem Wald!'

Joseph von Eichendorff, 1788–1857

Song for voice and piano by Robert Schumann, 1840
(*Liederkreis*)

das Waldesgespräch *conversation in a wood*; *2* **was** *what, what for*; *4* **heim**
home; *5* **der Männer** *of men* (genitive plural of **der Mann**); *6* **gebrochen**
broken; *7* **Wohl...hin** *the sound of the hunting horn strays here and there*;
9 **geschmückt** *decorated*; **das Roß** *horse, steed*; **das Weib** *woman*; *10* **der**
Leib *body*; *12* **die Lorelei** (proper name), a character in German folk
legend; *14* **schauen** *to look*

9

Ein Ausflug ins Grüne

Heute ist ein Feiertag, und wir gehen nicht zur Arbeit.
Wir machen einen Ausflug ins Grüne. Es ist halb acht
morgens, und wir sind schon unterwegs. Wir fahren mit
dem Zug und steigen in einem kleinen Dorf aus. Von dort
5 aus wollen wir auf einen Berg steigen, denn oben auf dem
Berg ist eine alte Burg.

Wir gehen durch das Dorf, über eine Brücke und am
Flußufer entlang, und dann beginnen wir zu steigen. Der
Weg wird steil, und es wird uns warm. Der Weg führt in
10 einen Wald, und hier ist es kühl im Schatten der Bäume.
Es ist auch wunderbar still, und wir hören nur die Vögel
zwitschern. Nun kommen wir zu grünen Wiesen und
erreichen die Burg.

Hier oben ist zum Glück eine Gaststätte. Wir haben
15 Durst, gehen hinein und bestellen etwas zu trinken: ein
Glas Apfelsaft, ein Glas Tee mit Zitrone und zwei Bier.
Wir sitzen draußen und genießen die herrliche Aussicht
auf den Fluß, das Tal, das Dorf, den Wald und die ganze
Umgebung.

der Ausflug *outing, trip*; *1* **der Feiertag** *public holiday*; *4* **aussteigen** *to get out*; **das Dorf** *village*; *5* **steigen** *to climb*; *6* **die Burg** *castle, ruins*; *8* **der Fluß** *river*; *9* **der Weg** *way, path*; *12* **die Wiese** *meadow*; *14* **zum Glück** *fortunately*; *15* **bestellen** *to order*; *17* **draußen** *outside*; **die Aussicht** *view*; *18/19* **die Umgebung** *surroundings*

The genitive case
This case is used to indicate possession. In English we use 's or *of*.
In German the possessor is in the genitive case:

Der Mantel des Mannes ist neu. *The man's coat is new.*
Der Komponist der Oper ist sehr berühmt.
The composer of the opera is very famous.

Die Fahrräder der Jungen sind blau.
The boys' bicycles are blue.

The article changes in all three genders in the genitive case; there is also a change in the plural:

nominative singular		genitive singular	
der König	ein König	des Königs	eines Königs
die Frau	eine Frau	der Frau	einer Frau
das Kind	ein Kind	des Kindes	eines Kindes

nominative plural	genitive plural
die Männer	der Männer
keine Männer	keiner Männer

As a general rule **-es** is added to masculine and neuter nouns after a stressed syllable:

das Geschenk	des Geschenkes
der Tag	des Tages

and **-s** is added to masculine and neuter nouns after an unstressed syllable:

der König	des Königs
der Bahnhof	des Bahnhofs

-s can also be added to proper names when there is no article:

Hier ist Katharinas Zimmer. *Here is Katharina's room.*
Viele Werke Telemanns sind noch unbekannt.
Many works by Telemann are still unknown.

Remember that weak nouns (see p. 50) end in **-n** or **-en** in all cases except the nominative singular:

	singular	plural
nominative	der Junge	die Jungen
accusative	den Jungen	die Jungen
genitive	des Jungen	der Jungen
dative	dem Jungen	den Jungen

The full declension of nouns is given on p.254.

Prepositions that govern the genitive case

The genitive case is also necessary after certain prepositions. The most common are:

außerhalb	outside
innerhalb	*inside, within*
statt	*instead of*
trotz	*in spite of*
während	*during*
wegen	*on account of*

Er schläft während des Vortrags. *He sleeps during the lecture.*

Mixed declension nouns

A few nouns add **-n** or **-en** throughout just like weak nouns but also add **-s** in the genitive singular. One of these is **der Gedanke** *thought, idea:*

	singular	plural
nominative	**der Gedanke**	**die Gedanken**
accusative	**den Gedanken**	**die Gedanken**
genitive	**des Gedankens**	**der Gedanken**
dative	**dem Gedanken**	**den Gedanken**

Similarly:
das Herz *heart*
der Glaube *faith*
der Name *name*

Wer?

Notice the declension of **wer?** *who?*

nominative	**wer?**	*who?*
accusative	**wen?**	*whom?*
genitive	**wessen?**	*whose?*
dative	**wem?**	*to whom?*

Wer bist du? *Who are you?*
Wen liebst du? *Whom do you love?*
Wessen Buch ist das? *Whose book is that?*
Wem gibst du das Buch? *To whom are you giving the book?*

Was?

Was? *What?* is used in the nominative and accusative cases:

Was ist das? *What is that?*
Was machst du? *What are you doing?*

The prefix wo-

When the interrogative pronoun is used with a preposition and refers to a thing, the prefix **wo-** is added to the preposition:

womit *with what*
wovon *from what*
wodurch *through what*

The prefix **wor-** is added if the preposition begins with a vowel:

worauf *on what*
worunter *under what*
woraus *out of what*

Womit schreibt er? *What is he writing with?*
Woran denkst du? *What are you thinking about?*
Wovon sprechen Sie? *What are you talking about?*

EXERCISES

Complete these sentences with a suitable word and/or ending:

1 Wegen...Wetter- bleiben wir zu Hause.
2 Ich vergesse immer den Namen dies- Mann-.
3 'Sie werden innerhalb ein- Woche wieder gesund', sagt der Arzt.
4 Ich fahre das Auto mein- Bruder-.
5 Während...Sommerferien arbeiten wir nicht.
6 Am Ufer...Rhein- sind viele Burgruinen.
7 Ich wohne in der Wohnung mein- Schwester.
8 ...hat heute Geburtstag?
9 ...gibst du das Geld?
10 Wir spielen mit dem Ball. ...spielst du?

Answer these questions:

11 Wo ist die alte Burg?
12 Wohin führt der Weg?
13 Was hören sie im Wald?
14 Wo sitzt die Familie und trinkt?
15 Was kann man von oben sehen?

Translate:

16 He plays during the morning.
17 We are walking to the church in spite of the weather.
18 They live outside the town.
19 We are enjoying the wonderful view.
20 Whose bicycle is in the garden?

Die Lorelei

Ich weiß nicht, was soll es bedeuten,
Daß ich so traurig bin;
Ein Märchen aus alten Zeiten,
Das kommt mir nicht aus dem Sinn.

5 Die Luft ist kühl und es dunkelt,
Und ruhig fließt der Rhein;
Der Gipfel des Berges funkelt
In Abendsonnenschein.

Die schönste Jungfrau sitzet
10 Dort oben wunderbar,
Ihr goldnes Geschmeide blitzet,
Sie kämmt ihr goldnes Haar.

Sie kämmt es mit goldenem Kamme,
Und singt ein Lied dabei;
15 Das hat eine wundersame,
Gewaltige Melodei.

Den Schiffer im kleinen Schiffe
Ergreift es mit wildem Weh;
Er schaut nicht die Felsenriffe,
20 Er schaut nur hinauf in die Höh'.

Ich glaube, die Wellen verschlingen
Am Ende Schiffer und Kahn;
Und das hat mit ihrem Singen
Die Lorelei getan.

Heinrich Heine, 1797–1856

Song for voice and piano by Franz Liszt, 1841

die Lorelei (proper name), a character in German folk legend; *1* bedeuten *to mean, signify*; *4* das kommt...Sinn *I cannot get out of my mind*; *7* funkeln *to sparkle*; *11* das Geschmeide *jewellery*; *14* dabei *at the same time*; *15* wundersam *wonderful*; *16* gewaltig *powerful*; *18* ergreifen *to take hold of*; es *it* (refers here to ein Lied in line 14); das Weh *woe, sorrow*; *19* das Felsenriff *rocky reef*; *20* hinauf *upwards*; *21* verschlingen *to devour*; *22* der Kahn *small boat*; *24* getan *done* (past participle of tun)

Die Lorelei
According to legend it was high on this promontory, on the bank of the
Rhine, that the beautiful Lorelei sat combing her golden hair. Boatmen
were so entranced by her singing that they were lured to shipwreck and
death on the rocks below.

10

Fröhliche Weihnachten und ein glückliches Neues Jahr!

Es ist Winter und Heiligabend. Die Stimmung ist heiter und feierlich, denn die Familie Müller feiert Weihnachten. Die Geschenke liegen um den Weihnachtsbaum und die Kinder können kaum erwarten, sie auszupacken. Die
5 ganze Familie ist muskalisch. Helga bekommt eine Blockflöte von ihrer Tante, einen Notenständer von ihren Großeltern und Noten von ihren Eltern. Sie freut sich natürlich sehr. Ihr Bruder bekommt ein Buch von seinem Onkel, eine Schallplatte von den Großeltern und eine
10 Gitarre von seinen Eltern. Herr Müller ist Dirigent, er bekommt die Partitur der *Matthäus-Passion* von Bach. Seine Frau bekommt den Klavierauszug, denn sie singt im Chor. Alle freuen sich sehr über ihre Geschenke. Um Mitternacht geht die Familie in die Kirche und singt
15 Weihnachtslieder. Am nächsten Tag ruhen sich alle aus und essen und trinken viel. Zu Weihnachten ist es bei den meisten Familien so.

1 **die Stimmung** *atmosphere, mood*; **heiter** *cheerful*; *2* **feierlich** *festive*; **feiern** *to celebrate*; *5/6* **die Blockflöte** *recorder*; *6* **der Notenständer** *music stand*; *7* **die Noten** (pl) *music*; **sich freuen** *to be pleased*; *11* **die Partitur** *full score*; *12* **der Klavierauszug** *vocal score*; *15* **sich ausruhen** *to rest, relax*

Reflexive verbs

There are more reflexive verbs in German than in English, so some are not translated into English in reflexive form:

sich waschen *to wash oneself*
sich entscheiden *to decide*

The reflexive pronoun comes after the verb, which is conjugated in the normal way:

sich **freuen** *to be pleased*
ich   **freue mich**
du   **freust dich**
er   **freut sich**
wir   **freuen uns**
ihr   **freut euch**
Sie   **freuen sich**
sie   **freuen sich**

The imperative of a reflexive verb is formed thus:

sich setzen   *to sit down*
Setz dich!   *Sit down!*
Setzen wir uns! *Let us sit down!*
Setzt euch!   *Sit down!*
Setzen Sie sich! *Sit down!*

Here are some common reflexive verbs:

sich befinden *to be situated*
sich entscheiden *to decide*
sich freuen *to be pleased*
sich interessieren *to be interested*
sich treffen *to meet*
sich unterhalten *to converse*

Possessive adjectives

mein	*my*	**unser**	*our*
dein	*your*	**eu(e)r**	*your*
sein	*his*	**Ihr**	*your*
ihr	*her*	**ihr**	*their*
sein	*its*		

These possessive adjectives take the same endings as **ein** and **kein**:

Er gibt unseren Kindern die Geschenke.
He gives the presents to our children.
Sie bekommt Geld von ihrer Tante.
She receives money from her aunt.
Wo sind eure Spielzeuge, Kinder?
Where are your toys, children?
Er öffnet sein Geschenk. *He opens his present.*

EXERCISES

Complete with a reflexive pronoun:

1 Er freut ... in Italien zu sein.
2 Ich interessiere ... nicht für neue Musik.
3 Treffen wir ... vor dem Bahnhof.
4 Das Kind wäscht ... im Badezimmer.
5 Setzen Sie ... bitte.

Complete with a possessive adjective:

6 Er schenkt ... Freundin einen Ring.
7 Sie gibt ... Tante ein Buch.
8 Sie sind mit ... Geschenken zufrieden.
9 Er kann ... Fahrrad nicht reparieren.
10 Wo sind ... Bücher, Kinder?

Answer these questions:

11 Wo liegen die Geschenke?
12 Was bekommt Helga von ihren Eltern?
13 Was bekommt ihr Bruder von seinen Eltern?
14 Wann geht die Familie in die Kirche?
15 Was singen sie in der Kirche?

Translate:

16 The castle is situated on the mountain.
17 They are having a conversation in the restaurant.
18 We are very pleased.
19 The children like the Christmas tree.
20 Merry Christmas and a Happy New Year!

Erlkönig
A fine illustration of Goethe's ballad. (Engraving by C. A. Schwerdtge-
burth, after H. Ramberg.)

Erlkönig

Wer reitet so spät durch Nacht und Wind?
Es ist der Vater mit seinem Kind;
Er hat den Knaben wohl in dem Arm,
Er faßt ihn sicher, er hält ihn warm.

5 *'Mein Sohn, was birgst du so bang dein Gesicht?'*
'Siehst, Vater, du den Erlkönig nicht?
Den Erlenkönig mit Kron' und Schweif?'
'Mein Sohn, es ist ein Nebelstreif.'

'Du liebes Kind, komm, geh mit mir!
10 Gar schöne Spiele spiel' ich mit dir;
Manch' bunte Blumen sind an dem Strand,
Meine Mutter hat manch gülden Gewand.'

'Mein Vater, mein Vater, und hörest du nicht,
Was Erlenkönig mir leise verspricht?'
15 'Sei ruhig, bleibe ruhig, mein Kind;
In dürren Blättern säuselt der Wind.'

'Willst, feiner Knabe, du mit mir gehn?
Meine Töchter sollen dich warten schön;
Meine Töchter führen den nächtlichen Reihn,
20 Und wiegen und tanzen und singen dich ein.'

'Mein Vater, mein Vater, und siehst du nicht dort
Erlkönigs Töchter am düstern Ort?'
'Mein Sohn, mein Sohn, ich seh' es genau:
Es scheinen die alten Weiden so grau.'

25 'Ich liebe dich, mich reizt deine schöne Gestalt;
Und bist du nicht willig, so brauch ich Gewalt.'
'Mein Vater, mein Vater, jetzt faßt er mich an!
Erlkönig hat mir ein Leids getan!'

Dem Vater grauset's, er reitet geschwind,
30 Er hält in Armen das ächzende Kind,
Erreicht den Hof mit Müh' und Not;
In seinen Armen das Kind war tot.

Johann Wolfgang Goethe, 1749–1832

Songs for voice and piano by Franz Schubert, 1815;
Carl Loewe, 1818

der Erlkönig *Erlking*, a mythical, evil spirit, king of the elves; *4* **fassen** *to grasp*; *5* **was** *what, what for*; **bergen** *to hide*; *7* **die Kron'** *crown* (contraction of **Krone**); **der Schweif** *train*; *8* **der Nebelstreif** *streak of mist*; *10* **gar schöne Spiele** *many beautiful games*; *11* **manch'** *a good many* (contraction of **manche**); *12* **das Gewand** *garment*; *16* **dürr** *dry*; *18* **sollen dich warten schön** *will wait on you*; *19* **den nächtlichen Reihn** *nocturnal dance*; *20* **einwiegen** *to rock to sleep*; *22* **düster** *gloomy*; *24* **die Weide** *willow*; *25* **reizen** *to enchant*; *26* **brauchen** *to use, need*; **die Gewalt** *force, violence*; *28* **das Leid** *wrong, harm*; **hat...getan** *has done*; *29* **dem Vater grauset's** *the father is horrified* (elision of **grauset es**); *30* **ächzen** *to groan*; *31* **die Müh'** *trouble*; **die Not** *urgency, distress*.

11

Über Wozzeck

This extract about Alban Berg's opera *Wozzeck* gives the orchestration of the main orchestra, the chamber orchestra and the small ensemble which plays on stage in Act 2, scene 4.

Alban Berg verwendet in seiner Oper einen mächtigen Instrumentalenkörper. 4 Flöten (1 Piccolo), 4 Oboen (1 Englischhorn), 4 B-Klarinetten (1 in C und 2 in Es), 1 Baßklarinette, 3 Fagotte, 1 Kontrafagott, 4 Hörner, 4
5 Trompeten, 4 Posaunen (einschließlich 1 Tenor- und 3 Baßposaunen), 1 Baßtuba, Streichinstrumente, Harfe und eine starke Schlagzeuggruppe mit 2 Paar Kesselpauken, Tam-Tam, Triangel, Xylophon und Celesta. In der dritten Szene des zweiten Aktes benutzt der Komponist ein
10 Kammerorchester, das unabhängig von dem großen Orchester und zusammen mit diesem spielt. Dieses kleine Orchester hat dieselbe Besetzung, die Schönberg in seiner Kammersymphonie verwendet und zwar 1 Flöte (mit Piccolo), 1 Oboe, 1 Englischhorn, 1 Es-Klarinette, 1
15 C-Klarinette, 1 Baßklarinette, 1 Fagott, 1 Kontrafagott, 2 Hörner, 2 Violinen, 2 Viola, 1 Violoncello und zwei Kontrabässe. Für die Wirtshausszene (vierte Szene des zweiten Aktes) plaziert Berg auf der Bühne ein Ensemble, das aus 2 oder 4 einen Ton höher gestimmten Violinen, 1
20 C-Klarinette, Akkordeon, Gitarre und Baßtuba besteht. In der dritten Szene des letzten Aktes wird ein verstimmtes Klavier eingeführt.

Konrad Vogelsang

1 **verwenden** *to use, employ*; **mächtig** *powerful*; *5* **einschließlich** *including*; *10* **das** *which* (relative pronoun); *12* **die Besetzung** *instrumentation*; *13* **zwar** *namely*; *17* **das Wirtshaus** *inn, tavern*; *19* **das** *which* (relative pronoun); **gestimmt** *tuned*; *19/20* **bestehen aus** *to consist of*; *21* **verstimmt** *out of tune*; *21/22* **wird ... eingeführt** *is introduced*;

74

Separable verbs

These verbs are made up of a verb and a prefix. The prefix is usually a preposition but it can also be a noun or a verb. The prefix is stressed when spoken.

Here are some common separable verbs:

aussteigen *to get out, off*	**stattfinden** *to take place*
ankommen *to arrive*	**teilnehmen** *to take part*
abfahren *to depart*	**spazierengehen** *to go for a walk*
anfangen *to begin*	**aufstehen** *to get up*
aufhören *to stop*	**aufmachen** *to open*
aussehen *to look like*	**zumachen** *to close*

In a simple sentence the verb is conjugated in the usual way and the prefix comes at the end:

Wir steigen in München aus. *We get off in Munich.*
Der Zug kommt pünktlich an. *The train arrives on time.*

After a modal verb the prefix remains with the infinitive at the end:

Wir müssen in München aussteigen.
We must get off in Munich.
Das Stück soll gleich anfangen.
The play is to begin straight away.

After any other verb the **zu**, which usually precedes the infinitive, comes between the two parts:

Die Kinder, beginnen ihre Geschenke auszupacken.
The children being to unpack their presents.
Er versucht, das Fenster aufzumachen.
He is trying to open the window.

Inseparable verbs

These verbs are made up of a verb and a prefix, but these prefixes are not stressed when spoken, they do not exist on their own as independent words and they are never separated from the infinitive. The inseparable prefixes are: **be-, emp-, ent-, er-, ge-, miß-, ver-, zer-**.

Here are some common inseparable verbs:

verstehen *to understand*	**sich befinden** *to be situated*
erhalten *to receive*	**empfehlen** *to recommend*
verreisen *to go away, travel*	**geschehen** *to happen*

Wir erhalten einen langen Brief.
We receive a long letter.
Ich kann Ihnen dieses Hotel empfehlen.
I can recommend this hotel to you.
Er versucht den Lehrer zu verstehen.
He is trying to understand the teacher.

Some verbs with prepositional prefixes are inseparable:

Er übersetzt das Gedicht. *He translates the poem.*

Hin and her

Hin denotes movement away, and **her** denotes movement towards the person concerned:

wohin? *where to?, whither?*
woher? *where from?, whence?*

It is common to find **hin** and **her** at the end of a sentence:

Wo gehst du hin? *Where are you going to?*
Wo kommst du her? *Where do you come from?*

Hin and **her** are frequently found attached to separable prefixes, and they still have directional force:

Geh hinein! *Go in!*
Komm heraus! *Come out!*
Er steigt den Berg hinauf. *He climbs up the mountain.*
Er kommt das Tal herunter. *He comes down the valley.*

EXERCISES

Rewrite these sentences using the correct forms of the verb and making any necessary changes in word order:

1 Er (aufstehen) um acht Uhr morgens.
2 Ich (einkaufen) immer auf dem Markt.
3 Wann (abfahren) der Zug?
4 Es (aufhören) zu regnen.
5 Die Hochzeit (stattfinden) im Dom.
6 Wir (verreisen) jedes Jahr im August.
7 Sie hofft, nächstes Jahr ihr Studium in Berlin (anfangen).
8 Die Kinder dürfen wegen des Wetters nicht (spazierengehen).
9 Du mußt hier (aussteigen).
10 Wann sollen wir in Köln (ankommen)?

Translate:

11 Der Student erhält ein Stipendium von der Regierung.
12 Wir können Ihren Eltern dieses Hotel empfehlen.
13 Was geschieht in der Stadt?
14 Die Burg befindet sich auf dem Gipfel des Berges.
15 Sie läuft schnell die Treppe hinunter.
16 Komm herauf! Die Aussicht ist wunderbar.
17 Dieses Gebäude sieht wie eine Schule aus.
18 Er hofft, an dem Wettbewerb teilnehmen zu können.
19 Die Blechbläser unterstützen das Thema in den Streichern.
20 Die Holzbläser und die Streicher nehmen an dem Hauptthema teil.

Die Nacht

Aus dem Walde tritt die Nacht,
Aus den Bäumen schleicht sie leise,
Schaut sich um in weitem Kreise,
Nun gib acht.

5   *Alle Lichter dieser Welt,*
Alle Blumen, alle Farben
Löscht sie aus und stiehlt die Garben
Weg vom Feld.

Alles nimmt sie, was nur hold,
10   *Nimmt das Silber weg des Stroms,*
Nimmt vom Kupferdach des Doms
Weg das Gold.

Ausgeplündert steht der Strauch,
Rücke näher, Seel' an Seele;
15   *O die Nacht, mir bangt, sie stehle*
Dich mir auch.

Hermann von Gilm, 1812–64

Song for voice and piano by Richard Strauss, 1885

1 **Walde** *wood* (the **-e** ending is an archaic form of the dative singular);
3 **sich umschauen** *to look around*; *4* **achtgeben** *to take heed*; *7* **auslöschen**
to extinguish; *8* **weg** *away*; *9* **was nur hold** *that is lovely*; *10* **wegnehmen**
to take away; *13* **ausgeplündert** *ravaged*; *15* **mir bangt** *I fear*; **sie stehle**
lest she steal (subjunctive)

77

12

Die englischen Lautenisten

Um 1600, zur Zeit Shakespeares, war die Laute das bevorzugte Instrument der englischen Liederkomponisten. Einer der bedeutendsten Komponisten jener Zeit, John Dowland, war als Lautenvirtuose bekannt, seine
5 Abhandlung *Short Treatise on Lute-playing* ist eine der besten Einführungen in diese Kunst. Dowland und die zeitgenössischen Liederkomponisten Ford, Campion und Robert Jones bekamen die gemeinsame Bezeichnung 'Lautenistenschule'. Die Musik der englischen Laute-
10 nisten ist uns nicht in der üblichen Notenschrift überliefert, sondern in Tabulaturen, das ist eine Notierung, bei der nicht die Töne, sondern die Fingerstellungen auf dem Lautengriffbrett dargestellt sind.

N. Lloyd

der Lautenist *lutenist*; *1* **war** *was*; *2* **bevorzugt** *preferred*; *5* **die Abhandlung** *treatise*; *7* **zeitgenössisch** *contemporary*; *8* **bekamen** *acquired*; **die gemeinsame Bezeichnung** *the general description*; *10* **die Notenschrift** *manuscript*; **überliefert** *handed down*; *11* **die Notierung** *notation*; **bei der** *in which*; *12* **dargestellt sind** *are shown*

The future tense

The future tense is formed with the present tense of **werden** and an infinitive:

ich werde singen	*I shall sing*
du wirst singen	*you will sing*
er wird singen	*he will sing*
wir werden singen	*we shall sing*
ihr werdet singen	*you will sing*
Sie werden singen	*you will sing*
sie werden singen	*they will sing*

The infinitive comes at the end of the main clause:

Was wirst du machen? *What will you do?*
Wir werden in der Hauptstadt wohnen.
We shall live in the capital.

When a modal verb is used in the future tense there will be two infinitives at the end:

Er wird den Film verstehen können.
He will be able to understand the film.

In fact the future tense is little used in German, especially when the sentence contains a time phrase that suggests the future. Then the present tense is preferred:

Morgen fahren wir nach Hause.
Tomorrow we are going home.

Comparative and superlative of adjectives

The comparative and superlative forms of German adjectives are similar to those in English in that they add **-er** and **-st** endings:

klein *small*
kleiner *smaller*
kleinst *smallest*

Gabriele ist schön. *Gabriele is beautiful.*
Maria ist schöner. *Maria is more beautiful.*
Elisabeth ist die schönste Frau im Zimmer.
Elisabeth is the most beautiful woman in the room.

When the superlative adjective comes after the noun, it takes the form **am schönsten**:

Der Wald ist im Herbst am schönsten.
The wood is most beautiful in the autumn.

Many adjectives modify the vowel in the comparative and superlative forms:

jung *young*	**jünger** *younger*	**jüngst** *youngest*
alt *old*	**älter** *older*	**ältest** *oldest*
kurz *short*	**kürzer** *shorter*	**kürzest** *shortest*
groß *big*	**größer** *bigger*	**größt** *biggest*

Der kürzeste Weg ist durch die Stadtmitte.
The shortest way is through the town centre.

Here are some irregular forms:

gut	*good*	**besser**	*better*	**best**	*best*
viel	*many*	**mehr**	*more*	**meist**	*most*
hoch	*high*	**höher**	*higher*	**höchst**	*highest*
nah	*near*	**näher**	*nearer*	**nächst**	*nearest, next*

Die meisten Schüler lernen Englisch.
Most schoolchildren learn English.

Notice these constructions:

Sie ist älter als er. *She is older than he is.*
Er ist nicht so alt wie sie. *He is not as old as she is.*
Du wirst immer schöner. *You get more and more beautiful.*

Comparative and superlative of adverbs

These forms are just like those of adjectives:

schnell *fast*
schneller *faster*
am schnellsten *fastest*

Mein Auto fährt schnell. *My car goes fast.*
Dein Auto fährt schneller. *Your car goes faster.*
Sein Auto fährt am schnellsten. *His car goes the fastest.*

The forms of **gern** are irregular:

gern
lieber
am liebsten

Ich trinke gern Wasser. *I like drinking water.*
Ich trinke lieber Tee. *I prefer drinking tea.*
Ich trinke am liebsten Wein. *I like drinking wine best of all.*

EXERCISES

Put into the future tense:

1 Was machst du?
2 Kostet die Reise viel Geld?
3 Wir fahren erst am Montag zurück.
4 Ich sage es dir noch einmal.
5 Kannst du vielleicht mit uns spielen?

Complete these sentences:

6 Meine Schwester ist... als ich.
7 Im Winter ist das Wetter... als im Sommer.
8 Gehen Sie abends... ins Kino oder ins Theater?
9 Der Montblanc ist... als der Snowdon, aber nicht so hoch... der Everest.
10 Ich trinke Tee... als Wasser, aber nicht... gern... Wein.
11 Auf den Autobahnen passieren... Unfälle als auf den Landstraßen.
12 Sie spielt das erste Stück gut, aber das zweite spielt sie....
13 Ein Arzt verdient... als ein Lehrer.
14 Dieser Rotwein schmeckt... als der Weißwein.
15 New York ist... als Paris, aber nicht... groß... London.

Translate:

16 Die Arbeiter verlangen immer mehr Geld.
17 Das blonde Mädchen spielt am besten.
18 Dies ist das schönste Tal der Gegend.
19 Lauf so schnell wie möglich und gib dem Mann diesen Brief!
20 Der Ton wird immer lauter.

Morgen

Und morgen wird die Sonne wieder scheinen
Und auf dem Wege, den ich gehen werde,
Wird uns, die Glücklichen, sie wieder einen
Inmitten dieser sonnenatmenden Erde...

5 *Und zu dem Strand, dem weiten, wogenblauen,*
Werden wir still und langsam niedersteigen,
Stumm werden wir uns in die Augen schauen,
Und auf uns sinkt des Glückes stummes Schweigen...

John Henry Mackay, 1864–1933

Song for voice and piano by Richard Strauss, 1894

morgen *tomorrow*; *2* **den** *which* (relative pronoun); *3* **die Glücklichen** *the happy ones*; **sie** *it* (refers to **die Sonne** in line 1); **einen** *to unite*; *4* **sonnenatmend** *sun-breathing*; *5* **wogenblau** *wave-blue*; *6* **niedersteigen** *to climb down*; *8* **stummes Schweigen** *speechless silence*

13

Stille Nacht

The carol *Stille Nacht* was first sung at a Christmas service in Austria in 1818. It was the result of a collaboration between a curate and a schoolmaster, and has become the best-known German carol.

Zur Christmette des Jahres 1818 sangen in der St Nikolaus-Kirche zu Oberndorf bei Salzburg der Hilfspriester Joseph Mohr und der Lehrer Franz Gruber zum ersten Mal das Lied *Stille Nacht, heilige Nacht.* Es
5 war eine glückliche Fügung, daß diese beiden Männer, die in benachbarten Ortschaften ihren Dienst versahen, in ihrer gemeinsamen Liebe zur Musik auf den Gedanken kamen, ein Lied für das Weihnachtsfest zu verfassen.
Mohr übergab seinem Freund Gruber am vierund-
10 zwanzigsten Dezember ein Gedicht mit sechs Strophen und bat ihm, diesen Text für zwei Solostimmen und Chor mit Gitarrebegleitung zu vertonen. Gruber entsprach dem Wunsch noch am gleichen Tag. Als die beiden
Urheber das Lied zum nächtlichen Gottesdienst
15 anstimmten, die Gemeinde die Schlußverse wiederholte und Mohr mit der Gitarre begleitete, ahnte niemand, daß diese schlichten Worte und die volkstümlich-innige Weise einmal zum berühmtesten Weihnachtslied in aller Welt werden sollten.

Robert Wolf

1 **die Christmette** *midnight mass* (dialect form of **Christmesse**); St *Saint* (contraction of **Sankt**); 2/3 **der Hilfspriester** *curate*; 5 **eine glückliche Fügung** *a happy chance*; 6 **die** *who*; **den Dienst versehen** *to work*; 9 **übergeben** *to hand over*; 13 **einem Wunsch entsprechen** *to comply with a request*; **als** *when*; 13/14 **der Urheber** *writer*; 15 **anstimmen** *to begin to sing*; **die Gemeinde** *congregation*; 17 **die volkstümlich-innige Weise** *heartfelt melody*; 18 **einmal** *one day*; 19 **werden sollten** *would become*

The imperfect tense

This tense is sometimes called the simple past tense. It is used for narrative in spoken and written German and corresponds to the English forms *I played, I was playing, I used to play.*

Regular weak verbs

The imperfect tense of regular weak verbs is formed by adding endings to the stem of the infinitive in the following way:

	spielen
ich	spielte
du	spieltest
er	spielte
wir	spielten
ihr	spieltet
Sie	spielten
sie	spielten

Verbs whose stem ends in **t** or **d** add **e** before these endings for ease of pronunciation:

	warten	*to wait*
ich	wartete	*I waited*
du	wartetest	*you waited*
er	wartete	*he waited*
wir	warteten	*we waited*
ihr	wartetet	*you waited*
Sie	warteten	*you waited*
sie	warteten	*they waited*

Strong verbs

Remember that the characteristic of strong verbs in the present tense is that they show a vowel change in the **du** and **er** forms (see pp. 40-1). In the imperfect tense there is a change in all forms and endings are added to the new stem in the following way:

	singen		
		wir	sangen
ich	sang	ihr	sangt
du	sangst	Sie	sangen
er	sang	sie	sangen

The change in the vowel is frequently the same as in English:

beginnen	**ich begann**	*I began*
geben	**ich gab**	*I gave*
sprechen	**ich sprach**	*I spoke*
sehen	**ich sah**	*I saw*
sitzen	**ich saß**	*I sat*
finden	**ich fand**	*I found*
trinken	**ich trank**	*I drank*
kommen	**ich kam**	*I came*
gehen	**ich ging**	*I went*

From this list it is clear that some verbs that do not show a vowel change in the present tense (e.g. **kommen**) are in fact strong verbs, and have a change of stem in the imperfect tense.

Modal verbs

These verbs are easily recognizable in the imperfect tense. They add the same endings to the infinitive stem as weak verbs, but if the stem carries an Umlaut this is lost:

können	**ich konnte**
sollen	**ich sollte**
müssen	**ich mußte**
dürfen	**ich durfte**
wollen	**ich wollte**
mögen	**ich mochte**

Irregular verbs

	sein	**haben**	**werden**
ich	**war**	**hatte**	**wurde**
du	**warst**	**hattest**	**wurdest**
er	**war**	**hatte**	**wurde**
wir	**waren**	**hatten**	**wurden**
ihr	**wart**	**hattet**	**wurdet**
Sie	**waren**	**hatten**	**wurden**
sie	**waren**	**hatten**	**wurden**

In the imperfect tense a few irregular verbs show a change in the stem like strong verbs, but take the same endings as weak verbs:

bringen	ich brachte	*I brought*
denken	ich dachte	*I thought*
wissen	ich wußte	*I knew*

A table of strong and irregular verbs can be found on pp. 256–262. They are listed in dictionaries as it is not possible to guess the changes.

EXERCISES

Put the following sentences into the imperfect tense:

1 Mendelssohn schreibt sehr interessante Briefe.
2 Sie grüßt ihre Nachbarin.
3 Ich weiß den Namen des Mädchens nicht.
4 Sie spielt den ganzen Vormittag.
5 Was sagst du?
6 Der Professor spricht mit dem Amerikaner.
7 Die Vorstellung beginnt pünktlich.
8 Die Kellnerin bringt das Bier.
9 Wann fährt der Zug ab?
10 Sie gehen durch den Park.
11 Der Student arbeitet in seinem Zimmer.
12 Der Bischof gibt dem Bettler einige Münzen.
13 Er kommt sehr spät an.
14 Der Ton wird allmählich stärker.
15 Sie ist krank und kann nicht aufstehen.
16 Ich muß das ganze Wochenende arbeiten.
17 Sie will ihm ein Geschenk kaufen.
18 Es wird dunkel im Wald, denn es kommt ein Gewitter.
19 Sie hat eine sehr wertvolle Geige.
20 Wir müssen nach Wien fahren.
21 Wir dürfen spät nach Hause kommen.
22 Er nimmt an dem Wettbewerb teil.
23 Ich kenne die Stadt nicht.
24 Wo bist du?

Stille Nacht

Stille Nacht! Heilige Nacht!
Alles schläft; einsam wacht
Nur das traute heilige Paar.
Holder Knab im lockigen Haar,
5 Schlaf' in himmlischer Ruh!
Schlaf' in himmlischer Ruh!

Stille Nacht! Heilige Nacht!
Hirten erst kundgemacht
Durch der Engel Alleluja,
10 Tönt es laut bei Ferne und Nah;
Jesus, der Retter ist da!
Jesus, der Retter ist da!

Still Nacht! Heilige Nacht!
Gottes Sohn, o wie lacht
15 Lieb' aus deinem göttlichen Mund
Da uns schlägt die rettende Stund,
Jesus in deiner Geburt!
Jesus in deiner Geburt!

Joseph Mohr, 1792–1848

Carol for two voices and guitar by Franz Gruber, 1818

2 **wachen** *to be awake*; 3 **traut** *dear*; 4 **hold** *sweet*; **lockig** *curly*; 8 **Hirten erst kundgemacht** *first made known to the shepherds*; 9 **der Engel** *angels'* (genitive plural); 15 **Lieb'** *love* (contraction of **Liebe**); 16 **da uns schlägt die rettende Stund** *as the hour of deliverance chimes for us*

14

Brief Mahlers an Anna von Mildenburg

In a letter to Anna von Mildenburg Mahler describes a journey to a
bell foundry in search of bells for his second symphony.

Berlin, 8. Dezember 1895

Ich brauche zu meiner Symphonie (der Zweiten), wie
Du weißt, am Ende des letzten Satzes Glockentöne,
welche jedoch durch kein musikalisches Instrument
5 ausgeführt werden können. Ich dachte daher von
vornherein an einen Glockengießer, daß der allein mir
helfen könnte. Einen solchen fand ich nun endlich; um
seine Werkstatt zu erreichen, muß man per Bahn
ungefähr eine halbe Stunde weit fahren. In der Gegend
10 des Grunewald liegt sie. Ich machte mich nun in aller
Frühe auf, und es war herrlich eingeschneit. Als ich in
Zehlendorf, so heißt der Ort, ankam und durch Tannen
und Fichten, ganz von Schnee bedeckt, meinen Weg
suchte, alles ganz ländlich, eine hübsche Kirche im
15 Wintersonnenschein fröhlich funkelnd, da wurde mir
wieder weit ums Herz, und ich sah, wie frei und froh der
Mensch sofort wird, wenn er aus dem unnatürlichen und
unruhevollen Getriebe der großen Stadt zurückkehrt in
das stille Haus der Natur. Nach längerem Suchen fand ich
20 die Gießerei; mich empfing ein schlichter alter Herr mit
schönem weißem Haar und Bart. Alles war mir so lieb und
schön. Ich sprach mit ihm, er war mir Ungeduldigem
freilich etwas weitschweifig und langsam. Er zeigte mir
herrliche Glocken, unter andern eine große, mächtige, die
25 er auf Bestellung des deutschen Kaisers für den neuen
Dom gegossen. Der Klang war geheimnisvoll mächtig. So
etwas Ähnliches hatte ich mir für mein Werk gedacht.

Gustav Mahler, 1860–1911

4 **welche** *which* (relative pronoun); 5 **ausgeführt werden können** *can be
performed*; 5/6 **von vornherein** *from the outset*; 6 **der Glockengießer** *bell*

founder; **daß der allein** *that he alone*; *7* **könnte** *could*; *10* **Grunewald** (proper name), a region outside Berlin; **sich aufmachen** *to set off*; *11* **eingeschneit** *snowy*; *15* **funkelnd** *sparkling* (present participle); *15/16* **wurde mir wieder weit ums Herz** *I became lighthearted again*; *18* **das Getriebe** *bustle*; *20* **die Gießerei** *foundry*; *22* **mir Ungeduldigem** *to me, impatient as I am* (noun in apposition to **mir**); *23* **etwas** *somewhat*; **weitschweifig** *long-winded*; *24* **die** *which* (relative pronoun); *26* **gegossen** *cast*; *26/27* **so etwas Ähnliches** *something similar*; *27* **hatte gedacht** *had thought*

Anna von Mildenburg as Brünnhilde
The Austrian operatic soprano (1872–1947) made her début in 1895 at the Hamburg Opera, where she met Mahler, who was chief conductor there, and whose mistress she became. She was an eminent Wagnerian singer and performed in Vienna and at Covent Garden.

Coordinating conjunctions

When the conjunctions **und, oder, aber, denn** and **sondern** are used in a sentence there is no change in the word order:

Karl ist zehn Jahre alt und Peter ist acht.
Karl is ten years old and Peter is eight.
Kommst du mit oder bleibst du hier?
Are you coming with us or staying here?
Sie ist für Musik sehr begabt, aber sie kann kein Deutsch.
She is very gifted in music, but she knows no German.
Sie kann heute nicht singen, denn sie ist krank.
She cannot sing today, for she is ill.
Er ist nicht verheiratet sondern ledig.
He is not married, but single.

Notice that **sondern** is used for *but* after a negative when there is a contradiction between two ideas.

Coordinating phrases

Some conjunctions are made up of two parts, just as in English:

nicht nur ... sondern auch *not only ... but also*
sowohl ... als auch *both ... and*
entweder ... oder *either ... or*
weder ... noch *neither ... nor*
je ... desto *the more ... the more*
bald ... bald *first ... then*
teils ... teils *partly ... partly*

Sie ist nicht nur hübsch sondern auch intelligent.
She is not only pretty, but also intelligent.
Sowohl die Eltern als auch die Großeltern waren dabei.
Both the parents and the grandparents were there.
Sie können entweder Russisch oder Italienisch lernen.
They can learn either Russian or Italian.
Ohne Brille kann sie weder lesen noch fernsehen.
Without spectacles she can neither read nor watch television.
Bald regnet es, bald scheint die Sonne.
First it rains, then the sun shines.
Wir fahren teils mit dem Zug, und teils mit dem Schiff.
We are going partly by train and partly by boat.

Subordinating conjunctions

Here are the most common conjunctions that introduce subordinate clauses:

als *as, when*	**ob** *whether*
bevor *before*	**obgleich, obwohl** *although*
bis *until*	**seitdem** *since*
da *as*	**sobald** *as soon as*
damit *so that* (purpose)	**so daß** *so that (result)*
daß *that*	**während** *while*
falls *in case*	**weil** *because*
indem *while, by*	**wenn** *if, whenever,*
(doing something)	*when*
nachdem *after*	**wo** *where*

A subordinate clause is one that depends on a main clause for its sense; the main clause makes sense on its own. The subordinate clause is introduced by a conjunction, and in German the verb comes at the end of this clause. The two clauses are separated by a comma.

Er ist glücklich, obwohl er kein Geld hat.
He is happy, although he has no money.
Ich trage einen Regenmantel, weil es stark regnet.
I am wearing a raincoat because it is raining hard.
Ich glaube nicht, daß er uns verstehen kann.
I do not think that he can understand us.

As in English, either clause may precede the other:

Obwohl er kein Geld hat, ist er glücklich.
Although he has no money, he is happy.

When the subordinate clause begins a sentence the main verb comes before its subject. The verb maintains its place as second idea in the sentence as a whole, the subordinate clause being the first idea:

Wenn du morgen kommst, gebe ich dir das Buch.
When you come tomorrow I shall give you the book.

EXERCISES

Complete these sentences:

1 Nicht er,...seine Frau spielt Bratsche.
2 Seit der Reformation ist Deutschland...lutherisch...katholisch.
3 Sie trinkt keinen Alkohol,...Wein...Bier.
4 Ich verstehe ihn gut...ich kann etwas Französisch.
5 Der Doktor besitzt...ein Haus in der Stadt...ein Ferienhaus auf dem Lande.

Join these sentences with the conjunction given, and make the necessary changes in word order; remember that either clause may precede the other:

6 Das Baby weint. Es hat Hunger. (wenn)
7 Ich fahre lieber mit dem Zug. Es geht am schnellsten. (weil)
8 Er spielt seine Schallplatten. Ich versuche zu lesen. (während)
9 Wir warten hier. Er kommt noch. (falls)
10 Ich muß nach Hause gehen. Ich möchte länger bleiben. (obwohl)
11 Sind Sie sicher? Der Zug fährt bald ab. (daß)
12 Wir haben abends nichts zu tun. Wir gehen ins Kino. (wenn)
13 Er sprach. Das Telefon klingelte.
14 Er ging aus dem Haus. Es fing zu regnen an. (sobald)
15 Du machst ihm eine Freude. Du besuchst ihn. (indem)
16 Sie sah ihn. Sie lächelte freundlich. (als)
17 Ich kaufte mir einen Stadtplan. Ich kannte die Stadt nicht. (da)
18 Er besuchte die Universität. Er hat studiert. (wo)
19 Er spricht deutlich. Die Ausländer können ihn verstehen. (damit)
20 Wir werden den Gipfel erreichen. Es wird dunkel. (bevor)

Ich atmet' einen linden Duft

Ich atmet' einen linden Duft.
Im Zimmer stand
Ein Zweig der Linde
Ein Angebinde
5 Von lieber Hand.
Wie lieblich war der Lindenduft!

Wie lieblich ist der Lindenduft!
Das Lindenreis
Brachst du gelinde;
10 Ich atme leis'
Im Duft der Linde
Der Liebe linden Duft.

Friedrich Rückert, 1788–1866

Song for voice and piano or orchestra by Gustav Mahler, 1905
(*Rückert Lieder*)

1 **Ich atmet'** *I breathed* (contraction of the imperfect); **lind** *balmy, gentle* (the word has a double meaning here as it describes the scent of a lime tree); *3* **die Linde** *lime tree*; *4* **das Angebinde** *gift*; *8* **das Lindenreis** *branch of lime*; *9* **gelinde** *gently*; *10* **leis'** *gently* (contraction of **leise**); *11* **der Linde** *of the lime* (genitive singular); *12* **der Liebe** *of love* (genitive singular)

15

Die Neue Zeitschrift für Musik

Schumann reports on the founding of his music journal.

Zu Ende des Jahres 1833 fand sich in Leipzig, allabendlich und wie zufällig, eine Anzahl meist jüngerer Musiker zusammen, zunächst zu geselliger Versammlung, nicht minder aber auch zum Austausch der Gedanken über die
5 Kunst, die ihnen Speise und Trank des Lebens war, — die Musik. Man kann nicht sagen, daß die damaligen musikalischen Zustände Deutschlands sehr erfreulich waren. Auf der Bühne herrschte noch Rossini, auf den Klavieren fast ausschließlich Herz und Hünten. Und doch waren
10 nur erst wenige Jahren verflossen, daß Beethoven, K.M.v. Weber und Franz Schubert unter uns lebten. Zwar Mendelssohns Stern war im Aufsteigen und verlauteten von einem Polen Chopin wunderbare Dinge, — aber eine nachhaltigere Wirkung äußerten diese erst später. Da fuhr
15 eines Tages der Gedanke durch die Brauseköpfe: laßt uns nicht müßig zusehen, greift an, daß es besser werde, greift an, daß die Poesie der Kunst wieder zu Ehren komme. So entstanden die ersten Blätter einer neuen Zeitschrift für Musik.

Robert Schumann, 1810–56

1/3 **sich zusammenfinden** *to meet up*; *1* **allabendlich** *every evening*; *2* **wie zufällig** *as if by chance*; *3/4* **nicht minder aber auch** *but also*; *6* **damalig** *at that time*; *9* **Herz und Hünten** (proper names), Heinrich Herz and Franz Hünten were pianists; *9/10* **waren verflossen** *had passed*; *11* **zwar** *admittedly*; *12* **im Aufsteigen** *in the ascendant*; **verlauten** *to be heard*; *13/14* **aber eine nachhaltigere Wirkung äußerten diese erst später** *but these did not show a lasting effect until later*; *15* **der Brausekopf** *hothead*; *16* **greift an** *set to*; **werde** *might become* (subjunctive); *17/18* **wieder zu Ehren komme** *might again be respected* (subjunctive)

Relative pronouns

Some subordinate clauses are linked to the main clause by a relative pronoun; they are called relative clauses. The relative pronoun agrees with its antecedent in number and gender, but takes the case from its function in the clause it introduces.

The relative pronouns are:

	masculine	feminine	neuter	plural
nominative	**der**	**die**	**das**	**die**
accusative	**den**	**die**	**das**	**die**
genitive	**dessen**	**deren**	**dessen**	**deren**
dative	**dem**	**der**	**dem**	**denen**

Here are some sentences containing relative pronouns. Notice that in these clauses the word order is the same as in other subordinate clauses with the verb at the end. The two clauses are separated by a comma. The relative pronoun is never omitted in German, as it often is in English.

Der Wagen, den Sie fahren, ist sehr alt.
The car that you drive is very old.
Die Kinder, die im Park spielen, sind lebhaft.
The children who are playing in the park are lively.
Das Kind, dessen Spielzeug kaputt ist, weint.
The child, whose toy is broken, is crying.
Die Frau, der ich helfe, ist blind.
The woman whom I help is blind.
Der Student, mit dem du sprachst, ist sehr klug.
The student with whom you were talking is very clever.

Welcher as a relative pronoun

Sometimes the appropriate form of **welcher** is preferred:

Das ist das Brot, welches das Mädchen kaufte.
That is the bread which the girl bought.

The use of **welches** here avoids repetition of **das**.

Was as a relative pronoun

Was is used after indefinite antecedents:

Alles, was er sagte, stimmte. *Everything he said was true.*

Er sagte nichts, was ich nicht schon wußte.
He said nothing that I did not already know.

Impersonal verbs and phrases

The sentences below show the use of verbs in the third person with **es** as the subject. This feature of the German language is usually translated by a different construction in English:

Es klopft. *Someone is knocking.*
Es freut mich. *I am pleased.*
Er ist mir kalt. *I am cold.*
Es tut mir weh. *It hurts me.*
Es tut mir leid. *I am sorry.*
Es gefällt mir. *I like it.*
Es macht mir Spaß. *I enjoy myself.*
Wie geht es Ihnen? *How are you?*
Es geht mir gut. *I am well.*

Sometimes **es** precedes a verb that has another subject. The **es** seems redundant, but it has the poetic effect of delaying the subject. There are many examples in older literary texts:

Es braust das Meer. *The sea roars.*
Es scheinen die alten Weiden so grau.
The old willows shine so grey.
Es ruhen die Gassen. *The streets are so quiet.*

The present participle

The present participle is formed by adding **d** to the infinitive:

lachen	*to laugh*	**lachend**	*laughing*
singen	*to sing*	**singend**	*singing*
schlafen	*to sleep*	**schlafend**	*sleeping*

Sie kam mir lachend entgegen.
She came towards me laughing.

EXERCISES

Complete these sentences with a relative pronoun:
1 Der Polizist, ... im Wagen wartet, trägt eine Pistole.
2 Der Film, ... wir gestern sahen, war uninteressant.
3 Alles, ... wir essen, ist ganz frisch.

4 Der Baum, ... wir dort sehen, ist eine Linde.
5 Das Opernhaus, in ... wir *Fidelio* sahen, ist sehr modern.
6 Die Terrasse, auf ... wir sitzen, ist schön sonnig.
7 Ich möchte etwas erzählen, ... dich amüsieren wird.
8 Die Dame, ... Kinder Deutsch sprechen, ist Engländerin.
9 Die Soldaten, ... der König dankt, blieben treu.
10 Das Buch, ... er kaufte, kostete dreißig Mark [DM30].

Translate:

11 Es tut mir leid, ich kann nicht mitfahren.
12 Gefällt es dir hier in Deutschland?
13 Wie geht es Ihnen?
14 Ist Ihnen zu kalt?
15 Diese Musik gefällt uns.

Der Nußbaum

Es grünet ein Nußbaum vor dem Haus,
Duftig, luftig breitet er blättrig die Blätter aus,
Viel liebliche Blüten stehen dran;
Linde Winde kommen, sie herzlich zu umfahn.
5 *Es flüstern je zwei zu zwei gepaart,*
Neigend, beugend zierlich zum Kusse die Häuptchen zart.
Sie flüstern von einem Mägdlein, das
Dächte die Nächte und Tage lang, wußte, ach, selber nicht was.
Sie flüstern, wer mag verstehen so gar
10 *Leise Weis'? Flüstern von Bräut'gam und nächstem Jahr.*
Das Mägdlein horchet, es rauscht im Baum;
Sehnend, wähnend sinkt es lächelnd in Schlaf und Traum.

Julius Mosen, 1803–67

Song for voice and piano by Robert Schumann, 1840

2 **blättrig** *leafy, leafily*; 3 **dran** *on it* (contraction of **daran**); 4 **umfahn** *to embrace* (archaic form of **umfangen**); 5 **gepaart** *in pairs*; 6 **zum Kusse** *for a kiss*; 8 **dächte** *thought*; 9/10 **so gar leise Weis'** *so soft a song*; 12 **wähnen** *to wonder*

16

Die Zauberflöte

Tamino, a prince, has been saved from a serpent by three ladies, who have killed the beast. Not knowing who has saved his life, Tamino encounters Papageno, a bird catcher and a strange-looking fellow.

Erster Aufzug, zweiter Auftritt

TAMINO:

Sag' mir, du lustiger Freund, wer du bist!

PAPAGENO:

Wer ich bin? (Dumme Frage.) Ein Mensch wie du. Wenn ich dich nun fragte, wer du bist?

TAMINO:

5 So würde ich dir antworten, daß ich ein Prinz bin.

PAPAGENO:

Was?

TAMINO:

Mein Vater ist Fürst, der über viele Länder und Menschen herrscht; darum nennt man mich Prinz.

PAPAGENO:

Länder? Menschen? Prinz? Gibt's außer diesen
10 Bergen auch noch Länder und Menschen?

TAMINO:

Viele Tausende!

PAPAGENO:

Da ließ' sich eine Spekulation mit meinen Vögeln machen.

TAMINO:

Wie lebst du?

PAPAGENO:

Von Essen und Trinken wie alle Menschen. Ich fange für
15 die sternflammende Königin verschiedene Vögel; dafür erhalt' ich täglich Speis' und Trank von ihr.

TAMINO:

Sternflammende Königin?

Emanuel Schikaneder as Papageno
Schikaneder, the librettist of *Die Zauberflöte*, sang the role of the
bird-catcher Papageno in the first performance of Mozart's opera in
Vienna in 1791. (Engraving by Ignaz Alberti, 1791.)

PAPAGENO:

Wie er mich so starr anblickt! Warum siehst du so
verdächtig und schelmisch nach mir?

TAMINO:

20 Weil — weil ich zweifle, ob du ein Mensch bist.

PAPAGENO:

Wie war das?

TAMINO:

Nach deinen Federn, die dich bedecken, halt' ich dich
für...

PAPAGENO:

Doch für keinen Vogel? Bleib' zurück, sag' ich, und traue
25 mir nicht; denn ich habe Riesenkraft.

TAMINO:

Riesenkraft? Also warst du mein Erretter, der diese giftige
Schlange bekämpfte?

PAPAGENO:

Schlange? Ist sie tot oder lebendig?

TAMINO:

Freund, wie hast du dieses Ungeheuer bekämpft? Du bist
30 ohne Waffen!

PAPAGENO:

Brauch' keine!

TAMINO:

Du hast sie also erdrosselt?

PAPAGENO:

Erdrosselt! Bin in meinem Leben nicht so stark gewesen
als heute.

Libretto by Emanuel Schikaneder, 1748–1812

Opera by Wolfgang Amadeus Mozart, 1791

5 **ich würde antworten** *I should answer*; 8 **darum** *for that reason*; 9 **außer**
apart from; 12 **da ließ'** ...**machen** *that would be good business for my birds*;
15 **die sternflammende Königin** *the starry queen*; 18 **starr anblicken** *to
stare at*; 19 **schelmisch** *insolently*; 22 **nach** *from*; 22/3 **halten für** *to consider
to be, to take for*; 26 **der Erretter** *rescuer*; 27 **die Schlange** *serpent*; 29 **das
Ungeheuer** *monster*; 32 **erdrosseln** *to strangle*

The perfect tense

The perfect tense is formed with the present tense of **haben** or
sein and the past participle, which comes at the end of the main
clause. Most verbs use the auxiliary **haben**, but some verbs,
especially those of movement, use **sein**:

Ich habe gespielt *I have played*
Ich bin gefahren *I have travelled*

The perfect tense is the predominant past tense in spoken
German. In written German, as a narrative tense, the imperfect is

99

preferred. The German perfect tense can be appropriately translated into English as a past tense with or without *have*:

Ich habe eine Zeitung gekauft.	*I have bought a newspaper.*
	I bought a newspaper.
Er hat seinen Schirm verloren.	*He has lost his umbrella.*
	He lost his umbrella.
Wir sind in die Stadt gegangen.	*We have been into town.*
	We went into town.
Was haben Sie gesagt?	*What have you said?*
	What did you say?

The past participle of regular weak verbs

The prefix **ge-** and the ending **-t** are added to the infinitive stem:

spielen	**gespielt**
kaufen	**gekauft**
lieben	**geliebt**

The full tense is thus:

Ich habe gespielt. *I have played.*

The past participle of strong verbs

These verbs usually show a vowel change in the stem and have the prefix **ge-** and the ending **-en**:

singen	**gesungen**
fahren	**gefahren**
nehmen	**genommen**

The full tense is thus:

Ich habe genommen. *I have taken.*

Points to watch in the formation of participles of weak and strong verbs

Verbs with an inseparable prefix do not add **ge-**:

verstehen   **verstanden**
Ich habe verstanden. *I have understood.*

Verbs whose stem ends in **t** or **d** add the ending **-et**:

arbeiten   **gearbeitet**
Ich habe gearbeitet. *I have worked.*

Separable verbs have the prefix **ge-** between the two parts:

aufstehen   **aufgestanden**
Ich bin aufgestanden. *I have got up.*

Irregular forms of the past participle are given in most dictionaries. Notice particularly:

haben   **ich habe gehabt**
sein   **ich bin gewesen**
werden   **ich bin geworden**

The verb table on pp. 256–262 shows strong and irregular past participles and whether the auxiliary is **haben** or **sein**.

The past participle of modal verbs

Modal verbs are rarely used on their own, but when they are used like this in the perfect tense the past participles are easily recognized by the prefix **ge-** and the ending **-t**:

können gekonnt   **müssen gemußt**   **sollen gesollt**
dürfen gedurft   **wollen gewollt**   **mögen gemocht**

Modal verbs are much more commonly used in conjunction with another verb, and then the past participles look exactly like the infinitives:

Sie hat das Buch lesen wollen.
She has wanted to read the book.
Er hat das Lied auswendig lernen müssen.
He has had to learn the song from memory.

Word order in the perfect tense

Notice the word order in these sentences:

main clause:

Wir sind pünktlich angekommen. *We arrived on time.*

main clause and subordinate clause:

Wir sind pünktlich angekommen, weil wir schnell gefahren sind. *We arrived on time, because we drove fast.*

subordinate clause and main clause:

Weil wir schnell gefahren sind, sind wir pünktlich angekommen. *Because we drove fast, we arrived on time.*

main clause with a modal verb:

Er hat DM400 für den Flugschein bezahlen müssen.
He had to pay DM400 for the airline ticket.

main clause and subordinate clause with modal verb:

Ich weiß, daß er DM400 für den Flugschein hat bezahlen müssen.
I know that he had to pay DM400 for the airline ticket.

EXERCISES

Put these sentences into the perfect tense:

1 Die Sängerin singt drei Lieder.
2 Der Tourist kommt aus Schweden.
3 Was machst du hier in England?
4 Der Fremde versteht den Film nicht ganz.
5 Es wird kalt.
6 Wir haben schlechtes Wetter.
7 Mozart verbringt die ersten Jahre seines Lebens in Salzburg.
8 Es wird kühl, weil die Sonne untergeht.
9 Wo bist du?
10 Er spielt seine Schallplatten, während ich ein Buch lese.
11 Sie hat Angst, sobald sie ihn sieht.
12 Die Vorstellung gefällt uns gut.
13 Sie können uns nicht helfen.
14 Was wollen Sie von ihm?
15 Das Orchester spielt unter der Leitung von Bruno Walter.

Der Doppelgänger

Still ist die Nacht, es ruhen die Gassen,
in diesem Hause wohnte mein Schatz;
sie hat schon längst die Stadt verlassen,
doch steht noch das Haus auf demselben Platz.
5 Da steht auch ein Mensch und starrt in die Höhe,
und ringt die Hände vor Schmerzensgewalt;
mir graust es, wenn ich sein Antlitz sehe,
der Mond zeigt mir mein eig'ne Gestalt!
Du Doppelgänger, du bleicher Geselle!
10 Was äffst du nach mein Liebesleid,
das mich gequält auf dieser Stelle
so manche Nacht in alter Zeit?

Heinrich Heine, 1797–1856

Song for voice and piano by Franz Schubert, 1828
('Schwanengesang')

3 **schon längst** *long ago*; 6 **vor Schmerzensgewalt** *from the force of pain*;
7 **mir graust es** *I shudder*; 10 **was äffst du nach mein Liebesleid** *why do
you imitate my pain in love*

17

Die Matthäus-Passion

EVANGELIST:
Aber am ersten Tage der süßen Brote traten die Jünger zu
Jesu, und sprachen zu ihm:

CHOR:
Wo willst du, daß wir dir bereiten das Osterlamm zu
essen?

EVANGELIST:
5 Er sprach:

JESUS:
Gehet hin in die Stadt zu Einem, und sprecht zu ihm: 'Der
Meister läßt dir sagen, "Meine Zeit ist hier, ich will bei dir
die Ostern halten mit meinen Jüngern."'

EVANGELIST:
Und die Jünger taten, wie ihnen Jesus befohlen hatte, und
10 bereiteten das Osterlamm. Und am Abend setzte er sich
zu Tische mit den Zwölfen; und da sie aßen sprach er:

JESUS:
Wahrlich, ich sage euch, einer unter euch wird mich
verraten.

EVANGELIST:
Und sie wurden sehr betrübt, und huben an, ein Jeglicher
15 unter ihnen, und sagen zu ihm:

CHOR:
Herr, bin ich's?

CHORAL:
>   Ich bin's, ich sollte büßen,
>   An Händen und an Füßen
>   Gebunden in der Höll'.
20 Die Geißeln und die Banden,
>   Und was du ausgestanden,
>   Das hat verdienet meine Seel'.

EVANGELIST:
Er antwortete und sprach:

Thomaskirche and Thomasschule
The church and school of St Thomas, Leipzig, where J. S. Bach was
Kantor from 1723 until his death in 1750. It was here that the *St Matthew
Passion* was written and first performed.

JESUS:

Der mit der Hand mit mir in die Schüssel tauchet, der
25 wird mich verraten. Des Menschen Sohn gehet zwar
dahin, wie von ihm geschrieben stehet; doch wehe dem
Menschen, durch welchen des Menschen Sohn verraten
wird. Es wäre ihm besser, daß derselbige Mensch noch
nie geboren wäre.

EVANGELIST:

30 Da antwortete Judas, der ihn verriet, und sprach:

JUDAS:

Bin ich's, Rabbi?

EVANGELIST:

Er sprach zu ihm:

JESUS:

Du sagest's.

EVANGELIST:

Da sie aber aßen, nahm Jesus das Brot, dankete, und
35 brach's, und gab's den Jüngern und sprach:

JESUS:

Nehmet, esset, das ist mein Leib.

EVANGELIST:

Und er nahm den Kelch, und dankete, gab ihnen den,
und sprach:

JESUS:

Trinket alle daraus; das ist mein Blut des neuen Testa-
40 ments, welches vergossen wird für Viele, zur Vergebung
der Sünden. Ich sage euch, ich werde von nun an nicht
mehr von diesem Gewächs des Weinstocks trinken, bis an
den Tag, da ich's neu trinken werde mit euch in meines
Vaters Reich.

Bible text, *Matthew* xxvi 17–29, translated by Martin Luther
1483–1546; chorale, stanza 5 of *O Welt, sieh hier dein Leben* by
Paul Gerhardt, 1607–76

Passion oratorio for soloists, double choir and double
orchestra by Johann Sebastian Bach, 1727

1 **die Tage der süßen Brote** *feast of the unleavened bread*; *3* **das
Osterlamm** *feast of the Passover*; *7* **sagen lassen** *to tell*; *8* **die Ostern**
Passover; *14* **sie huben an** *they began* (archaic form of the imperfect of
anheben); *14/15* **ein Jeglicher unter ihnen** *each and every one of them*; *17*

büßen *to atone*; *20* **die Geißeln** *scourges*; **die Banden** *bonds*; *21* **ausstehen** *to endure*; *24* **der** *he who*; *26* **wehe** *woe*; *27/28* **wird verraten** *is betrayed* (present passive of **verraten**); *28* **wäre** *would be* (imperfect subjunctive of **sein**); *37* **der Kelch** *goblet*; *40* **wird vergossen** *is shed* (present passive of **vergießen**); *42* **das Gewächs des Weinstocks** *the plant of the vine*

The pluperfect tense

The pluperfect tense is formed with the imperfect tense of **haben** or **sein** and the past participle. The use of the pluperfect tense is generally the same in German and English and is translated thus:

Ich hatte gespielt. *I had played.*
Er war weit gefahren. *He had driven a long way.*

The word order is the same for this tense as for the perfect tense (see p. 101–2):

Er war schon weggegangen, als ich ankam.
He had already gone away when I arrived.
Wir warteten, bis er zu spielen aufgehört hatte, und dann verließen wir den Saal.
We waited until he had stopped playing, and then we left the hall.

The future perfect tense

This tense is rare in German, as it is in English. It is formed with the future of **haben** or **sein** and the past participle:

Ich werde bald gespielt haben. *I shall soon have played.*
Er wird schon weggegangen sein. *He will already have left.*

The gerund

The gerund is formed in German from the infinitive of the verb. It is a noun, has a capital letter and is neuter:

Das Rauchen ist im Hörsaal verboten.
Smoking is forbidden in the lecture hall.

Correspondence

There follow some examples of the conventions of letter writing in German, with the appropriate English equivalents:

Sehr geehrter Herr! *Dear Sir*
Sehr geehrte gnädige Frau! *Dear Madam*
Sehr geehrte Damen und Herren! *Dear Sir or Madam*
Sehr geehrter Herr Professor Baehr! *Dear Professor Baehr*

This is the way to begin a formal letter to somebody whom you do not know. Either an exclamation mark or a comma is correct here.

A less formal way is more appropriate if you have met the person, know his name, or know him well:

Lieber Herr Professor Braun! *Dear Professor Braun*
Liebe Frau Braun! *Dear Mrs Braun*
Lieber Klaus! *Dear Klaus*
Liebe Elisabeth! *Dear Elisabeth*

In a letter the familiar forms **du, dir, dich, ihr, euch, dein, ihr,** etc. are always written with a capital letter:

Vielen Dank für Deinen Brief. *Many thanks for your letter.*

The date is either written in numerals, or in the accusative case:

London, 10.10.84
London, den 10. Oktober 1984

Here are some phrases with which to finish a letter:

Hochachtungsvoll	*Yours faithfully*
Mit freundlichen Grüßen	*Yours sincerely*
Mit herzlichen Grüßen	*With best wishes*
Viele liebe Grüße von Deinem Klaus	*With love from Klaus*

The postcode (**die Postleitzahl**) is numerical and is written before the name of the town or city. The codes for the big German cities are:

1000 Berlin	**5000 Köln**
2000 Hamburg	**6000 Frankfurt**
3000 Hannover	**7000 Stuttgart**
4000 Düsseldorf	**8000 München**

It is therefore possible to ascertain from the postcode in which region of Germany a town is situated: **5300 Bonn, 5340 Bad Honnef, 5484 Bad Breisig** are all in the vicinity of Cologne.

The address on the envelope should be in the following form:

Herrn
Johann Schmidt
Lessingstraße 22
5300 Bonn

Notice that **Herrn** is in the accusative case.

It is usual to write the sender's name and address on the back of the envelope, or on the front top left corner, and here the title **Herr, Frau, Fraülein** is omitted.

EXERCISES

Put these sentences into the pluperfect tense:

1 Er schreibt mir einen Brief.
2 Was sagt er?
3 Wir gehen sehr weit.
4 Ich verstehe ihn nicht.
5 Die erste Aufführung findet in der Thomaskirche statt.
6 Ich will am Wochenende verreisen.

Put these sentences into the future perfect tense:

7 Wir sehen ihn am Samstag.
8 Er vergißt das Gespräch.
9 Sie fahren schon weg.
10 Die Aufführung ist außerordentlich gut.

Translate:

11 Dear Richard.
12 Dear Helga.
13 Dear Professor Schmidt.
14 Dear Sir.
15 Yours sincerely.
16 With best wishes.

Fürchte dich nicht

Fürchte dich nicht, ich bin bei dir, weiche nicht, denn ich
bin dein Gott. Ich stärke dich, ich helfe dir auch, ich
erhalte dich durch die rechte Hand meiner Gerechtigkeit. Fürchte dich nicht, ich habe dich bei deinem Namen
5 gerufen, ich habe dich erlöset, du bist mein.

Herr, mein Hirt, Brunn aller Freuden!
Du bist mein,
Ich bin dein,
Niemand kann uns scheiden.
10 *Ich bin dein, weil du dein Leben*
Und dein Blut,
Mir zu gut,
In den Tod gegeben

Du bist mein, weil ich dich fasse,
15 *Und dich nicht,*
O mein Licht
Aus dem Herzen lasse!
Laß mich hingelangen,
Wo du mich,
20 *Und ich dich*
Ewig werd' umfangen.

Bible text, *Isaiah* xli 10, xliii 1, translated by Martin Luther,
1483–1546; chorale, stanzas 11 and 12 of *Warum sollt ich mich
denn grämen* by Paul Gerhardt, 1607–76

Motet in eight parts by Johann Sebastian Bach, 1726

1 **sich fürchten** *to* *fear*; **weichen** *to* *depart*; *3/4* **die Gerechtigkeit**
righteousness; *5* **erlösen** *to redeem*; *6* **der Hirt** *shepherd*; *12* **mir zu gut** *for
my good*; *18* **hingelangen** *to reach the place*; *21* **umfangen** *to embrace*

Erinnerungen an Beethoven

Czerny tells in his memoirs (1842) of his first visit to Beethoven when
he was ten years old.

Beethoven selber war in einer Jacke von langhaarigem
dunkelgrauem Zeuge und gleichen Beinkleidern
gekleidet. Das pechschwarze Haar sträubte sich zottig um
seinen Kopf. Der seit einigen Tagen nicht rasierte Bart
5 schwärzte den unteren Teil seines Gesichts. Auch
bemerkte ich sogleich, daß er in beiden Ohren Baumwolle
hatte, welche in eine gelbe Flüssigkeit getaucht schien.
    Doch war damals an ihm nicht die geringste
Harthörigkeit bemerkbar. Ich mußte sogleich etwas
10 spielen, und da ich mich zu sehr scheute, mit einer von
seinen Compositionen anzufangen, so spielte ich das
Mozart'sche große C-dur Concert (KV 503). Beethoven
wurde bald aufmerksam, näherte sich meinem Stuhle und
spielte bei den Stellen, wo ich nur accompagnierende
15 Passagen hatte, mit der linken Hand die
Orchestermelodie mit. Seine Hände waren sehr mit
Haaren bewachsen, und die Finger, besonders an den
Spitzen, sehr breit. Die Zufriedenheit, die er äußerte,
machte mir Mut die eben erschienene Sonate Pathétique
20 und endlich die Adelaïde vorzutragen, welche mein Vater
mit seiner recht guten Tenorstimme sang. Als ich
vollendet hatte, wendete sich Beethoven zu meinem Vater
und sagte: 'Der Knabe hat Talent, ich selber will ihn
unterrichten und nehme ihn als meinen Schüler an.
25 Schicken Sie ihn wöchentlich einigemal zu mir. Vor allem
aber verschaffen Sie ihm Emanuel Bachs Lehrbuch über
die wahre Art das Clavier zu spielen, das er schon das
nächste Mal mitbringen muß.'
    In den ersten Lektionen beschäftigte mich Beethoven
30 ausschließlich nur mit den Scalen in allen Tonarten, zeigte

111

mir die damals den meisten Spielern noch unbekannte
einzig richtige Haltung der Hände, der Finger und
vorzüglich den Gebrauch des Daumens.

Er machte mich vorzüglich auf das Legato auf-
35 merksam, das er selber in einer so unübertrefflichen Art in
seiner Machte hatte und das zu jener Zeit alle anderen
Pianisten auf dem Fortepiano für unausführbar hielten.

Carl Czerny, 1791–1857

die Erinnerung *memory*; *2* **das Zeug** *material*; *3* **sich sträuben** *to stand on end*; *5* **schwärzen** *to blacken*; *7* **getaucht schien** *seemed to be soaked*; *8/9* **die Harthörigkeit** *deafness*; *10* **sich scheuen** *to be afraid*; *12* **KV (Köchel-Verzeichnis)** *K (Köchel catalogue)*; *17* **bewachsen** *covered*; *19* **Mut machen** *to encourage*; *20* **vortragen** *to perform*; *25* **vor allem** *above all*; *27* **die Art** *way*; *30* **ausschließlich** *exclusively*; *31/32* **die einzig richtige Haltung** *the only correct position*; *33* **vorzüglich** *especially*; *37/38* **halten für** *to consider to be*

Adjectives

Adjectives that follow the noun are not inflected: they do not
agree with the noun.

> **Der König ist reich.**
> **Die Königin ist reich.**
> **Das Mädchen ist reich.**

Adjectives that precede the noun are inflected, and the adjectival
endings are in accordance with three declensions:

1 After the definite article **der** and words that decline like it,
dieser, welcher, jener, jeder:

	Masc. Sing.	Fem. Sing.	Neut. Sing.
nom.	der alte Mann	die schöne Frau	das kleine Buch
acc.	den alten Mann	die schöne Frau	das kleine Buch
gen.	des alten Mannes	der schönen Frau	des kleinen Buches
dat.	dem alten Mann	der schönen Frau	dem kleinen Buch

2 After the indefinite article **ein** and words that decline like it,
kein, mein, dein, etc.:

	Masc. Sing.	Fem. Sing.	Neut. Sing.
nom.	ein brauner Tisch	eine neue Stadt	ein hübsches Mädchen
acc.	einen braunen Tisch	eine neue Stadt	ein hübsches Mädchen
gen.	eines braunen Tisches	einer neuen Stadt	eines hübschen Mädchens
dat.	einem braunen Tisch	einer neuen Stadt	einem hübschen Mädchen

112

3 When the adjective precedes the noun but there is no article:

	Masc. Sing.	Fem. Sing.	Neut. Sing.
nom.	roter Wein	warme Suppe	kaltes Wasser
acc.	roten Wein	warme Suppe	kaltes Wasser
gen.	roten Weins	warmer Suppe	kalten Wassers
dat.	rotem Wein	warmer Suppe	kaltem Wasser

Notice that in declensions 1 and 2 all adjectives below the bold line end in **-en**, as do the plurals.

	Plural 1	Plural 2	Plural 3
nom.	die reichen Leute	keine guten Männer	gute Freunde
acc.	die reichen Leute	keine guten Männer	gute Freunde
gen.	der reichen Leute	keiner guten Männer	guter Freunde
dat.	den reichen Leuten	keinen guten Männern	guten Freunden

Ordinal numbers

The ending **-te** is added to numbers up to nineteen:

der zweite *second*
der neunte *ninth*

except for:

der erste *first*
der dritte *third*
der siebte *seventh*
der achte *eighth*

The ending **-ste** is added to numbers twenty and above:

der zwanzigste *twentieth*
der zweiunddreißigste *thirty-second*

Ordinal numbers have the usual adjectival endings:

Er ist ihr viertes Kind. *He is her fourth child.*
Er ist am zehnten August geboren.
He was born on the tenth of August.

Adjectives formed from place names

Adjectives formed from place names usually add **-er** and no further ending:

der Kölner Dom *Cologne Cathedral*
die Berliner Philharmonika *the Berlin Philharmonic*
die Wiener Staatsoper *the Vienna State Opera*

Participles used adjectivally

When used before a noun the present participle has the appropriate adjectival ending:

Sie hat das schlafende Kind auf dem Schoß.
She has the sleeping child on her lap.

The past participle also has the usual adjectival endings when it precedes the noun:

Die Polizei hat mein gestohlenes Auto gefunden.
The police have found my stolen car.

Prepositional phrases used adjectivally

A common feature of literary German is the appearance of prepositional phrases between the article and the noun. This construction is best translated into English by a subordinate clause:

Der vom ganzen Volk verehrte und geliebte König ist jetzt gestorben.
The king, who was respected and loved by all the people, is now dead.

Ein and possessive adjectives used as pronouns

These words take the endings of **dieser** when they act as pronouns:

einer der Männer *one of the men*
eine der Frauen *one of the women*
eines der Kinder *one of the children*
Mein Buch ist rot, deines ist blaue.
My book is red, yours is blue.
Dein Bruder ist älter als meiner.
Your brother is older than mine.

Hören, sehen, lassen

These verbs are often followed by an infinitive without **zu**. The sentence construction is therefore similar to that of modal verbs:

Wir hörten ihn wegfahren. *We heard him drive away.*

Ich sah ihn kommen. *I saw him coming.*
Sie ließ ihn dort stehen. *She left him standing there.*

As with modal verbs (see p. 102) the past participles look just like the infinitives:

Sie hat uns kommen sehen. *She has seen us coming.*
Sie hatte ihn dort stehen lassen.
She had left him standing there.

EXERCISES

Translate:

1 Wir laufen durch den grünen Wald.
2 Eines der Mädchen hat blonde Haare.
3 Wir wohnen am Ende einer langen Straße.
4 Kühler Apfelsaft schmeckt gut.
5 Bei heißem Wetter gehe ich gern schwimmen.
6 Der Geschmack roten Weins ist köstlich.
7 Er ißt ein gekochtes Ei zum Frühstück.
8 Sie grüßte das lachende Kind.
9 Sie haben mich weinen sehen.
10 Wir hörten die Vögel im Walde zwitschern.

Complete these sentences:

11 Die italienisch- Touristen stehen vor d- berühmt- Dom.
12 Wir steigen bis zur alt- Burg hinauf.
13 Ihr Freund hat ihr ein- golden- Ring geschenkt.
14 Der Wirt hat uns ein- ausgezeichnet- Wein angeboten.
15 Der Briefträger hat ein gelb- Fahrrad.
16 Wir leben im zwanzigst- Jahrhundert.
17 Der Wettbewerb findet am erst- Juni in unser- klein- Dorf statt.
18 Sie hängt das frisch gewaschen- Hemd in den Kleiderschrank.
19 Sie stand weinend vor dem brennend- Haus.
20 Trotz strömend- Regens gingen Hunderte von Arbeitern auf die Straßen.

Adelaïde

Einsam wandelt dein Freund im Frühlingsgarten,
Mild vom lieblichen Zauberlicht umflossen,
Das durch wankende Blütenzweige zittert,
Adelaïde!

5 In der spiegelnden Flut, im Schnee der Alpen,
In des sinkenden Tages Goldgewölken,
Im Gefilde der Sterne strahlt dein Bildnis,
Adelaïde!

Abendlüfte im zarten Laube flüstern,
10 Silberglöckchen des Mais im Grase säuseln,
Wellen rauschen und Nachtigallen flöten:
Adelaïde!

Einst, o Wunder! entblüht auf meinem Grabe
Eine Blume der Asche meines Herzens;
15 Deutlich schimmert auf jedem Purpurblättchen:
Adelaïde!

Friedrich von Matthisson, 1761–1831

Song for voice and piano by Ludwig van Beethoven, 1794-5

2 **umflossen** *surrounded*; 5 **spiegeln** *to sparkle*; 6 **das Gewölk** *clouds*; 7 **das Gefilde** *realm*; 13 **einst** *one day*; **entblühen** *to flower*; 15 **das Purpurblättchen** *crimson petal*

19

Brief Mozarts an seinen Vater

Mozart reports on the second performance of *Die Entführung aus dem Serail*.

Wien, den 20. Juli 1782

Mon très cher Père!

Ich hoffe, Sie werden meinen letzten Brief, worin ich Ihnen die gute Aufnahme meiner Oper berichtet habe,
5 richtig erhalten haben. Gestern ist sie zum zweiten Male gegeben worden.

    Könnten Sie wohl vermuten, daß gestern noch eine stärkere Kabale war als am ersten Abend? Der ganze erste Akt ist verzischet worden. Aber das laute Bravo-Rufen
10 unter den Arien konnten sie doch nicht verhindern.

Das Burgtheater, Vienna
In this great theatre Mozart's operas *Die Entführung aus dem Serail* (1782), *Le nozze di Figaro* (1786) and *Così fan tutte* (1790) were first performed. (Engraving by Carl Postl, 1810.)

117

Meine Hoffnung war also das Schlußterzett. Da machte aber das Unglück den Fischer fehlen — durch das fehlte auch der Dauer (Pedrillo) — und Adamberger allein konnte auch nicht alles ersetzen — mithin ging der ganze
15 Effekt davon verloren, und wurde für diesmal nicht repetiert. Ich war so in Wut, daß ich mich nicht kannte, wie auch Adamberger, und sagte gleich, daß ich die Opera nicht geben lasse, ohne vorher eine kleine Probe (für die Sänger) zu machen. Im zweiten Akt wurden die
20 beiden Duette wie das erste Mal, und dazu das Rondeau von Belmonte 'Wenn der Freude Tränen fließen' wiederholet. Das Theater war noch fast voller als das erste Mal. Den Tag vorher konnte man keine gesperrten Sitze mehr haben, weder auf dem Noble-Parterre noch im 3. Stock;
25 und auch keine Loge mehr. Die Opera hat in den zwei Tagen 1200 Gulden getragen.

Wolfgang Amadeus Mozart, 1756–91

4 **berichten** *to tell*; *5/6* **ist gegeben worden** *was performed*; *8* **die Kabale** *uproar*; *9* **ist verzischet worden** *was hissed*; *10* **sie** *they*, those people hissing; *11/12* **da machte das Unglück den Fischer fehlen** *by bad luck Fischer made a mistake*; **Fischer** (proper name), the singer taking the part of Osmin; *13* **Dauer** (proper name), the singer taking the part of Pedrillo; **Adamberger** (proper name), the singer taking the part of Belmonte; *14* **ersetzen** *to make up for*; *17* **wie auch** *as was*; **gleich** *straight away*; *20* **wie das erste Mal** *as at the first performance*; *23* **keine gesperrten Sitze** *no reserved seats*; *24* **das Noble-Parterre** *the expensive stalls*; **3. Stock** *gallery*; *25* **die Loge** *box*; *26* **tragen** *to bring in*

The passive

The passive form of the verb is widely used in German and English. Here is an example using an active verb, **essen** *to eat*:

Das Mädchen ißt den Kuchen. *The girl eats the cake.*

and an example using the same verb in the passive:

Der Kuchen wird von dem Mädchen gegessen.
The cake is being eaten by the girl.

Notice that the present passive is formed with the present tense of **werden** and the past participle, which comes at the end.

The use of **werden** as an auxiliary, and the presence of a past participle makes the passive easy to recognize:

present	**Der Kuchen wird gegessen.**
	The cake is being eaten.
future	**Der Kuchen wird gegessen werden.**
	The cake will be eaten.
imperfect	**Der Kuchen wurde gegessen.**
	The cake was eaten.
perfect	**Der Kuchen ist gegessen worden.**
	The cake has been eaten.
pluperfect	**Der Kuchen war gegessen worden.**
	The cake had been eaten.

Notice that in the perfect and pluperfect passive the past participle of **werden** is **worden**, not **geworden**.

Modal verbs

The passive of modal verbs can be recognized by **werden** and a past participle:

Der Junge muß um acht geweckt werden.
The boy must be woken at eight.

Von, durch, mit after a passive verb

After a passive verb **von**, **durch** or **mit** will be used in German for the English by: **von** indicates human agency; **durch** indicates non-human agency; and **mit** indicates the means.

Der Kuchen wird von dem Mädchen gegessen.
The cake is being eaten by the girl.
Das Gebäude wurde durch den Wind beschädigt.
The building was damaged by the wind.
Das Papier wurde mit einem Messer geschnitten.
The paper was cut with a knife.

Man used to express the passive

Man *one* is used frequently in German where the passive is preferred in English:

Man sah ihn weglaufen. *He was seen running away.*

Sein with **zu** and the infinitive to express the passive

The passive can also be constructed using **sein** followed by **zu** and the infinitive of the main verb:

Viele Autos sind in der Stadtmitte zu sehen.
Many cars are to be seen in the town centre.

Lassen with the infinitive to express the passive

Lassen, which means *to let*, *to allow*, and which is always followed by an infinitive (without **zu**), can have a passive sense:

Ich lasse mir ein Haus bauen. *I am having a house built.*
Das läßt sich leicht verstehen. *That can easily be understood.*

EXERCISES

Translate:

1 Wann wurde dieses Gebäude gebaut?
2 Ludwig van Beethoven wurde in Bonn geboren.
3 Viele Komponisten werden von ihren Zeitgenossen nicht anerkannt.
4 In Deutschland werden die Geschenke am Heiligen Abend ausgepackt.
5 Zu Karneval wurde viel getanzt und gesungen.
6 Wegen seiner Krankheit ist ihm das Rauchen verboten worden.
7 Leider ist dieses schöne Haus nicht zu kaufen.
8 *Die Matthäus-Passion* von Bach war hundert Jahre lang nicht zu hören.
9 Männer und Frauen sollen bei gleicher Arbeit gleich bezahlt werden.
10 Ich lasse mir die Haare schneiden.

Auch kleine Dinge können uns entzücken

Auch kleine Dinge können uns entzücken,
Auch kleine Dinge können teuer sein.
Bedenkt, wie gern wir uns mit Perlen schmücken;
Sie werden schwer bezahlt und sind nur klein.
5 *Bedenkt, wie klein ist die Olivenfrucht,*
Und wird um ihre Güte doch gesucht.
Denkt an die Rose nur, wie klein sie ist,
Und duftet doch so lieblich, wie ihr wißt.

Anonymous poem from the *Italienisches Liederbuch* (1860) translated by Paul Heyse

Song for voice and piano by Hugo Wolf, 1891 (*Italienisches Liederbuch*)

1 **auch** *even*; *4* **werden schwer bezahlt** *are dearly paid for*; *6* **um ihre Güte** *for its goodness*

Paulus an die Korinther

Wenn ich mit Menschen- und mit Engelszungen redete,
und hätte der Liebe nicht, so wär ich ein tönend Erz, oder
eine klingende Schelle. Und wenn ich weissagen könnte,
und wüßte alle Geheimnisse und alle Erkenntnis; und
5 hätte allen Glauben, also daß ich Berge versetzte und
hätte der Liebe nicht, so wäre ich nichts. Und wenn ich
alle meine Habe den Armen gäbe, und ließe meinen Leib

Johannes Brahms
This composite photograph shows the figure of Brahms superimposed on
the background of his music room in the Karlsgasse, Vienna. On the wall
is a bust of Beethoven. The picture was perhaps devised to illustrate the
awe in which Brahms held his great predecessor. He is reported to have
said to a friend in the early 1870s: 'Ich werde nie eine Symphonie
komponieren! Du hast keinen Begriff davon, wie es unsereinem zu Mute
ist, wenn er immer so einen Riesen hinter sich marschieren hört.'

brennen und hätte der Liebe nicht, so wäre mir's nichts nütze. Wir sehen jetzt durch einen Spiegel in einem 10 dunkeln Worte; dann aber von Angesicht zu Angesichte. Jetzt erkenne ich's stückweise; dann aber werd ich's erkennen, gleich wie ich erkennet bin. Nun aber bleibet Glaube, Hoffnung, Liebe, diese drei; aber die Liebe ist die größeste unter ihnen.

Bible text, *1 Corinthians xiii:* 1-3, 12-13, translated by Martin Luther, 1483–1546

Song for voice and piano by Johannes Brahms, 1896 (*Vier ernste Gesänge*)

1 **Menschen(zungen)** *tongues of men*; *2* **tönend Erz** *sounding brass*; *3* **die Schelle** *bell*; **weissagen** *to prophesy*; *5* **der Glaube** *faith*; **versetzen** *to move*; *7* **die Habe** *possessions*; **der Leib** *body*; *8/9* **wäre mir's nichts nütze** *would be of no use to me*; *9* **der Spiegel** *glass*; *10* **das Angesicht** *face*; *11* **erkennen** *to understand*; **stückweise** *little by little*; *12* **gleich wie** *just as*

The subjunctive

The verbs presented in the lessons so far have all been in the indicative mood. This lesson introduces the basic forms and uses of verbs in the subjunctive mood. The fundamental difference between these two forms of the verb is that the indicative expresses certainty and fact whereas the subjunctive expresses uncertainty and hypothesis. The sentences below, the first in the indicative and the second in the subjunctive, show this difference;

Wenn das Wetter gut ist, können Sie die Berge sehen.
When the weather is good, you can see the mountains.
Wenn das Wetter gut wäre, könnten Sie die Berge sehen.
If the weather were good, you could see the mountains.

There is a tendency in spoken German not to use the subjunctive and many of the subjunctive forms found in older literature sound stilted today. There is a preference for the indicative, just as there is in English. But some subjunctive forms are in everyday use and have already been introduced in Lesson 5:

Ich hätte gern zwei Brötchen. *I would like two rolls.*
Ich möchte zwei Kilo Äpfel. *I would like two kilos of apples.*

The subjunctive is also used in reported speech or indirect questions:

> **Er sagte, er hätte mich nicht gesehen.**
> *He said he had not seen me.*
> **Er fragte, ob Sie krank wären.**
> *He asked whether you were ill.*

and after **als** and **als ob** *as if:*

> **Sie sehen aus, als ob Sie krank wären.**
> *You look as if you were ill.*
> **Er sah aus, als hätte er Fieber.**
> *He looked as if he had a temperature.*

The present subjunctive

To form the present subjunctive of both weak and strong verbs, endings are added to the stem of the infinitive in the following way:

	spielen		nehmen
ich	spiele	ich	nehme
du	spielest	du	nehmest
er	spiele	er	nehme
wir	spielen	wir	nehmen
ihr	spielet	ihr	nehmet
Sie	spielen	Sie	nehmen
sie	spielen	sie	nehmen

It is the third person singular form that is most often used and this is easily recognized by the **-e** ending (**er spiele, er komme, er könne, er habe, er werde, er singe**).

The present subjunctive of **sein** *to be* is irregular:

ich	sei
du	seist
er	sei
wir	seien
ihr	seiet
Sie	seien
sie	seien

The imperfect subjunctive

The imperfect subjunctive is not strictly a past tense. It is the form most often used for hypothetical and conditional expressions:

Ich hätte gern zwei Kilo Äpfel.
I should like two kilos of apples.

Ich wäre froh, wenn Sie morgen kämen.
I should be pleased if you would come tomorrow.

The imperfect subjunctive form of weak verbs is the same as the indicative (see p. 83). The imperfect subjunctive of strong verbs adds subjunctive endings to the imperfect stem (see p. 83–4) and the vowels **a**, **o** and **u** are modified with an Umlaut:

	kommen
ich	käme
du	kämest
er	käme
wir	kämen
ihr	kämet
Sie	kämen
sie	kämen

The irregular verbs **haben**, **sein**, and **werden** follow this pattern and are in frequent use:

infinitive	imperfect	imperfect subjunctive
haben	**hatte**	**hätte**
sein	**war**	**wäre**
werden	**wurde**	**würde**

Here are some more examples of verbs in the imperfect subjunctive:

geben	**gab**	**gäbe**
gehen	**ging**	**ginge**
sprechen	**sprach**	**spräche**
fahren	**fuhr**	**führe**
müssen	**mußte**	**müßte**
dürfen	**durfte**	**dürfte**

Imperfect subjunctive forms are given in the verb table on pp. 256–262.

Some subjunctive forms sound stilted today and they are often replaced in spoken German by **würde** and the infinitive. This form is easy to recognize and corresponds to the English *should/would* or *should have/would have*.

Wenn ich Zeit hätte, würde ich gerne mitfahren.

If I had the time, I should like to go with you.

Compound tenses in the subjunctive

Compound tenses are formed in the usual way, except that the auxiliaries **sein, haben** and **werden** are in the subjunctive:

future	**er werde gehen**
perfect	**er habe gespielt**
	er sei gegangen
pluperfect	**er hätte gespielt**
	er wäre gegangen

Ich hätte geschrieben, wenn ich deine Adresse gewußt hätte.
I should have written if I had known your address.
Wir wären gern geflogen, aber der Flug war ausverkauft.
We should have liked to fly, but the flight was sold out.

EXERCISES

Translate:

1 Wo würden Sie gern studieren?
2 Er lag auf der Erde, als ob er tot wäre.
3 Er glaubte, er würde ein Stipendium bekommen.
4 Wenn wir nur allein wären!
5 Was möchten Sie trinken?
6 Ich hätte gern Auskunft über einen Flug nach Paris.
7 Ich dachte, Sie wären krank.
8 Er sagte, er würde nicht spielen.
9 Das hätte er mir gestern sagen sollen.
10 Wenn ich Zeit hätte, würde ich das Schloß besichtigen.
11 Wenn ich Zeit gehabt hätte, hätte ich das Schloß besichtigt.
12 Wir müssen nach Hause fahren, obwohl wir länger bleiben möchten.
13 Wäre es besser, wenn Studenten von ihren Eltern unabhängig wären?
14 Was würden Sie tun, wenn Sie arbeitslos wären?
15 Würden Sie berufstätig bleiben, wenn Sie Kinder hätten?

Und wüßten's die Blumen, die kleinen

Und wüßten's die Blumen, die kleinen,
Wie tief verwundet mein Herz,
Sie würden mit mir weinen,
Zu heilen meinen Schmerz.

5 Und wüßten's die Nachtigallen,
Wie ich so traurig und krank,
Sie ließen fröhlich erschallen
Erquickenden Gesang.

Und wüßten sie mein Wehe,
10 Die goldenen Sternelein,
Sie kämen aus ihrer Höhe,
Und sprächen Trost mir ein.

Sie alle können's nicht wissen,
Nur eine kennt meinen Schmerz;
15 Sie hat ja selbst zerrissen,
Zerrissen mir das Herz.

Heinrich Heine, 1797–1856

Songs for voice and piano by Robert Schumann, 1840 (*Dichterliebe*); Felix Mendelssohn

1 **wüßten** *if they knew* (imperfect subjunctive of **wissen**); 2 **verwundet** *wounded*; 7 **erschallen lassen** *to let ring out*; 8 **erquickend** *refreshing*; 11 **aus ihrer Höhe** *from the heights*; 14 **eine** *one person*; 15 **selbst** *herself*; 16 **zerrissen** *torn*

3 *TEXTS*

Gustav Mahler
Photograph taken in 1892 during the period when he was chief conductor
at the Hamburg Opera.

Wo die schönen Trompeten blasen

Wer ist denn draußen und wer klopfet an,
Der mich so leise, so leise wecken kann?
Das ist der Herzallerliebste dein,
Steh auf und laß mich zu dir ein!

5 *Was soll ich hier nun länger stehn?*
  Ich seh die Morgenröt aufgehn,
  Die Morgenröt, zwei helle Stern.
  Bei meinem Schatz da wär ich gern,
  Bei meinem Herzallerliebe.
10 *Das Mädchen stand auf und ließ ihn ein;*
  Sie heißt ihn auch willkommen sein.
  Willkommen, lieber Knabe mein,
  So lang hast du gestanden!

131

Sie reicht' ihm auch die schneeweiße Hand.
15 Von ferne sang die Nachtigall;
Das Mädchen fing zu weinen an.

Ach weine nicht, du Liebste mein,
Aufs Jahr sollst du mein eigen sein.
Mein eigen sollst du werden gewiß,
20 Wie's keine sonst auf Erden ist.
O Lieb auf grüner Erden.

Ich zieh in Krieg auf grüne Heid',
Die grüne Heide, die ist so weit.
Allwo dort die schönen Trompeten blasen,
25 Da ist mein Haus, von grünem Rasen.

Text by the composer, based on an anonymous poem from the anthology *Des Knaben Wunderhorn* (1805–8), edited by Achim von Arnim and Clemens Brentano

Song for voice and piano or orchestra by Gustav Mahler, 1898 (*Des Knaben Wunderhorn*)

2 **der** *who* (relative pronoun); *5* **was** *what for, why*; *8* **wär ich gern** *I should like to be*; *11* **willkommen heißen** *to welcome*; *13* **hast du gestanden** *you have stood*; *18* **aufs Jahr** *in a year*; *20* **keine sonst** *no one else*; *22* **ziehen** *to go*; **die Heide** *heath*; *24* **allwo** *everywhere*

Weihnachtshistorie

Historia von der freuden- und gnadenreichen Geburt Gottes und Mariens Sohnes Jesu Christi

Herod sends the Wise Men to Bethlehem to seek the new-born child.

EVANGELIST:
Da berief Herodes die Weisen heimlich und erlernete mit Fleiß von ihnen, wann der Stern erschienen wäre, und weisete sie gen Bethlehem und sprach:
HERODES:
Ziehet hin, und forschet fleißig nach dem Kindlein, und

Heinrich Schütz
Schütz, the Hofkapellmeister at Dresden, is shown directing his singers in the court chapel, *c.*1670. Musicians are playing in the gallery below the organ loft. (Engraving, published 1676.)

5 wenn ihr's findet, so saget mir es wieder, daß ich auch komme und es anbete.

EVANGELIST:

Als sie nun den König gehöret hatten, zogen sie hin, und siehe, der Stern, den sie im Morgenlande gesehen hatten, ging vor ihnen hin, bis daß er kam und stund oben
10 über da das Kindlein war. Da sie den Stern sahen, wurden sie hoch erfreuet und gingen in das Haus und funden das Kindlein mit Maria seiner Mutter und fielen nieder und beteten es an und täten ihre Schätze auf und schenkten ihm Gold, Weihrauch und Myrrhen. Und Gott befahl

15 ihnen im Traum, daß sie sich nicht sollten wieder zu
Herodes lenken, und sie zogen durch einen andern Weg
wieder in ihr Land.

Da sie aber hinweggezogen waren, siehe, da erschien der
Engel des Herren dem Joseph im Traum und sprach:

ENGEL:

20 Stehe auf Joseph. Stehe auf und nimm das Kindlein und
seine Mutter zu dir und fleuch ins Ägyptenland, und
bleibe da, bis ich dir sage, denn es ist vorhanden, daß
Herodes das Kindlein suche, dasselbe umzubringen.

EVANGELIST:

Und er stund auf und nahm das Kindlein und seine
25 Mutter zu sich bei der Nacht und entfloh ins Ägyptenland
und blieb allda bis nach dem Tode Herodes, auf das erfüllt
würde, das der Herr durch den Propheten geredet hat,
der da spricht: 'Aus Ägypten habe ich meinen Sohn
gerufen.'

30 Da nun Herodes sahe, daß er von den Weisen betrogen
war, ward er sehr zornig und schickte aus und ließ alle
Kinder zu Bethlehem töten und an ihren Grenzen, die da
zweijährig und darunter waren nach der Zeit, die er mit
Fleiß von den Weisen erlernet hatte. Da ist erfüllet, das
35 gesagt ist durch den Propheten Jeremias, der da spricht:
'Auf dem Gebirge hat man ein Geschrei gehöret, viel
Klagens, Weinens und Heulens, Rahel beweinete ihre
Kinder und wollte sich nicht trösten lassen, denn es war
aus mit ihnen.'

Bible text, *Matthew* ii 7–18, translated by Martin Luther,
1483–1546

Oratorio by Heinrich Schütz, 1664

1 **berufen** *to summon*; *1/2* **mit Fleiß** *diligently*; *3* **gen** *towards* (archaic form
of **gegen**); *4* **ziehen** *to go*; **forschen** *to search*; *8* **siehe** *behold*; *9* **ging vor
ihnen hin** *went before them*; *11* **funden** *found* (archaic form of the
imperfect of **finden**); *13* **täten auf** *opened* (archaic form of the imperfect
of **auftun**); *16* **lenken** *to make one's way*; *21* **fleuch** *flee* (archaic form of the
singular imperative of **fliehen**); *22* **vorhanden** *at hand*;
24 **stund** *stood* (archaic form of the imperfect of **stehen**); *25* **entfliehen**
to escape; *31* **ward** *became* (archaic form of the imperfect of **werden**);
36 **das Gebirge** *mountains*; *38/39* **es war aus mit ihnen** *they were dead*

134

Hänsel und Gretel

3. Aufzug: 'Das Knusperhäuschen'

Tiefer Wald. Der Morgen bricht an. Taumännchen tritt auf und schüttelt aus einer Glockenblume Tautropfen auf die schlafenden Kinder.

TAUMÄNNCHEN:
Der kleine Taumann heiß' ich,
5 und mit der Sonne reis' ich,
von Ost bis Westen weiß ich
wer faul ist und wer fleißig —
kling, klang, kling, klang!
Ich komm mit gold'nem Sonnenschein
10 und strahl in eure Äugelein,
und weck mit kühlem Taue,
was schläft auf Flur und Aue.
Dann springet auf, wer munter
in früher Morgenstunde,
15 denn sie hat Gold im Munde.
Drum auf, ihr Schläfer, erwachet.
Der lichte Tag schon lachet!
Drum auf, ihr Schläfer, erwacht!
[Eilt singend davon; die Kinder regen sich ein wenig auf, während
20 *Hänsel sich auf die andere Seite legt, um weiter zu schlafen.]*

GRETEL:
Wo bin ich? Wach ich? Ist es ein Traum?
Hier lieg' ich unterm Tannenbaum!
Hoch in den Zweigen da lispelt es leise,
Vöglein singen so süße Weise.
25 Wohl früh schon waren sie aufgewacht
und haben ihr Morgenliedchen dargebracht.
Ihr liebe Vöglein, liebe Vöglein,
guten Morgen!
[wendet sich zu Hänsel]
30 Sieh da, der faule Siebenschläfer!
Wart nur, dich weck' ich!
[springt auf]
Tirelireli! 'S ist nicht mehr früh!
Die Lerche hat's gesungen

35 und hoch sich aufgeschwungen.
Tirelireli!

HÄNSEL [*plötzlich in die Höhe springend*]:
Kikeriki! 'S ist noch früh!
Ja, hab's wohl vernommen,
40 der Morgen ist gekommen.
Kikeriki! Ü-ü-ü!

GRETEL:
Tirelireli!

HÄNSEL:
Mir ist so wohl, ich weiß nicht wie;
so gut wie heute schlief ich noch nie.

GRETEL:
45 Doch höre nur. Hier, unter'm Baum,
hatt' ich 'nen wunderschönen Traum.

HÄNSEL:
Richtig! Auch mir träumte was!

GRETEL:
Mir träumt, ich hört' ein
Rauschen und Klingen,
50 wie Chöre der Engel ein himmlisches Singen;
lichte Wölkchen im rosigen Schein
wallten und wogten ins Dunkel hinein.
Siehe, helle ward's mit einem Male,
licht durchflossen vom Himmelsstrahle;
55 eine goldene Leiter sah ich sich neigen,
Engel hernieder steigen,
gar holde Englein mit goldenen Flügelein —

HÄNSEL:
Vierzehn müssen's gewesen sein!

GRETEL:
Hast du denn alles dies auch gesehn?

HÄNSEL:
60 Freilich! 'S war wunderschön,
und dorthin sah ich sie gehn!

[*Er wendet sich nach dem Hintergrunde: in diesem Augenblicke
zerreißt der letzte Nebelschleier. An Stelle des Tannengehölzes
erscheint glitzernd im Strahle der aufgegangenen Sonne das
65 Knusperhäuschen am Ilsensteine. Links davon in einiger Entfernung
befindet sich ein Backofen, diesem rechts gegenüber ein großer Käfig.*]

GRETEL:

Bleib stehn! Bleib stehn!

HÄNSEL:

O Himmel, welch Wunder ist hier geschehn!
Nein, so was hab ich mein Tag nicht gesehn!

70 *[Beide blicken wie verzaubert auf das Knusperhäuschen.]*

GRETEL:

Wie duftet's von dorten,
o schau nur diese Pracht!
Von Kuchen und Torten...

HÄNSEL, GRETEL:

...ein Häuslein gemacht!

75 Mit Fladen und Torten
ist's hoch überdacht!
Die Fenster wahrhaftig
wie Zucker so blank,
Rosinen gar saftig
80 den Giebel entlang!
Und — traun!
Rings zu schaun
gar ein Lebkuchen-Zaun!
O herrlich Schlößchen,
85 wie bist du schmuck und fein!
Welch' Wald-Prinzeßchen
mag da wohl drinnen sein!
Ach, wär' doch zu Hause
die Wald-Prinzessin fein
90 sie lüde zum Schmause
bei Kuchen und Wein,
zum herrlichsten Schmause
uns beide freundlich ein!

HÄNSEL:

Alles bleibt still,
95 nichts regt sich da drinnen!
Komm, laß uns hineingehn!

GRETEL:

Bist du bei Sinnen?
Hänsel, wie magst du so dreist nur sein?
Wer weiß, wer da drin wohl
100 im Häuschen fein?

HÄNSEL:
Oh, sieh, nur sieh, wie das
Häuschen uns lacht!
Ha! Die Englein haben's uns hergebracht!

GRETEL:
Die Englein? Ja, so wird es wohl sein!

HÄNSEL:
105 Ja, Gretel, sie laden freundlich uns ein!
Komm, wir knuspern ein
wenig vom Häuschen!

HÄNSEL, GRETEL:
Komm, ja, knuspern wir,
wie zwei Nagemäuschen!

110 [Sie hüpfen Hand in Hand nach dem Hintergrunde und schleichen
dann vorsichtig auf den Zehen bis an das Häuschen. Nach einigem
Zögern bricht Hänsel ein Stückchen Kuchen heraus.]

Libretto by Adelheide Wette (sister of the composer), based
on a fairytale from the collection *Kinder- und Hausmärchen*
(1812–14) by the brothers Grimm

Opera for children by Engelbert Humperdinck, 1893

das **Knusperhäuschen** *gingerbread house* (from **knuspern** *to crunch,
nibble*); *1* das **Taumännchen** *Dew man*; *5* **reisen** *to travel*; *12* die **Flur**
field; **die Aue** *meadow*; *13* **wer munter** *whoever is cheerful*; *16* **drum auf** *so
get up*; *23* **lispeln** *to whisper*; *26* **dargebracht** *offered*; *30* **der
Siebenschläfer** *sleepy-head* (literally *dormouse*); *38* **kikeriki** *cock-a-doodle-
doo*; *52* **wallen** *to float*; **wogen** *to drift*; *53* **ward's** *it became* (archaic form of
es wurde); **mit einem Male** *all at once*; *54* **durchflossen** *penetrated*;
55 **sich neigen** *to descend*; *57* **gar** *very*; *63* **zerreißen** *to disperse*; das
Tannengehölz *clump of fir trees*; *65* **der Ilsenstein** (proper name), *the
witch's abode*; *75* **der Fladen** *round flat cake*; *76* **überdacht** *covered*;
78 **blank** *shiny*; *81* **traun** *to imagine* (contracted form of **trauen**);
83 **der Lebkuchen** *gingerbread*; *85* **schmuck** *neat*; *87* **mag da wohl
drinnen sein** *might be inside*; *90/93* **einladen** *to invite*; *92* **zum Schmause**
to the feast; *97* **Bist du bei Sinnen?** *Are you crazy?*; *98* **dreist** *bold*;
103 **hergebracht** *provided*; *109* das **Nagemäuschen** *nibbling mouse*;
111 **nach einigem Zögern** *after some hesitation*

138

Fidelio, oder Die eheliche Liebe

Leonore, disguised as Fidelio, has gone with Rocco the jailer into the dungeon where Florestan, her husband, is near to death.

2. Aufzug, 2. Auftritt

LEONORE:

Er erwacht!

ROCCO:

Er erwacht sagst du? Ohne Zweifel wird er wieder tausend Fragen an mich stellen. Ich muß allein mit ihm reden. *[nach einer kleinen Pause zu Florestan]* Nun, Ihr habt
5 wieder einige Augenblicke geruht?

FLORESTAN:

Geruht? Wie fände ich Ruhe?

LEONORE *[für sich]*:

Diese Stimme! — Wenn ich nur einen Augenblick sein Gesicht sehen könnte.

FLORESTAN:

10 Werdet Ihr immer bei meinen Klagen taub sein, grausamer Mann?
[Mit den letzten Worten wendet er sein Gesicht gegen Leonore.]

LEONORE *[für sich]*:

Gott! Er ist's!

ROCCO:

Was verlangt Ihr denn von mir? Ich vollziehe die Befehle, die man mir gibt; das ist mein Amt, meine Pflicht.

FLORESTAN:

15 Sagt mir endlich einmal, wer ist Gouverneur dieses Gefängnisses?

ROCCO:

Der Gouverneur dieses Gefängnisses ist Don Pizarro.

FLORESTAN:

Pizarro! O schickt so bald als möglich nach Sevilla, fragt nach Leonore Florestan —

LEONORE:

20 Gott! Er ahnt nicht, daß sie jetzt sein Grab gräbt!

FLORESTAN:

Sagt ihr, daß ich hier in Ketten liege.

Fidelio
The three scenes, in which Providence is always present, show Fidelio
and Rocco digging the grave, Florestan in the dungeon, and Leonora and
Florestan reunited. (Fresco by Moritz von Schwind, 1804–71, in the
foyer of the Vienna Staatsoper.)

ROCCO:
Es ist unmöglich, sag ich Euch.

FLORESTAN:
Wenn ich verdammt bin, hier mein Leben zu enden, o so
laßt mich nicht langsam verschmachten.

LEONORE:
25 O Gott! Wer kann das ertragen?

FLORESTAN:
Aus Barmherzigkeit, gib mir nur einen Tropfen Wasser.
Das ist ja so wenig.

ROCCO:
Ich kann Euch nicht verschaffen, was Ihr verlangt. Alles
was ich Euch anbieten kann, ist ein Restchen Wein, das
30 ich in meinem Kruge habe. — Fidelio!

LEONORE [*den Krug in größter Eile bringend*]:
Da ist er! Da ist er!

FLORESTAN [*Leonore betrachtend*]:
Wer ist das?

ROCCO:

Mein Schließer und in wenigen Tagen mein Eidam. *[Er reicht Florestan den Krug.]* Trinkt! Es ist freilich nur wenig
35 Wein, aber ich gebe ihn Euch gern. *[zu Leonore]* Du bist ja ganz in Bewegung?

LEONORE *[in größter Verwirrung]*:

Wer sollte es nicht sein? Ihr selbst, Meister Rocco —

ROCCO:

Es ist wahr, der Mensch hat so eine Stimme ...

LEONORE:

Jawohl, sie dringt in die Tiefe des Herzens.

FLORESTAN:

40 Euch werde Lohn in bessern Welten,
Der Himmel hat Euch mir geschickt.
O Dank! Ihr habt mich süß erquickt;
Ich kann die Wohltat nicht vergelten.

ROCCO *[leise zu Leonore, die er beiseite zieht]*:

Ich labt' ihn gern, den armen Mann,
45 Es ist ja bald um ihn getan.

LEONORE *[für sich]*:

Wie heftig pochet dieses Herz,
Es wogt in Freud' und scharfem Schmerz.

FLORESTAN *[für sich]*:

Bewegt seh ich den Jüngling hier,
Und Rührung zeigt auch dieser Mann.
50 O Gott, du sendest Hoffnung mir,
Daß ich sie noch gewinnen kann.

LEONORE:

Die hehre, bange Stunde winkt,
Die Tod mir oder Rettung bringt.

ROCCO:

Ich tu, was meine Pflicht gebeut,
55 Doch haß ich alle Grausamkeit.

LEONORE *[leise zu Rocco, indem sie ein Stück Brot aus der Tasche zieht]*:

Dies Stückchen Brot — ja, seit zwei Tagen
Trag ich es immer schon bei mir.

ROCCO:

Ich möchte gern, doch sag ich dir,
Das hieße wirklich zu viel wagen.

LEONORE:
60 Ach! *[schmeichelnd]*
Ihr labtet gern den armen Mann.

ROCCO:
Das geht nicht an, das geht nicht an.

LEONORE:
Es ist ja bald um ihn getan.

ROCCO:
So sei es — ja, so sei's — du kannst es wagen.

LEONORE:
65 Da, nimm Brot — du armer Mann!

FLORESTAN:
O Dank dir, Dank! O Dank! O Dank!
Euch werde Lohn in bessern Welten,
Der Himmel hat Euch mir geschickt.
O Dank! Ihr habt mich süß erquickt,
70 Ich kann die Wohltat nicht vergelten.

LEONORE:
Der Himmel schicke Rettung dir,
Dann wird mir hoher Lohn gewährt.

ROCCO:
Mich rührte oft dein Leiden hier,
Doch Hilfe war mir streng verwehrt.
75 Ich labt' ihn gern, den armen Mann,
Es ist ja bald um ihn getan.

LEONORE:
O mehr, als ich ertragen kann!

FLORESTAN:
O daß ich Euch nicht lohnen kann! *[Er ißt das Brot.]*

ROCCO:
Alles ist bereit. Ich gehe, das Signal zu geben.

LEONORE:
80 O Gott, gib mir Mut und Stärke!

FLORESTAN:
Wo geht er hin? *[Rocco öffnet die Türen und gibt durch einen starken Pfiff das Zeichen.]* Ist das der Vorbote meines Todes?

LEONORE:
Nein, nein! Beruhige dich, lieber Gefangener.

FLORESTAN:
O meine Leonore! So soll ich dich nie wieder sehen?

LEONORE:

85 Mein ganzes Herz reißt mich zu ihm hin! *[zu Florestan]* Sei
ruhig, sag ich dir! Vergiß nicht, was du auch hören und
sehen magst, daß überall eine Vorsehung ist. — Ja, ja, es
gibt eine Vorsehung!

Libretto by Joseph Sonnleithner, 1766–1835, based on
Bouilly's *Léonore, ou L'amour conjugal*

Opera by Ludwig van Beethoven, 1805

4 **Ihr** *you* (archaic form of polite address in the singular); 6 **fände** *I might
find* (imperfect subjunctive); 7 **für sich** *aside*; 10 **die Klage** *complaint*;
14 **das Amt** *job*; 18 **fragen nach** *to enquire after*; 20 **ahnen** *to suspect*;
23 **verdammen** *to condemn*; 24 **verschmachten** *to languish*; 29 **ein
Restchen** *a little*; 33 **der Schließer** *jailer*; **der Eidam** *son-in-law*; 36 **in
Bewegung sein** *to be agitated*; 37 **Wer sollte es nicht sein?** *Who would not
be?*; 39 **dringen** *to penetrate*; 40 **euch werde Lohn** *may you be rewarded*;
43 **vergelten** *to repay*; 44 **ich labt' ihn gern** *I would gladly refresh him*;
45 **um ihn getan** *over for him*; 47 **wogen** *to heave*; 49 **die Rührung**
emotion; 52 **hehr** *sublime*; 54 **gebeut** *demands* (archaic form of the
third person singular of **gebieten**); 59 **das hieße** *that would be*; 62 **das
geht nicht an** *that is out of the question*; 72 **gewähren** *to grant*;
74 **verwehren** *to deny*; 82 **der Vorbote** *forewarning*; 86 **was auch**
whatever; 88 **die Vorsehung** *providence*

Lieder eines fahrenden Gesellen

I

Wenn mein Schatz Hochzeit macht,
Hab ich meinen traurigen Tag!
Geh ich in mein Kämmerlein, dunkles Kämmerlein!
Weine! Weine! um meinen Schatz, um meinen lieben Schatz!

5 *Blümlein blau! Verdorre nicht!*
Vöglein süß! Du singst auf grüner Heide!
Ach! Wie ist die Welt so schön! Ziküth!

Singet nicht, blühet nicht! Lenz ist ja vorbei!
Alles Singen ist nun aus!

10 Des Abends, wenn ich schlafen geh,
    Denk ich an mein Leid, an meine Leide!

1 **der Schatz** *treasure, sweetheart*; *4* **um** *for*; *7* **Ziküth!** onomatopoeic word illustrating bird sound; *8* **der Lenz** *spring*; *9* **ist aus** *is over*

II

    Ging heut morgen übers Feld,
    Tau noch auf den Gräsern hing;
    Sprach zu mir der lustge Fink:
    'Ei, du! Gelt? Guten Morgen! Ei gelt? Du!
 5 Wird's nicht eine schöne Welt? schöne Welt!?
    Zink! Zink! schön und flink!
    Wie mir doch die Welt gefällt!'

    Auch die Glockenblum am Feld
    Hat mir lustig, guter Ding
10 Mit dem Glöckchen klinge, kling,
    Ihren Morgengruß geschellt:
    'Wird's nicht eine schöne Welt? schöne Welt!?
    Kling! Kling! Schönes Ding!
    Wie mir doch die Welt gefällt! Hei-a!'

15 Und da fing im Sonnenschein
    Gleich die Welt zu funkeln an;
    Alles, alles, Ton und Farbe gewann im Sonnenschein!
    Blum und Vogel, groß und klein!
    Guten Tag, guten Tag! Ist's nicht eine schöne Welt?
20 Ei du! Gelt!? Schöne Welt!?

    Nun fängt auch mein Glück wohl an?!
    Nein! Nein! Das ich mein, mir nimmer blühen kann!

3 **der Fink** *chaffinch*; *4* **Ei, du! Gelt?** *Hi you! How are you?*; *6* **Zink!** onomatopoeic word illustrating bird sound; **flink** *nimble*; *9/11* **hat geschellt** *has rung out*; *9* **guter Ding** *in good spirits*; *15/16* **anfangen** *to begin*; *16* **gleich** *at once*; *17* **Ton und Farbe gewinnen** *to acquire tone and colour*; *22* **meinen** *to think*

III

Ich hab ein glühend Messer, ein Messer in meiner Brust.
O weh! o weh!
Das schneidt so tief in jede Freud und jede Lust, so tief!
Ach, was ist das für ein böser Gast!
5 Nimmer hält er Ruh, nimmer hält er Rast,
Nicht bei Tag, noch bei Nacht, wenn ich schlief!
O weh! o weh!

Wenn ich in den Himmel seh,
Seh ich zwei blaue Augen stehn!
10 O weh! o weh!
Wenn ich im gelben Felde geh,
Seh ich von fern das blonde Haar im Winde wehn!
O weh! o weh!

Wenn ich aus dem Traum auffahr
15 Und höre klingen ihr silbern Lachen,
O weh! o weh!
Ich wollt, ich läg auf der schwarzen Bahr,
Könnt nimmer die Augen aufmachen!

3 **die Lust** *pleasure*; 4 **was für ein** *what sort of*; 14 **auffahren** *to wake with a start*; 17 **ich läg** *if I were lying* (subjunctive); **die Bahr** *bier*; 18 **könnt** *could* (subjunctive)

IV

Die zwei blauen Augen von meinem Schatz,
Die haben mich in die weite Welt geschickt.
Da mußt ich Abschied nehmen vom allerliebsten Platz!
O Augen, blau! Warum habt ihr mich angeblickt?
5 Nun hab ich ewig Leid und Grämen!

Ich bin ausgegangen in stiller Nacht,
In stiller Nacht wohl über die dunkle Heide.
Hat mir niemand ade gesagt, ade!
Mein Gesell war Lieb und Leide!
10 Auf der Straße stand ein Lindenbaum,
Da hab ich zum erstenmal im Schlaf geruht!

Unter dem Lindenbaum der hat
Seine Blüten über mich geschneit,
Da wußt ich nicht, wie das Leben tut,
15 *War alles, ach alles wieder gut!*
Alles! Alles! Lieb und Leid!
Und Welt und Traum!

2 **die** *they*; 3 **mußt** *must* (contracted form of the imperfect **mußte**); 5 **das Grämen** *grieving*; 8 **ade** *adieu*; 11 **zum erstenmal** *for the first time*; 12 **der** *which* (relative pronoun); 14 **wie das Leben tut** *life's ways*

Texts by the composer, based on anonymous poems from the anthology *Des Knaben Wunderhorn* (1805–8), edited by Achim von Arnim and Clemens Brentano

Songs for voice and orchestra by Gustav Mahler, 1898 (*Lieder eines fahrenden Gesellen*)

Wozzeck

Marie has been receiving the attentions of the Drum Major, and he has given her some earrings. While she is admiring herself, Wozzeck, a common soldier, comes home to her and their child. It is the earrings that first suggest to Wozzeck that Marie has been unfaithful to him. Some days later, convinced of her infidelity, Wozzeck takes Marie out of the town and stops by a pond.

2. Akt, 1. Szene: Mariens Stube

Marie sitzt mit ihrem Kind auf dem Schoß, hält ein Stückchen Spiegel in der Hand und besieht sich darin.

MARIE:

Was die Steine glänzen! Was sind's für welche? Was hat er gesagt? *[zu ihrem Buben, der sich bewegt hat]* Schlaf, Bub! Drück
5 die Augen zu, fest. *[Das Kind versteckt die Augen hinter den Händen.]* Noch fester! Bleib so! Still, oder er holt dich! *[singt]*
    Mädel, mach's Lädel zu!
    's kommt ein Zigeunerbu'
    Führt dich an seiner Hand'
10   Fort ins Zigeunerland.

146

Wozzeck in Vienna, 1930
Playbill for the first performance of Berg's opera *Wozzeck* in his native city. After the Berlin première in 1925, *Wozzeck* enjoyed immense success in opera houses throughout Europe.

[*Marie besieht sich wieder im Spiegel.*] 'S ist gewiß Gold!
Unsereins hat nur ein Eckchen in der Welt und ein
Stückchen Spiegel. Und doch ich hab' einen so roten
Mund, als die großen Madamen mit ihren Spiegeln von
15 oben bis unten, und ihren schönen Herrn, die ihnen die
Hände küssen; aber ich bin nur ein armes Weibsbild! [*Das
Kind richtet sich auf.*] Still! Bub! Die Augen zu! [*blinkt mit dem
Spiegel*] Das Schlafengelchen, wie's an der Wand läuft.
Mach die Augen zu! Oder es sieht dir hinein, das du blind
20 wirst.
[*Wozzeck tritt herein, hinter Marie. Sie fährt plötzlich auf, mit den
Händen nach den Ohren.*]
WOZZECK:
Was hast du?
MARIE:
Nix!
WOZZECK:
25 Unter deinen Fingern glänzt's ja.
MARIE:
Ein Ohrringlein, hab's gefunden!
WOZZECK:
Ich hab' so was noch nicht gefunden, zwei auf einmal.
MARIE:
Bin ich ein schlecht Mensch?
WOZZECK:
'S ist gut Marie. — Was der Bub immer schläft. Greif' ihm
30 unter's Ärmchen, der Stuhl drückt ihn. Die hellen
Tropfen stehn ihm auf der Stirn; nichts als Arbeit unter
der Sonne, sogar Schweiß im Schlaf. Wir arme Leut! Da
ist wieder Geld, Marie, die Löhnung und was vom
Hauptmann und vom Doktor.
MARIE:
35 Gott vergelt's Franz.
WOZZECK:
Ich muß fort, Marie. Adies! [*ab*]
MARIE [*allein*]:
Ich bin doch ein schlecht Mensch. Ich könnt' mich
erstechen. Ach! was Welt? Geht doch Alles zum Teufel,
Mann und Weib und Kind!

3. Aufzug, 2. Szene: Waldweg am Teich

40 *Es dunkelt.*

MARIE:

Dort links geht's in die Stadt. 's ist noch weit. Komm schneller.

WOZZECK:

Du sollst da bleiben, Marie. Komm, setz' dich.

MARIE:

Aber ich muß fort.

WOZZECK:

45 Komm. Bist weit gegangen, Marie. Sollst dir die Füße nicht mehr wund laufen. 's ist still hier! Und so dunkel. Weißt noch, Marie, wie lang es jetzt ist, daß wir uns kennen?

MARIE:

Zu Pfingsten, drei Jahre.

WOZZECK:

50 Und was meinst, wie lang es noch dauern wird?

MARIE:

Ich muß fort.

WOZZECK:

Fürchst dich Marie? Und bist doch fromm? *[lacht]* Und gut! Und treu! Was du für süße Lippen hast, Marie! *[küßt sie]* Den Himmel gäb' ich drum und die Seligkeit, wenn ich

55 dich noch oft so küssen dürft! Aber ich darf nicht! Was zitterst?

MARIE:

Der Nachttau fällt.

WOZZECK *[flüstert vor sich hin]*:

Wer kalt ist, den friert nicht mehr! Dich wird beim Morgentau nicht frieren.

MARIE:

60 Was sagst du da?

WOZZECK:

Nix

MARIE:

Wie der Mond rot aufgeht!

WOZZECK:

Wie ein blutig Eisen! *[zieht ein Messer]*

MARIE:
Was zitterst? *[springt auf]* Was willst?

WOZZECK:

65 Ich nicht, Marie! Und kein Andrer auch nicht!

[Packt sie an und stößt ihr das Messer in den Hals.]

MARIE:

Hilfe!

WOZZECK *[beugt sich über sie]:*

Tot!

[Richtet sich scheu auf und stürzt geräuchlos davon.]

Libretto by the composer, adapted from the play *Woyzeck*, 1836, by Georg Büchner, 1813–37

Opera by Alban Berg, 1925

4 **der Bub** *lad* (south German); *5* **fest** *tight*; *7* **das Lädel** *shutter* (dialect form of **Laden**); *12* **unsereins** *the likes of us*; *16* **das Weibsbild** *wench*; *21* **auffahren** *to start*; *24* **nix** *nothing* (dialect form of **nichts**); *33* **die Löhnung** *wage*; *35* **Gott vergelt's** *God bless*; *36* **ab** *exit*; *45/46* **sich die Füße wund laufen** *to become footsore*; *54* **die Seligkeit** *salvation*; *63* **blutig** *blood-red*; *65* **Und kein Andrer auch nicht!** *Then no other either!*; *66* **anpacken** *to grab*; *69* **scheu** *cautiously*; **stürzen** *to dash*

Kompositionen für die Laute

In this introduction of 1921 to the lute compositions of J. S. Bach the writer explains the change in lute notation from tablature to the two-stave system initiated by Bach.

Die Quellen der Kompositionen Johann Sebastian Bachs für die Laute lassen sich in drei Arten gliedern: 1. Autographe, 2. originaltreue Kopien, 3. Bearbeitungen von fremder Hand.

5 Autograph sind: Praeludium mit Fuge (Es-Dur), Suite III (g-Moll) und Suite IV (E-Dur).

Kopien, die von zuverlässigen Abschreibern — Schülern oder Freunden Bachs — stammen: Praeludium (c-Moll), Suite I (e-Moll) und Suite II (c-Moll).

10 Bearbeitungen von fremder Hand besitzen wir in Form von Lautentabulaturen (französische Tabulaturnotierung)

aus der nachbachschen Zeit. Auf der Stadtbibliothek in Leipzig befinden sich drei derartige Tabulaturen. Sie stellen Bearbeitungen der Suiten II und III und der Einzel-
15 fuge dar.

In der Notierungsweise stimmen die Autographe und Kopien der Lautenkompositionen Bachs fast durchweg überein: sie benutzen den Diskant- und Baßschlüssel — also ein Doppelsystem nach Cembaloart. Das muß für die
20 Zeit zwischen 1700–1750, in welchen Jahren Bachs Lautenkompositionen entstanden sind, als etwas sehr Auffallendes bezeichnet werden. Damals bedienten sich die Lautenisten aller Länder der von Denis Gaultier (um 1600) festgelegten neufranzösischen Lautentabulatur. Wir
25 können den Grund für diese sicherlich beabsichtigte Sonderart der Lautennotierung Bachs nur darin finden, daß er einesteils den nicht mehr fernen Untergang der Tabulaturen vorausahnte und durch die Anwendung einer neuen Normalnotierung seine Lautenstücke vor
30 dem frühzeitigen Veralten und Vergessenwerden bewahren wollte — und daß er anderteils die Mehrzahl seiner Stücke je nach Wahl für die Laute oder das Cembalo bestimmt hat, wie er ja auch viele Stücke für Klavier oder Orgel geschrieben. Einen Fingerzeig in der
35 zuletzt angedeuteten Richtung gibt uns der autographe Titel des Praeludium mit Fuge (Es-Dur), in welchem es heißt: 'Prelude pour la Luth o Cembal'.

Hans Dagobert Bruger

2 **sich gliedern lassen** *to be divided*; **die Art** *sort*; 3 **die Bearbeitung** *arrangement*; 7 **zuverlässig** *reliable*; 12 **aus der nachbachschen Zeit** *from the period after Bach*; 13 **derartig** *such*; 14/15 **darstellen** *to show*; 16/18 **übereinstimmen** *to correspond*; 18 **Diskant(schlüssel)** *treble clef*; 8 **das Doppelsystem** *double stave*; 21 **entstehen** *to originate*; 21/22 **etwas sehr Auffallendes bezeichnet werden** *be considered something very remarkable*; 24 **festgelegt** *established*; 25 **der Grund** *reason*; 27 **einesteils** *on the one hand*; 28 **vorausahnen** *to anticipate*; **die Anwendung** *use*; 30 **Veralten und Vergessenwerden** *becoming outdated and forgotten*; 31 **anderteils** *on the other hand*; 33 **bestimmen** *to intend*; 34 **der Fingerzeig** *indication*

151

Brief Mendelssohns an seine Mutter

On 19 July 1842 Mendelssohn wrote a long letter to his mother giving an enthusiastic account of music making at Buckingham Palace with Queen Victoria and Prince Albert.

Darauf bat ich aber, der Prinz möchte mir lieber erst etwas vorspielen, ich wollte damit in Deutschland recht renommieren; und da spielte er mir einen Choral auswendig mit Pedal so hübsch und rein und ohne
5 Fehler, daß mancher Organist sich was daraus nehmen konnte, und die Königin setzte sich daneben und hörte sehr vergnügt zu; darauf sollte ich spielen und fing meinen Chor aus dem Paulus 'Wie lieblich sind die Boten' an. Noch ehe ich den ersten Vers ausgespielt hatte, fingen
10 sie beide an, den Chor ordentlich mitzusingen, und der Prinz Albert zog mir nun so geschickt die Register zum ganzen Stück, erst eine Flöte dazu, dann beim Forte voll, beim C-Dur alles, dann machte er mit den Registern solch ein exzellentes Diminuendo und so fort bis zum Ende des
15 Stücks, und das alles auswendig, daß ich wirklich ganz entzückt davon war und mich herzlich freute.

Dann kam der Erbprinz von Gotha dazu, und es wurde wieder konversiert, und unter anderem sagte die Königin, ob ich neue Lieder komponiert hätte, und sie sänge die
20 gedruckten sehr gern. 'Du solltest ihm mal eins vorsingen', sagte Prinz Albert. Die Prinzeß von Gotha war unterdes noch dazugekommen, und so gingen wir durch die Korridors und Zimmer bis zu dem Wohnzimmer der Königin, wo neben dem Klavier ein gewaltig dickes
25 Schaukelpferd stand und zwei große Vogelbauer und Bilder an den Wänden und schön gebundene Bücher auf den Tischen und Noten auf dem Klavier. Die Herzogin von Kent kam dazu, und während sie sprachen, krame ich ein wenig unter den Noten und finde mein allererstes
30 Liederheft darunter. Da bat ich nun natürlich, sie möchte was daraus wählen, und sie tat es sehr freundlich, und was wählte sie? *Schöner und schöner*, sang es ganz allerliebst rein, streng im Takt und recht nett im Vortrag; nur wenn es nach 'der Prosa Last und Müh' nach D
35 heruntergeht und harmonisch heraufkommt, geriet sie

Mendelssohn playing to Queen Victoria and Prince Albert
The composer visited Britain many times between 1829 and 1847. In 1842 he was received at Buckingham Palace by the Queen and the Prince Consort. (Painting by Carl Röhling, 1900-01.)

beide Male nach Dis, und weil ich's ihr beide Male angab,
nahm sie das letztemal richtig D, wo es freilich hätte Dis
sein müssen. Aber bis auf dies Versehen war es wirklich
allerliebst, und das letzte lange G habe ich von keiner
40 Dilettantin besser und reiner und natürlicher gehört. Nun
mußte ich bekennen, daß Fanny das Lied gemacht hatte,
und sie bitten, mir auch eins von den wirklich Meinigen
zu singen. 'Wenn ich ihr recht helfen wollte, täte sie es
gern', sagte sie und sang: *Laß dich nur nichts dauern*,
45 wirklich ganz fehlerlos und mit wundernettem, gefühltem
Ausdruck. Ich dachte, zuviel Komplimente müsse man
bei solcher Gelegenheit nicht machen, und dankte bloß
sehr vielmal; als sie aber sagte: 'O, wenn ich mich nur
nicht so geängstigt hätte, ich habe sonst einen recht
50 langen Atem', da lobte ich sie recht tüchtig und mit dem
besten Gewissen von der Welt, denn gerade die Stelle mit
dem langen C am Schluß hatte sie so gut gemacht und die
nächsten drei Noten auf einem Atem herangebunden, wie
man es selten hört, und darum amüsierte mich's doppelt,
55 daß sie selbst davon anfing.

Hierauf sang Prinz Albert: *Es ist ein Schnitter, der heißt
Tod*, und dann sagte er, ich müßte ihnen aber noch vor der
Abreise was spielen, und gab mir als Themen den Choral,
den er vorhin auf der Orgel gespielt hatte, und den
60 Schnitter. Wäre es nun wie gewöhnlich gegangen, so
hätte ich zum Schluß recht abscheulich schlecht
phantasieren müssen, denn so geht's mir fast immer,
wenn es recht gut gehen soll, und dann hätte ich nichts
als Ärger von dem ganzen Morgen mitgenommen. Aber
65 gerade als ob ich ein recht hübsches, frohes Andenken
ohne allen Verdruß davon behalten sollte, so gelang mir
das Phantasieren so gut wie selten; ich war recht frisch im
Zug und spielte lange und hatte selbst Freude daran; daß
ich außer den beiden Themen auch noch die Lieder nahm,
70 die die Königin gesungen hatte, versteht sich; aber es kam
alles so natürlich hinein, daß ich gerne gar nicht aufgehört
hätte; und sie folgten mir mit einem Verständnis und
einer Aufmerksamkeit, daß mir besser dabei zumute war
als jemals, wenn ich vor Zuhörern phantasierte.

Felix Mendelssohn, 1809–47

3 **renommieren** *to boast;* *5/6* **sich was daraus nehmen konnte** *could learn something from it;* *8* **aus dem Paulus** *from [the oratorio] 'St Paul';* *11* **die Register ziehen** *to pull the organ stops;* *17* **der Erbprinz** *crown prince;* *20* **gedruckt** *printed;* *25* **das Vogelbauer** *birdcage;* *28* **kramen** *to rummage about;* *33* **allerliebst rein** *delightfully pure;* **der Vortrag** *presentation;* *35* **harmonisch** *chromatically;* **geriet** *went down;* *38* **bis auf** *apart from;* *40* **die Dilettantin** *amateur;* *41* **bekennen** *to admit;* **Fanny** Mendelssohn's sister published six of her songs with those of her brother; *42* **von den Meinigen** *of my own;* *53* **herangebunden** *taken in;* *55* **daß sie selbst davon anfing** *that she mentioned it;* *56* **der Schnitter** *reaper;* *62* **phantasieren** *to improvise;* *67* **der Verdruß** *disappointment;* *67/68* **frisch im Zug** *in the mood;* *70* **es versteht sich** *it goes without saying;* *73* **daß mir besser dabei zumute war** *that I felt happier about it*

Versuch über die wahre Art das Clavier zu spielen

In this extract from his *Versuch über die wahre Art das Clavier zu spielen* ('Treatise on the true art of playing the clavier', 1753) C. P. E. Bach compares the benefits of the harpsichord and the clavichord for the keyboard player.

Man hat außer vielen Arten der Claviere, welche teils wegen ihrer Mängel unbekannt geblieben, teils noch nicht überall eingeführt sind, hauptsächlich zwei Arten, nämlich die Flügel und Clavicorde, welche bis hieher den
5 meisten Beifall erhalten haben. Jene braucht man insgemein zu starken Musicken, diese zum allein spielen.
   Jeder Clavierist soll einen guten Flügel und auch ein gutes Clavicord haben, damit er auf beiden allerlei Sachen abwechselnd spielen könne. Wer mit einer guten Art auf
10 dem Clavicord spielen kann, wird solches auch auf dem Flügel zuwege bringen können, aber nicht umgekehrt. Man muß also das Clavicord zur Erlernung des guten Vortrags und den Flügel, um die gehörige Kraft in die Finger zu kriegen, brauchen. Spielt man beständig auf
15 dem Clavicord, so wird man viel Schwierigkeiten

antreffen, auf dem Flügel fortzukommen. Man gewöhnt sich bei beständigem Spiel auf dem Clavicord an, die Tasten gar zu sehr zu schmeicheln. Man kann sogar mit der Zeit, wenn man bloß auf einem Clavicord spielt, die
20 Stärke aus den Fingern verlieren, die man vorher hatte. Spielt man beständig auf dem Flügel, so gewöhnt man sich an in einer Farbe zu spielen, und der unterschiedene Anschlag, welchen bloß ein guter Clavicord-Spieler auf dem Flügel herausbringen kann, bleibt verborgen, so
25 wunderbar es auch scheint, indem man glauben sollte, alle Finger müßten auf einerlei Flügel einerlei Ton herausbringen. Man kann gar leicht die Probe machen, und zwei Personen, wovon der eine ein gutes Clavicord spielt, der andere aber bloß ein Flügel-Spieler ist, auf dem
30 letzteren Instrument ein Stück mit einerlei Manieren kurz hinter einander spielen lassen, und hernach urteilen, ob sie beide einerlei Wirkung hervorgebracht haben.

C. P. E. Bach, 1714–88

1 **außer** *apart from*; **die Art** *sort*; *2* **der Mangel** *deficiency*; *4* **bis hieher** *up to now*; *5* **der Beifall** *acclaim*; **jene** *the former*; *6* **zu starken Musicken** *for ensembles*; **diese** *the latter*; *8* **allerlei** *all sorts*; *9* **die Art** *style*; *11* **zuwege bringen** *to manage*; *13* **der Vortrag** *touch*; **gehörig** *necessary*; *16* **antreffen** *to encounter*; *16/17* **sich gewöhnen an** *to be accustomed*; *18* **schmeicheln** *to caress*; *18/19* **mit der Zeit** *in time*; *19* **bloß** *only*; *22* **die Farbe** *tone, colour*; *24* **verborgen** *unattained*; *24/5* **so wunderbar es auch scheint** *however strange that may seem*; *26* **einerlei** *the same*; *30* **die Manieren** *embellishments*; *30/31* **kurz hinter einander** *one after another*; *32* **die Wirkung** *effect*

Die Bürgschaft

This offensively anti-Jewish review of the first performance of Kurt Weill's opera *Die Bürgschaft* appeared in the Nazi newspaper *Völkischer Beobachter* on 9 March 1932.

Die Städtische Oper Charlottenburg beabsichtigt, in der ersten Hälfte des März dem Deutschtum einen Schlag ins Gesicht zu versetzen, und zwar mit der Uraufführung

Bertolt Brecht and Kurt Weill
The writer and composer are pictured together in 1927 at the start of their five-year collaboration, which was to produce *Mahagonny*, *Die Dreigroschenoper* and *Happy End*. On 28 February 1933, the day after the Reichstag fire, Brecht left Germany. Weill and his wife, Lotte Lenya, left for Paris some months later and finally settled in America. Brecht returned to East Berlin in 1949.

einer neuen Kurt Weill-Oper *Die Bürgschaft*. Man sieht
5 also, in Berlin nimmt man es nicht sonderlich ernst, wenn
man sich neuerdings national gebärdet und eine Reihe
guter deutscher Stücke zur Aufführung bringt; im
geeigneten Moment läßt man dann doch einen
Komponisten zu Worte kommen, der die Frechheit hatte,
10 dem deutschen Volke Werke wie die *Dreigroschenoper* und
Aufstieg und Fall der Stadt Mahagonny zu bieten, von den
anderen minderwertigen Werken, die er geschrieben hat,
einmal abgesehen. Dieser Jude hat doch erleben müssen,
wie die zuletzt genannte Oper in Leipzig zu einem
15 Krach führte. Auch sein schändliches Machwerk *Die
Dreigroschenoper* ist überall abgelehnt worden.
Infolgedessen ist es unbegreiflich, daß ein Autor, der
durch und durch undeutsche Werke liefert, an einem mit
dem Gelde deutscher Steuerzahler unterstützten Theater
20 wieder zu Worte kommt! Möge sich Israel an diesem
neuen Opus Weills erbauen.

157

1 **Charlottenburg** (proper name), a district in Berlin; 2 **das Deutschtum** *Germany and the Germans*; 3 **versetzen** *to deal*; 4 **Die Bürgschaft** *The pledge*, this work is entitled 'The hostage' in English; 5 **ernst nehmen** *to take seriously*; 6 **sich gebärden** *to behave*; 8/9 **läßt man einen Komponisten zu Worte kommen** *a composer is allowed to perform*; 11/13 **einmal abgesehen von** *not to mention*; 13 **hat erleben müssen** *had to experience*; 14 **der Krach** *trouble*; 15 **das Machwerk** *shabby piece of work*; 18 **durch und durch** *thoroughly*; **liefern** *to produce*; 20/21 **sich erbauen an** *to be uplifted by*

Surabaya Johnny

Happy End, a musical play written in 1928–9, is set in Chicago before World War I. Lilian Holiday, a young Salvation Army girl, sings this seductive song in an attempt to win over the gangster Bill and prevent him from taking part in a robbery.

Ich war jung, Gott, erst sechzehn Jahre
Du kamest von Burma herauf
Du sagtest, ich solle mit dir gehen
Du kämest für alles auf
5 *Ich fragte nach deiner Stellung*
Du sagtest so wahr ich hier steh
Du hättest zu tun mit der Eisenbahn
Und nicht zu tun mit der See.
Du sagtest viel, Johnny
10 *Kein Wort war wahr, Johnny*
Du hast mich betrogen, Johnny
Zur ersten Stund.
Ich hasse dich so, Johnny
Wie du da stehst und da grinst, Johnny
15 *Nimm doch die Pfeife aus dem Maul, du Hund!*
Surabaya Johnny, warum bist du so roh?
Surabaya Johnny, mein Gott, und ich liebe dich so.
Surabaya Johnny, warum bin ich nicht froh?
Du hast kein Herz Johnny, und ich liebe dich so.

20 *Zuerst war es immer Sonntag*
Das war bis ich mitging mit dir
Aber dann schon nach zwei Wochen

War dir nichts mehr recht an mir
Hinauf und hinab durch den Punjab
25 Den Fluß entlang bis zur See
Ich sehe schon aus im Spiegel
Wie eine Vierzigjährige!
Du wolltest nicht Liebe, Johnny
Du wolltest Geld, Johnny
30 Ich aber sah, Johnny
Nur auf deinen Mund
Du verlangtest alles, Johnny
Ich gab dir mehr Johnny
Nimm doch die Pfeife aus dem Maul, du Hund!
35 Surabaya Johnny ...

Ich hab es nicht beachtet,
Warum du den Namen hast
Doch an der ganzen langen Küste
Warst du ein bekannter Gast.
40 Eines Morgens in einem sixpencebett
Werd ich donnern hören die See
Und du gehst ohne etwas zu sagen
Und dein Schiff liegt unten am Kai
Du hast kein Herz, Johnny
45 Du bist ein Schuft, Johnny
Du gehst jetzt weg, Johnny
Sag mir den Grund
Ich liebe dich doch, Johnny
Wie am ersten Tag, Johnny
50 Nimm doch die Pfeife aus dem Maul, du Hund!
Surabaya Johnny ...

Bertolt Brecht, 1898–1956

Musical *Happy End* by Kurt Weill, 1928-9

---

4 **aufkommen für** *to take care of*; *12* **zur ersten Stund** *from the first moment*; *15* **das Maul** *mouth* (slang); *23* **war dir nichts mehr recht an mir** *nothing about me was right any more*; *26* **aussehen** *to look*; *36* **ich hab es nicht beachtet** *I did not consider*; *37* **warum du den Namen hast** *why you have this name*; *40* **in einem sixpencebett** *in a cheap bed*; *45* **der Schuft** *rogue*; *48* **doch** *nevertheless*

Pfeiferstuhl (musicians' gallery)
The musicians are playing (from left to right) treble shawm, cornett (?),
sackbut, tabor, shawm, sackbut and shawm, perhaps the instruments
Ludwig Senfl had in mind for his song *Mit Lust tritt ich an diesen Tanz*.
(Wall painting by Albrecht Dürer, 1471-1528, in the town hall of his
native city, Nürnberg.)

160

Mit Lust tritt ich an diesen Tanz

Mit Lust tritt ich an diesen Tanz,
ich hoff', mir werd' ein schöner Kranz
von einer hübschen Jungfraun fein:
drumb will ich ganz ihr eigen sein.

5 So tritt ich hie auf einen Stein:
Gott grüeß mir's zart Jungfräuelein,
und grüeß euch Gott allsambt geleich,
sie seien arm, arm oder reich!

Gott grüeß euch all in einer Gmein,
10 die Großen, darzue auch die Klein'n!
So ich ein' grüeß, die ander' nit,
so wär ich kein rechter Singer nit.

Anonymous, *c*1500

Song for voice and instruments by Ludwig Senfl (1486-1542), singer and later composer at the court of Maximilian I. The music was published posthumously in 1544.

1 **tritt ich an** *I join in* (archaic); *2* **mir werd'** *I shall get*; *4* **drumb** *for that*; **eigen** *own*; *5* **hie** *here*; *6* **Gott grüeß mir's** *I greet the*; *7* **grüeß euch Gott allsambt geleich** *I greet you one and all*; *8* **sie seien** *whether they be*; *9* **in einer Gmein** *gathered here*; *11* **So ich ein' grüeß** *if I greet one*; **nit** *not* (alternative form of **nicht**)

Gertrud

The opening of this novel contains a student's first impressions of life at a conservatory.

Endlich war ich frei, hatte die Schule hinter mir, den Eltern Lebewohl gesagt und ein neues Leben als Schüler des Konservatoriums in der Hauptstadt begonnen. Ich tat dies mit großen Erwartungen und war überzeugt
5 gewesen, ich würde in der Musikschule ein guter Schüler sein. Zu meinem peinlichen Erstaunen kam es aber anders. Ich hatte Mühe, dem Unterricht überall zu folgen, fand im Klavierunterricht, den ich jetzt nehmen mußte,

nur eine große Plage und sah bald mein ganzes Studium
10 wie einen unersteiglichen Berg vor mir liegen. Wohl war
ich nicht gesonnen nachzugeben, doch war ich enttäuscht
und befangen. Ich sah jetzt, daß ich bei aller
Bescheidenheit mich doch für eine Art von Genie gehalten
und die Mühen und Schwierigkeiten des Weges zur
15 Kunst bedenklich unterschätzt hatte. Dazu ward mir das
Komponieren gründlich verleidet, da ich jetzt bei der
geringsten Aufgabe nur Berge von Schwierigkeiten und
Regeln sah, meinem Gefühl durchaus mißtrauen lernte
und nicht mehr wußte, ob überhaupt ein Funke von
20 eigener Kraft in mir sei. So beschied ich mich, wurde klein
und traurig, ich tat meine Arbeit wenig anders, als ich sie
in meinem Kontor oder in einer andern Schule getan
hätte, fleißig und freudlos. Klagen durfte ich nicht, am
wenigsten in meinen Briefen nach Hause, sondern ging
25 den begonnenen Weg in stiller Enttäuschung weiter und
nahm mir vor, wenigstens ein ordentlicher Geiger zu
werden. Ich übte und übte, steckte Grobheiten und Spott
der Lehrer ein, sah manche andere, denen ich es nicht
zugetraut hätte, leicht vorwärtskommen und Lob ernten
30 und steckte meine Ziele immer niedriger. Denn auch mit
dem Geigen stand und ging es nicht so, daß ich darauf
hätte stolz sein können und etwa an ein Virtuosentum
denken dürfen. Es sah ganz so aus, als könne aus mir bei
gutem Fleiß zur Not ein brauchbarer Handwerker
35 werden, der in irgendeinem kleinen Orchester seine
bescheidene Geige ohne Schande und ohne Ehre spielt
und dafür sein Brot bekommt.

Hermann Hesse, 1877–1962

9 **die Plage** *torture*; 10 **unersteiglich** *insurmountable*; 11 **gesonnen**
inclined; **nachgeben** *to give in*; 12 **befangen** *diffident*; 13 **sich halten für** *to
consider oneself to be*; 15 **bedenklich** *seriously*; 15/16 **dazu ... verleidet** *and
I was thoroughly put off composition*; 20 **sich bescheiden** *to be content with
little*; 22 **das Kontor** *office*; 24/5 **weitergehen** *to continue*; 26 **sich
vornehmen** *to resolve* (with dative pronoun); **ordentlich** *reasonable*;
27/8 **einstecken** *to accept*; 29 **zutrauen** *to believe (somebody) capable of
(something)* (with dative); **vorwärtskommen** *to progress*; 30 **immer
niedriger** *lower and lower*; 32 **und etwa** *and for instance*; 34 **zur Not**
at a pinch

Der genügsame Liebhaber

This is the text of a cabaret song, one of the *Brettl Lieder* for voice and piano written in 1901 by Schoenberg. In that year Schoenberg moved from Vienna to Berlin to become director of music for the Überbrettl cabaret company.

Meine Freundin hat eine schwarze Katze
Mit weichem knisterndem Sammetfell,
Und ich, ich hab' eine blitzblanke Glatze,
Blitzblank und glatt und silberhell.

5 *Meine Freundin gehört zu den üppigen Frauen,*
Sie liegt auf dem Divan das ganze Jahr,
Beschäftigt das Fell ihrer Katze zu krauen,
Mein Gott ihr behagt halt das sammtweiche Haar.

Und komm' ich am Abend die Freundin besuchen,
10 *So liegt die Mieze im Schoße bei ihr,*
Und nascht mit ihr von dem Honigkuchen
Und schauert wenn ich leise ihr Haar berühr.

Und will ich mal zärtlich tun mit dem Schatze,
Und daß sie mir auch einmal 'Eitschi' macht,
15 *Dann stülp' ich die Katze auf meine Glatze,*
Dann streichelt die Freundin die Katze und lacht.

Hugo Salus, 1866–1929

Cabaret song for voice and piano by Arnold Schoenberg, 1901
(*Brettl Lieder*)

genügsam *modest, unassuming*; *2* knistern *to bristle*; der Sammet *velvet*; das Fell *fur*; *3* blitzblank *shining*; *7* beschäftigt *busy*; krauen *to fondle, stroke*; *8* ihr behagt halt *how it simply delights her* (behagen *to please, delight*, with the dative); *10* die Mieze *pussy*; *11* naschen *to nibble*; *12* schauern *to shudder*; berühren *to touch*; *13* zärtlich tun *to act tenderly*; der Schatz *treasure, sweetheart*; *14* Eitschi machen *to make a fuss of*; *15* stülpen *to clap on*

Biographische Notiz über Clara Wieck

Schumann describes the musical education of Clara Wieck. Schumann knew Clara when she was a young girl and he was taking piano lessons from her father.

Clara Wieck wurde am 13. September 1819 zu Leipzig geboren und erhielt von ihrem Vater, dem dortigen Klavierlehrer Friedrich Wieck, eine sorgfältige musikalische Erziehung. Ohne daß ihr früh sich entwickelndes Talent durch unmäßige Anstrengungen überzeitigt oder ihr ebenso zartes
5 als lebendiges Gefühl durch Ermüdung abgestumpft worden wäre, spielte sie dennoch schon in ihrem neunten Jahre mehrere Konzerte von Mozart und das a-Moll-Konzert von Hummel mit Orchesterbegleitung, aber nicht öffentlich, sondern nur vor auserwählten Kennern und teilnehmenden Freunden — und zwar auswendig.
10   Die Methode, nach der Clara Wieck von ihrem fünften Jahre an gebildet wurde, zeichnet sich unter andern Eigentümlichkeiten auch dadurch aus, daß der erste Unterricht ohne den Gebrauch der Noten gegeben wurde. Erst in ihrem siebenten Jahre, nachdem sie eine tüchtige Mechanik erlangt, Gehör und Taktgefühl ausgebildet, alle Tonarten und
15 Grundakkorde gelernt, Tonleitern in allen Richtungen geübt hatte und über 200 kleine eigens für sie geschriebene Etüden mit tadelloser Fertigkeit und Richtigkeit spielen und mit Leichtigkeit in alle Tonarten transponieren konnte, lernte sie bei solchen Vorkenntnissen natürlich mit ungemeiner Schnelligkeit die Noten kennen und lesen und spielte, mit Umgehung aller
20 Elementarübungsstücke, Etüden von Clementi, Cramer, Moscheles, Sonaten von Mozart, die leichteren und faßlicheren von Beethoven und andere Tonstücke, welche einesteils dem Geiste und der Phantasie eine tiefere, ernstere Richtung zu geben, und andererseits eine natürliche, regelrechte Applikatur zu fördern geeignet waren.

Robert Schumann, 1810–56

This is an example of the old style gothic type, see p. 245.

2 **dortig** there; 4 **die Anstrengung** demand; **überzeitigen** to spoil; 6 **abstumpfen** to dull; 8 **teilnehmend** sympathetic; 10 **nach der** according to which; 11 **sich auszeichnen** to distinguish oneself; 13 **die Mechanik** technique; 14 **ausbilden** to train; 16 **eigens** especially; **tadellos** faultless; 18 **die Vorkenntis** previous knowledge; 19 **mit Umgehung** avoiding; 21 **faßlich** accessible; 23 **die Phantasie** imagination; 25 **die Applikatur** technique; **fördern** to develop

Clara Wieck, 1819–96
The celebrated pianist, who made her début at the
age of nine, later became the wife of Robert
Schumann.

Vier letzte Lieder

These songs for high voice and orchestra were the last works of Richard Strauss. The order of composition, *Im Abendrot*, *Frühling*, *Beim Schlafengehen*, *September*, is not the usual one of performance. The collective title *Vier letzte Lieder* was given to the works by the publisher after the composer's death.

Frühling

In dämmrigen Grüften träumte ich lang
von deinen Bäumen und blauen Lüften,
von deinem Duft und Vogelsang.
Nun liegst du erschlossen in Gleiß und Zier

5 *von Licht übergossen wie ein Wunder vor mir.*
Du kennst mich wieder, du lockst mich zart.
Es zittert durch all meine Glieder
deine selige Gegenwart!

Hermann Hesse, 1877–1962

1 **dämmrig** *gloomy*; **die Gruft** *vault*; *4* **erschlossen** *opened up*; **Gleiß** *glistening* (noun formed from the verb **gleißen**); **die Zier** *adornment* (archaic form of **die Zierde**); *5* **von Licht übergossen** *bathed in light*

September

Der Garten trauert,
kühl sinkt in die Blumen der Regen.
Der Sommer schauert
still seinem Ende entgegen.

5 *Golden tropft Blatt um Blatt*
nieder vom hohen Akazienbaum,
Sommer lächelt erstaunt und matt
in den sterbenden Gartentraum.

Lange noch bei den Rosen
10 *bleibt er stehen, sehnt sich nach Ruh.*
Langsam tut er die (großen)*
müdgewordenen Augen zu.

Hermann Hesse, 1877–1962

3 **schauern** *to shiver*; 7 **matt** *weary*; 10 **stehenbleiben** *to remain*;
11/12 **zutun** *to close*; **die müdgewordenen Augen** *eyes that have become tired*
 * word omitted in the song

Beim Schlafengehen

Nun der Tag mich müd gemacht,
Soll mein sehnliches Verlangen
Freundlich die gestirnte Nacht
Wie ein müdes Kind empfangen.

5 *Hände, laßt von allem Tun,*
Stirn, vergiß du alles Denken,
Alle meine Sinne nun
Wollen sich in Schlummer senken.

Und die Seele unbewacht,
10 *Will in freien Flügen schweben,*
Um im Zauberkreis der Nacht
Tief und tausendfach zu leben.

Hermann Hesse, 1877–1962

2 **sehnlich** *ardent*; **das Verlangen** *longing*; 3 **die gestirnte Nacht** *the starry night* (subject of **soll empfangen**); 5 **laßt von allem Tun** *leave all your doing*; 9 **unbewacht** *unguarded*; 10 **in freien Flügen** *in free flight*; 11/12 **um zu leben** *(so as) to live*

Im Abendrot

Wir sind durch Not und Freude
gegangen Hand in Hand,
vom Wandern ruhen wir (heide)*
nun überm stillen Land.

5 *Rings sich die Täler neigen*
es dunkelt schon die Luft,
zwei Lerchen nur noch steigen
nachträumend in den Duft.

Tritt her und laß sie schwirren,
10 *bald ist es Schlafenszeit,*
daß wir uns nicht verirren
in dieser Einsamkeit.

O weiter, stiller Friede,
so tief im Abendrot.
15 *Wie sind wir wandermüde —*
ist dies etwa der Tod?

Joseph von Eichendorff, 1788–1857

1 **die Not** *distress*; *5* **rings** *all around*; **sich neigen** *to descend*; *8* **nachträumend** *dreaming*; *11* **sich verirren** *to go astray*; *16* **etwa** *perhaps*
* word omitted in the song

Songs for voice and orchestra by Richard Strauss, 1948
(*Vier letzte Lieder*)

Die Tagebücher

In 1870, Cosima describes in her diary the first Christmas after her
marriage to Wagner. On the morning of 25 December, her 33rd
birthday, she woke to the music of the *Tribschen Idyll*, which Wagner
had composed as a birthday gift. This work was later renamed
Siegfried Idyll.

Freitag 23ten Nichts zu berichten als Weihnachtsvor-
bereitungen. Ich fahre zur Stadt im Schlitten und kehre
halb erfroren heim. Abends putze ich den Baum aus.
Die Kinder arbeiten heimlich. Alles in großer Spannung.
5 *Samstag 24ten* Mein Tag gehört der Aufstellung der
Sachen, die ich mit Wehmut besorge; Bericht über unsre
Leute, in Pau gefangen und verhungernd, beherrscht
meine Stimmung, auch gedenke ich Hans! Um fünf Uhr
bringt R. Pr. Nietzsche von der Stadt mit, um 7 Uhr
10 zünden wir an. Es ist das erste Weihnachten, an welchem
ich R. nichts beschere und nichts von ihm erhalte — und
so ist es recht. Eine Depesche von Dr. Sulzer meldet, daß
er R.'s Einladung annimmt und morgen zu Mittag von
Bern herüberkommt. Alles ist zufrieden und froh. — Die
15 Kinder selig!

Richard Wagner with his second wife Cosima
Cosima, the daughter of Liszt, was formerly married to the conductor
Hans von Bülow, who conducted the first performances of *Tristan und
Isolde* (1865) and *Die Meistersinger von Nürnberg* (1868). Wagner and
Cosima were married in 1870.

Sonntag 25ten Von diesem Tag, meine Kinder, kann ich
euch nichts sagen, nichts von meinen Empfindungen,
nichts von meiner Stimmung, nichts, nichts. Dürr und
trocken will ich euch nur sagen, was geschah: Wie ich
20 aufwachte, vernahm mein Ohr einen Klang, immer voller
schwoll er an, nicht mehr im Traum durfte ich mich
wähnen, Musik erschallte, und welche Musik! Als sie
verklungen, trat R. mit den fünf Kindern zu mir ein und
überreichte mir die Partitur des 'Symphonischen
25 Geburtstagsgrußes' — in Tränen war ich, aber auch das
ganze Haus; auf der Treppe hatte R. sein Orchester
gestellt und so unser Tribschen auf ewig geweiht! Die
Tribscher Idylle so heißt das Werk. — Um Mittag kam Dr.
Sulzer, der bedeutendste wohl unter R.'s Freunden! Nach
30 dem Frühstück stellte das Orchester sich wieder ein, und
in der unteren Wohnung ertönte nun die Idylle wieder, zu
unserer aller Erschütterung; darauf Lohengrin's Brautzug,
das Septett von Beethoven, und zum Schluß noch einmal
die nie genug Gehörte! — Nun begriff ich R.'s heimliches
35 Arbeiten, nun auch des guten Richter's Trompete (er
schmetterte das Siegfried-Thema prachtvoll und hatte
eigens dazu Trompete gelernt), die ihm viele Ermahnun-
gen von mir zugezogen hat. 'Laß mich sterben', rief ich R.
zu. 'Es war leichter, für mich zu sterben als für mich zu
40 leben', erwiderte er mir.

Cosima Wagner, 1837–1930

3 **ausputzen** *to decorate*; *7* **Pau** (proper name) a town in France; *8* **Hans**
(proper name) Hans von Bülow, Cosima's former husband; *9* **R.** Richard
Wagner; **Pr.** *Professor*; *11* **bescheren** *to give a Christmas present*; *18* **dürr**
plainly; *21* **anschwellen** *to grow louder*; *21/2* **sich wähnen** *to imagine
oneself*; *27* **Tribschen** (proper name), the Wagners' villa near Lucerne,
Switzerland; *30* **sich einstellen** *to assemble*; *32* **die Erschütterung** *great
emotion*; **der Brautzug** *wedding procession*; *35* **Richter** (proper name),
Hans Richter, conductor; *36* **schmettern** *to blare out*; *37* **eigens
dazu** *especially for that purpose*; *37/8* **die Ermahnung** *admonishment*;
38 **zuziehen** *to earn*

Lebenserinnerungen

Louis Spohr the German composer, violinist and conductor went to Vienna and became acquainted with Beethoven. In this extract from his memoirs Spohr gives his impressions of Beethoven as a conductor. It is 1814, the year in which the revised version of *Fidelio* was performed in Vienna.

Nach meiner Ankunft in Wien suchte ich Beethoven sogleich auf, fand ihn aber nicht und ließ deshalb meine Karte zurück. Ich hoffte nun, ihn in einer der musikalischen Gesellschaften zu finden, zu denen ich häufig
5 eingeladen wurde, erfuhr aber bald, daß Beethoven sich, seitdem seine Taubheit so zugenommen, daß er Musik nicht mehr deutlich und im Zusammenhange hören könne, von allen Musikpartien zurückziehe und überhaupt sehr menschenscheu geworden sei. Ich versuchte
10 es daher nochmals mit einem Besuche; doch wieder vergebens. Endlich traf ich ihn ganz unerwartet in dem Speisehause, wohin ich jeden Mittag mit meiner Frau zu gehen pflegte. Ich hatte nun schon Konzert gegeben und zweimal mein Oratorium aufgeführt. Die Wiener Blätter
15 hatten günstig darüber berichtet. Beethoven wußte daher von mir, als ich mich vorstellte, und begrüßte mich ungewöhnlich freundlich. Wir setzten uns zusammen an einen Tisch, und Beethoven wurde sehr gesprächig, was die Tischgesellschaft sehr verwunderte, da er gewöhnlich
20 düster und wortkarg vor sich hinstarrte. Es war aber eine sauere Arbeit, sich ihm verständlich zu machen, da man so laut schreien mußte, daß es im dritten Zimmer zu hören war. Beethoven kam nun öfter in dieses Speisehaus und besuchte mich auch in meiner Wohnung. So wurden
25 wir bald gute Bekannte. Beethoven war ein wenig derb, um nicht zu sagen roh; doch blickte ein ehrliches Auge unter den buschigen Augenbrauen hervor.

Beethovens *Fidelio*, der 1804 oder 1805 unter ungünstigen Verhältnissen (es war die Zeit der Besetzung Wiens
30 durch die Franzosen) einen sehr geringen Erfolg gehabt hatte, wurde jetzt von den Regisseuren des Kärntnertortheaters wieder hervorgesucht und neu in Szene gesetzt. Beethoven hatte sich bewegen lassen, eine neue Ouver-

türe (die in E), ein Lied für den Kerkermeister und die große
35 Arie für Fidelio (mit den obligaten Hörnern) nachträglich
dazu zu schreiben, auch einige Veränderungen vorge-
nommen. In dieser neuen Gestalt machte nun die Oper
großes Glück und erlebte eine lange Reihe zahlreich
besuchter Aufführungen. Der Komponist wurde am
40 ersten Abend mehrere Male herausgerufen und war nun
wieder der Gegenstand allgemeinster Aufmerksamkeit.
Diesen günstigen Augenblick benutzten seine Freunde,
um für ihn ein Konzert im großen Redoutensaale zu
veranstalten, in welchem die neuesten Kompositionen
45 Beethovens zur Aufführung kommen sollten. Alles, was
geigen, blasen und singen konnte, wurde zur Mitwirkung
eingeladen, und es fehlte von den bedeutenden Künstlern
Wiens auch nicht einer. Ich und mein Orchester hatten
uns natürlich auch angeschlossen, und so sah ich Beetho-
50 ven zum ersten Male dirigieren. Soviel ich auch hatte
davon erzählen hören, so überraschte es mich doch in
hohem Grade. Beethoven hatte sich angewöhnt, dem
Orchester die Ausdruckszeichen durch allerlei sonderbare
Körperbewegungen anzudeuten. So oft ein Sforzando
55 vorkam, riß er beide Arme, die er vorher auf der Brust
kreuzte, mit Vehemenz auseinander. Bei dem Piano
bückte er sich nieder, und um so tiefer, je schwächer er es
wollte. Trat dann ein Crescendo ein, so richtete er sich
nach und nach wieder auf und sprang beim Eintritte des
60 Forte hoch in die Höhe. Auch schrie er manchmal, um die
Forte noch zu verstärken, mit hinein, ohne es zu wissen!

Louis Spohr, 1784–1859

4 **die Gesellschaft** *society*; 5 **erfahren** *to learn*; 6 **zunehmen** *to increase*;
5/8 **sich zurückziehen** *to withdraw*; 7 **im Zusammenhange** *as a whole*;
12/13 **zu gehen pflegte** *used to go*; 14 **die Wiener Blätter** *the Vienna
newspapers*; 20 **wortkarg** *taciturn*; 21 **sauer** *miserable*; 29 **die Besetzung**
occupation; 31 **der Regisseur** *director*; 32 **hervorsuchen** *to bring out*;
33 **sich bewegen lassen** *to be persuaded*; 35 **nachträglich** *subsequently*;
36/7 **vornehmen** *to carry out*; 38/9 **zahlreich besucht** *well attended*;
43 **der Redoutensaal** *ballroom*; 48 **auch nicht einer** *not even one*;
50 **soviel auch** *however much*; 57 **um so tiefer, je schwächer** *the lower,
the softer*; 59 **nach und nach** *gradually*

Arnold Schoenberg
A friend of Kokoschka and Kandinsky, Schoenberg was himself a
painter and exhibited with the 'Blaue Reiter' group. (Watercolour, 1917,
by the Austrian expressionist painter Egon Schiele, 1890–1918.)

Verklärte Nacht

> *Zwei Menschen gehn durch kahlen, kalten Hain;*
> *der Mond läuft mit, sie schaun hinein.*
> *Der Mond läuft über hohe Eichen*
> *kein Wölkchen trübt das Himmelslicht,*
> 5 *in das die schwarzen Zacken reichen.*
> *Die Stimme eines Weibes spricht:*
>
> *Ich trag ein Kind, und nit von Dir*
> *ich geh in Sünde neben Dir.*
> *Ich hab mich schwer an mir vergangen.*
> 10 *Ich glaubte nicht mehr an ein Glück*
> *und hatte doch ein schwer Verlangen*
> *nach Lebensinhalt, nach Mutterglück*
> *und Pflicht; da hab ich mich erfrecht,*

da ließ ich schaudernd mein Geschlecht
15 von einem fremden Mann umfangen,
und hab mich noch dafür gesegnet.
Nun hat das Leben sich gerächt:
nun bin ich Dir, o Dir begegnet.

Sie geht mit ungelenkem Schritt.
20 Sie schaut empor; der Mond läuft mit.
Ihr dunkler Blick ertrinkt in Licht.
Die Stimmes eines Mannes spricht:

Das Kind, das Du empfangen hast,
sei Deiner Seele keine Last,
25 o sieh, wie klar das Weltall schimmert!
Es ist ein Glanz um Alles her,
Du treibst mit mir auf kaltem Meer,
doch eine eigne Wärme flimmert
von Dir in mich, von mir in Dich.
30 Die wird das fremde Kind verklären
Du wirst es mir, von mir gebären;
Du hast den Glanz in mich gebracht,
Du hast mich selbst zum Kind gemacht.

Er faßt sie um die starken Hüften.
35 Ihr Atem küßt sich in den Lüften.
Zwei Menschen gehn durch hohe, helle Nacht.

Richard Dehmel, 1863–1920

String sextet by Arnold Schoenberg, 1899, based on the poem; arranged for string orchestra, 1917; revised 1943

verklärte Nacht *transfigured night*; *1* **der Hain** *grove*; *2* **läuft mit** *moves with (them)*; **schaun** *to look* (contraction of **schauen**); *4* **trüben** *to darken*; *5* **in das** *into which*; **die schwarzen Zacken** *the black treetops*; *7* **nit** *not* (alternative form of **nicht**); *9* **Ich hab mich schwer an mir vergangen.** *I have severely wronged myself.*; *10* **das Glück** *happiness*; *12* **der Lebensinhalt** *meaning of life*; *13* **sich erfrechen** *to dare*; *14/15* **ließ ich mein Geschlecht umfangen** *I let my body be embraced*; *16* **hab mich noch dafür gesegnet** *and have been blessed*; *19* **ungelenk** *awkward*; *21* **ertrinkt in Licht** *is drowned in light*; *24* **sei** *let it be* (present subjunctive); *25* **das Weltall** *universe*; *28* **eine eigne Wärme** *a particular warmth*; *33* **du hast den Glanz in mich gebracht** *you have caused an inner light to glow in me*

Die Zauberflöte

Papageno has a padlock on his mouth, as a punishment for lying. The Three Ladies, thinking he has learnt his lesson, take off the padlock. They present Tamino with a magic flute, which will protect him on his journey to Sarastro's castle. Papageno, who is to accompany Tamino, is given a glockenspiel.

1. Aufzug, 8. Auftritt

PAPAGENO: [deutet traurig auf das Schloß am Munde]:
Hm, hm, hm, hm.

TAMINO:
Der Arme kann von Strafe sagen,
denn seine Sprache ist dahin.

PAPAGENO:
5 Hm, hm, hm, hm.

TAMINO:
Ich kann nichts tun, als dich beklagen,
weil ich zu schwach zu helfen bin.

[die Drei Damen, die Vorigen]
1. DAME [zu Papageno]:
10 Die Königin begnadigt dich,
Erläßt die Strafe dir durch mich.
[Sie nimmt ihm das Schloß vom Munde.]

PAPAGENO:
Nun plaudert Papageno wieder.

2. DAME:
Ja, plaud're! Lüge nur nicht wieder!

PAPAGENO:
15 Ich lüge nimmermehr. Nein! Nein!

DIE 3 DAMEN:
Dies Schloß soll deine Warnung sein!

PAPAGENO:
Dies Schloß soll meine Warnung sein!

ALLE:
Bekämen doch die Lügner alle
Ein solches Schloß vor ihren Mund,
20 Statt Haß, Verleumdung, schwarzer Galle,
Bestünde Lieb' und Bruderbund.

1. DAME *[gibt Tamino eine goldne Flöte]:*
O Prinz, nimm dies Geschenk von mir!
Dies sendet unsre Fürstin dir.
25 Die Zauberflöte wird dich schützen,
Im größten Unglück unterstützen.
DIE 3 DAMEN:
Hiermit kannst du allmächtig handeln,
Der Menschen Leidenschaft verwandeln:
Der Traurige wird freudig sein,
30 Den Hagestolz nimmt Liebe ein.
ALLE:
Oh, so eine Flöte ist mehr als Gold und Kronen wert,
Denn durch sie wird Menschenglück
und Zufriedenheit vermehrt.
PAPAGENO:
Nun, ihr schönen Frauenzimmer,
35 Darf ich — so empfehl ich mich.
DIE 3 DAMEN:
Dich empfehlen kannst du immer
Doch bestimmt die Fürstin dich
Mit dem Prinzen ohn' Verweilen
Nach Sarastros Burg zu eilen.
PAPAGENO:
40 Nein, dafür bedank ich mich!
Von euch selbsten hörte ich,
Daß er wie ein Tigertier.
Sicher ließ ohn' alle Gnaden
Mich Sarastro rupfen, braten.
45 Setzte mich den Hunden für.
DIE 3 DAMEN:
Dich schützt der Prinz, trau ihm allein!
Dafür sollst du sein Diener sein.
PAPAGENO: *[für sich]:*
Das doch der Prinz beim Teufel wäre!
Mein Leben ist mir lieb;
50 Am Ende schleicht, bei meiner Ehre,
Er von mir wie ein Dieb.
1. DAME *[gibt Papageno ein Kästchen mit einem Glockenspiel]:*
Hier nimm dies Kleinod, es ist dein.
PAPAGENO:
Ei, ei! Was mag darinnen sein?

176

DIE 3 DAMEN:

55 Darinnen hörst du Glöckchen tönen.

PAPAGENO:

Werd' ich sie auch wohl spielen können?

DIE 3 DAMEN:

O ganz gewiß! Ja, ja, gewiß!

ALLE:

Silberglöckchen, Zauberflöten
Sind zu eurem Schutz vonnöten.

60 Lebet wohl, wir wollen gehn,
Lebet wohl, auf Wiedersehn!

TAMINO:

Doch, schöne Damen, saget an:

PAPAGENO:

Wie man die Burg wohl finden kann?

TAMINO, PAPAGENO:

Wie man die Burg wohl finden kann?

DIE 3 DAMEN:

65 Drei Knaben, jung, schön, hold und weise,
Umschweben euch auf eurer Reise;
Sie werden eure Führer sein,
Folgt ihrem Rate ganz allein.

TAMINO, PAPAGENO:

Drei Knaben, jung, schön, hold und weise,
70 Umschweben uns auf unsrer Reise.

ALLE:

So lebet wohl! Wir wollen gehn,
Lebt wohl, lebt wohl! Auf Wiedersehn!

Libretto by Emanuel Schikaneder, 1748–1812

Opera by Wolfgang Amadeus Mozart, 1791

---

1 **das Schloß** *padlock*; *4* **dahin** *gone*; *6* **beklagen** *to pity*; *8* **die Vorigen** *the same (characters as before)*; *11* **die Strafe erlassen** *to remit the punishment*; *18* **bekämen...alle** *if all liars were to receive* (imperfect subjunctive of **bekommen**); *20* **die Verleumdung** *slander*; **die Galle** *spite*; *21* **bestünde** *would prevail* (imperfect subjunctive of **bestehen**); *28* **der Menschen** *of men* (genitive plural); **verwandeln** *to transform*; *30* **der Hagestolz** *confirmed bachelor*; *33* **vermehren** *to increase*; *35* **sich empfehlen** *to take one's leave*; *37* **bestimmen** *to intend*; *38* **das Verweilen** *delay*; *40* **sich bedanken** *to thank*; *43/4* **ließ ... mich Sarastro rupfen, braten** *Sarastro would have me plucked and roasted*; *47* **dafür** *in return*; *49* **lieb** *dear*; *50* **schleichen** *to slip away*; *53* **das Kleinod** *treasure*; *59* **vonnöten** *necessary*; *60* **lebet wohl** *farewell*

Leutnant Gustl

This extract is the opening of the monologue *Leutnant Gustl*, published in 1900 in *Die Neue Freie Presse*, Vienna's popular newspaper. At the beginning of the story Leutnant Gustl, an officer in the Austro-Hungarian Imperial Army, is sitting through a choral concert.

Wie lange wird denn das noch dauern? Ich muß auf die Uhr schauen... schickt sich wahrscheinlich nicht in einem so ernsten Konzert. Aber wer sieht's denn? Wenn's einer sieht, so paßt er gerade so wenig auf, wie ich, und vor
5 dem brauch' ich mich nicht zu genieren... Erst Viertel auf zehn?... Mir kommt vor, ich sitz' schon drei Stunden in dem Konzert. Ich bin's halt nicht gewohnt... was ist es denn eigentlich? Ich muß das Programm anschauen... Ja, richtig: Oratorium? Ich hab' gemeint: Messe. Solche
10 Sachen gehören doch nur in die Kirche. Die Kirche hat auch das Gute, daß man jeden Augenblick fortgehen kann. — Wenn ich wenigstens einen Ecksitz hätt! — Also Geduld, Geduld! Auch Oratorien nehmen ein End'! Vielleicht ist es sehr schön, und ich bin nur nicht in der
15 Laune. Woher sollt' mir auch die Laune kommen? Wenn ich denke, daß ich hergekommen bin, um mich zu zerstreuen... Hätt' ich die Karte lieber dem Benedek geschenkt, dem machen solche Sachen Spaß; er spielt ja selber Violine. Aber da wär' der Kopetzky beleidigt
20 gewesen. Es war ja sehr lieb von ihm, wenigstens gut gemeint. Ein braver Kerl, der Kopetzky! Der einzige, auf den man sich verlassen kann... Seine Schwester singt ja mit, unter denen da oben. Mindestens hundert Jungfrauen, alle schwarz gekleidet; wie soll ich sie da
25 herausfinden? Weil sie mitsingt, hat er auch das Billett gehabt, der Kopetzky... Warum ist er denn nicht selber gegangen? — Sie singen übrigens sehr schön. Es ist sehr erhebend — sicher! Bravo! bravo!... Ja, applaudieren wir mit. Der neben mir klatscht wie verrückt. Ob's ihm
30 wirklich so gut gefällt? — Das Mädel drüben in der Loge ist sehr hübsch. Sieht sie mich an oder den Herrn dort mit dem blonden Vollbart?...

Arthur Schnitzler, 1862–1931

sich schicken *to be proper*; *4* aufpassen *to pay attention*; *5* sich genieren *to feel embarrassed*; *5/6* Viertel auf zehn *quarter past nine*; *6* vorkommen *to seem*; *7* halt *just* (dialect); *13* auch *even*; *16/17* sich zerstreuen *to amuse oneself*; *17/18* Hätt' ich lieber geschenkt *I should rather have given*; *18* dem machen solche Sachen Spaß *he enjoys such things*; *20/21* gut gemeint *well intentioned*; *22* sich verlassen auf *to rely on*; *23* unter denen *among those*; *28* erhebend *uplifting*; *29* der *the man*; *30* das Mädel *young woman* (Austrian dialect)

Altenberglieder

Two of Berg's *Altenberglieder* were first performed in Vienna in 1913, conducted by Schoenberg, but the riotous reception forced the performers to abandon the concert; this was due as much to the aphoristic, telegram-like style of Altenberg's texts as to Berg's music.

I

Seele, wie bist du schöner, tiefer, nach Schneestürmen.
Auch du hast sie, gleich der Natur.
Und über beiden liegt noch ein trüber Hauch, eh das Gewölk sich
*   verzog!*

II

Sahst du nach dem Gewitterregen den Wald?
Alles rastet, blinkt, und ist schöner als zuvor.
Siehe, Fraue, auch du brauchst Gewitterregen!

III

Über die Grenzen des All blicktest du sinnend hinaus;
Hattest nie Sorge um Hof und Haus!
Leben und Traum vom Leben — plötzlich ist alles aus.
Über die Grenzen des All blickst du noch sinnend hinaus.

IV

Nichts ist gekommen, nichts wird kommen für meine Seele.
Ich habe gewartet, gewartet, oh, gewartet!
Die Tage werden dahinschleichen und umsonst wehen meine
*   aschblonden, seidenen Haare um mein bleiches Antlitz!*

Peter Altenberg
The coffee-house poet was a member of Vienna's literary and artistic circle and a close friend of Alban and Helene Berg. (Oil painting, 1909, by the Austrian expressionist painter Oskar Kokoschka, 1886–1980.)

V

Hier ist Friede. Hier weine ich mich aus über alles!
Hier löst sich mein unfaßbares, unermeßliches Leid, das mir die
Seele verbrennt.
Siehe, hier sind keine Menschen, keine Ansiedlungen.
Hier ist Friede! Hier tropft Schnee leise in Wasserlachen.

Peter Altenberg, 1859–1919

Songs for voice and orchestra by Alban Berg, 1913

I *3* **und über beiden . . . Hauch** *both are overcast*
III *1* **das All** *universe*; **sinnend** *thoughtfully*; *2* **Hof und Haus** *house and home*; *3* **ist alles aus** *all is over*
IV *3* **dahinschleichen** *to pass slowly*; **umsonst** *in vain*
V *1* **sich ausweinen** *to cry one's heart out*; *2* **sich lösen** *to dissolve*; *3* **die Ansiedlung** *settlement*; *4* **die Lache** *pool*

Die Welt von Gestern, Erinnerungen eines Europäers

In this extract from his memoirs, Zweig describes the part played by the Jewish inhabitants of Vienna in the cultural life of the city at the turn of the century.

Nun ist Anpassung an das Milieu des Volkes oder des Landes, inmitten dessen sie wohnen, für Juden nicht nur eine äußere Schutzmaßnahme, sondern ein tief innerliches Bedürfnis. Ihr Verlangen nach Heimat, nach
5 Ruhe, nach Rast, nach Sicherheit, nach Unfremdheit drängt sie, sich der Kultur ihrer Umwelt leidenschaftlich zu verbinden. Seit mehr als zweihundert Jahren eingesessen in der Kaiserstadt, begegneten die Juden hier einem leichtlebigen, zur Konzilianz geneigten Volke. Und
10 sie begegneten sogar noch mehr in Wien; sie fanden hier

Emperor Franz Joseph, 1830–1916
Last emperor of the Austro-Hungarian Empire, which he ruled from the age of eighteen until his death at the age of eighty-six.

eine persönliche Aufgabe. In dem letzten Jahrhundert
hatte die Kunstpflege in Österreich ihre alten tradi-
tionellen Hüter und Protektoren verloren: das Kaiserhaus
und die Aristokratie. Während im achtzehnten
15 Jahrhundert Maria Theresia ihre Töchter von Gluck in
Musik unterweisen ließ, Joseph II. mit Mozart dessen
Opern als Kenner diskutierte, Leopold III. selbst
komponierte, hatten die späteren Kaiser Franz II. und
Ferdinand keinerlei Interesse an künstlerischen Dingen
20 mehr, und unser Kaiser Franz Joseph, der in seinen
achtzig Jahren nie ein Buch außer dem
Armeeschematismus gelesen oder auch nur in die Hand
genommen hat, bezeigte sogar eine ausgesprochene
Antipathie gegen Musik. Schon Wagner, Brahms und
25 Johann Strauß oder Hugo Wolf fanden bei ihnen nicht
mehr die geringste Stütze; um die philharmonischen
Konzerte auf der alten Höhe zu erhalten, den Malern, den
Bildhauern eine Existenz zu ermöglichen, mußte das
Bürgertum in die Bresche springen, und es war der Stolz,
30 der Ehrgeiz gerade des jüdischen Bürgertums, daß sie hier
in erster Reihe mittun konnten, den Ruhm der Wiener
Kultur im alten Glanz aufrechtzuerhalten. Sie liebten von
je diese Stadt und hatten sich mit innerster Seele hier
eingewohnt, aber erst durch ihre Liebe zur Wiener Kunst
35 fühlten sie sich voll heimatberechtigt und wahrhaft
Wiener geworden.

Stefan Zweig, 1881–1942

1 die **Anpassung** *adjustment*; *3* die **Schutzmaßnahme** *means of protection*;
4 das **Bedürfnis** *need*; *5* die **Unfremdheit** *belonging*; *8* **eingesessen**
established; *9* **leichtlebig** *easy-going*; **zur Konzilianz geneigt** *tolerant*;
12 die **Kunstpflege** *art patronage*; *14* **während** *whereas*; *16* **unterweisen**
lassen *to have instructed*; *16* **dessen** *his*; *22* der **Armeeschematismus**
army regulations; *24* **schon** *even*; *29* **in die Bresche springen** *to come to the*
rescue; *31* **in erster Reihe mittun** *to play a leading part*; *32/3* **von je** *from*
the beginning; *33/4* **sich einwohnen** *to settle down*; *35* **heimatberechtigt**
naturalized

Brief Hofmannsthals an Richard Strauss

Hofmannsthal reports to Strauss on completing the libretto of *Der Rosenkavalier*.

Rodaun, 6.VI. [1910]

Lieber Herr Doktor,
Ich erwarte stündlich aus Wien die typierte Reinschrift
von Akt III, die dann sogleich an Sie geht. Der Mittelteil
5 hält sich genau an die von Ihnen gewünschte
Linienführung. Mit dem lyrischen Schlußteil werden Sie,
hoffe ich, zufrieden sein. Erstens ist es kurz. Vom
Abgehen des Barons bis zum Fallen des Vorhangs etwa 12
Minuten. Noch kürzer dürfte es nicht sein, um der Figur
10 der Marschallin nicht ihre Bedeutung zu nehmen. Es ist
diese Figur, die das Publikum, namentlich die Frauen, als
Hauptfigur empfinden und mit der sie *gehen*. Ferner ist
es mir gelungen, den ganzen psychologischen Inhalt
des Schlußes in Nummern, Duett oder Terzett, unter-
15 zubringen, mit Ausnahme ganz kurzer Parlando-
stellen. Das ist sicher ein Vorteil, wenn der Schlußakt
nicht nur der lustigste, sondern auch der *singendste*

Richard Strauss and his librettist Hugo von Hofmannsthal
Their long collaboration produced *Der Rosenkavalier* (1911), *Adriadne
auf Naxos* (1912), *Die Frau ohne Schatten* (1919), *Die ägyptische Helene*
(1928) and *Arabella* (1933). (Silhouette by Willy Bithorn, 1914.)

ist. Für das allerletzte Duett, Quinquin-Sophie, war ich ja durch das von Ihnen gegebene Versschema sehr gebunden,
20 doch ist eine solche Gebundenheit an eine Melodie mir eigentlich sympathisch gewesen, weil ich darin etwas Mozartisches sehe und die Abkehr von der unleidlichen Wagnerischen Liebesbrüllerei ohne Grenzen, sowohl im Umfang als im Maß, — eine abstoßend barbarische,
25 fast tierische Sache, dieses Aufeinanderlosbrüllen zweier Geschöpfe in Liebesbrunst, wie er es praktiziert. Ich hoffe also, Sie sind zufrieden — mir war die Arbeit an dieser Sache so sympathisch, daß es mich fast traurig machte, *Vorhang* darunter schreiben zu müssen.

Hugo von Hofmannsthal, 1874–1929

3 **die Reinschrift** *fair copy*; *5* **sich halten an** *to keep to*; *5/6* **die Linienführung** *guideline*; *9* **noch kürzer** *any shorter*; *11* **namentlich** *particularly*; *12* **gehen** *to identify*; **ferner** *furthermore*; *13* **gelingen** *to succeed*; *15* **unterbringen** *to arrange*; *19* **das Versschema** *metric scheme*; *20* **gebunden** *tied*; *21* **sympathisch** *pleasing*; *22* **die Abkehr** *turning away*; *23* **die Liebesbrüllerei** *bawling of love*; *23/24* **sowohl im Umfang als im Maß** *both in volume and length*; *25* **das Aufeinanderlosbrüllen** *shrieking at each other*; *26* **die Liebesbrunst** *lust*

Die Unvollendete

This review was written in 1865 after the first performance of Schubert's Symphony no.8, the 'Unfinished'.

Nun folgt die Schubert'sche Novität, die einen außerordentlichen Enthusiasmus erregte. Es sind die beiden ersten Sätze (Allegro moderato, h-Moll und Andante, E-Dur) einer Symphonie, welche, seit vierzig
5 Jahren in Herrn Hüttenbrenner's Besitz, für gänzlich verschollen galt. Die uns vorliegende Originalpartitur, ganz von Schubert's Hand, trägt die Jahreszahl 1822 und enthält nebst den zwei ersten Sätzen noch den Anfang (neun Takte) des dritten, eines Scherzo in h-Moll.
10   Wir müssen uns mit den zwei Sätzen zufriedengeben, die, von Herbeck zu neuem Leben erweckt, auch neues

Leben in unsere Concertsäle brachten. Wenn nach den
paar einleitenden Takten Clarinette und Oboe einstimmig
ihren süßen Gesang über dem ruhigen Gemurmel der
15 Geigen anstimmen, da kennt auch jedes Kind den Com-
ponisten, und der halbunterdrückte Ausruf 'Schubert!'
summt flüsternd durch den Saal. Er ist noch kaum
eingetreten, aber es ist, als kennte man ihn am Tritt, an
seiner Art, die Türklinke zu öffnen. Erklingt nun gar auf
jenen
20 sehnsüchtigen Mollgesang das contrastirende G-Dur
Thema der Violoncelle, ein reizender Liedsatz von fast
ländlerartiger Behaglichkeit, da jauchzt jede Brust, als
stände Er nach langer Entfernung leibhaftig mitten unter
uns. Dieser ganze Satz ist ein süßer Melodienstrom, bei
25 aller Kraft und Genialität so krystallhell, daß man jedes
Steinchen auf dem Boden sehen kann. Und überall
die selbe Wärme, derselbe goldene, blättertreibende
Sonnenschein!

Eduard Hanslick, 1825–1904

1 **die Novität** *new work*; *6* **verschollen galt** *was thought to be lost*; *9* **der
Takt** *bar*; *10* **sich zufriedengeben** *to be content*; *11* **Herbeck** (proper
name), the conductor; *13* **einstimmig** *in unison*; *15* **anstimmen** *to begin to
play*; *16* **halbunterdrückt** *half suppressed*; *18* **als** *as if*; *19* **erklingt das
contrastirende G-Dur Thema** *when the contrasting G-major theme is
heard*; *20* **auf** *after*; *21* **der Liedsatz** *melody*; *22* **ländlerartig** *Ländler-like*, a
Ländler is a country dance in triple time; **die Behaglichkeit** *ease*; *23* **die
Entfernung** *absence*; **leibhaftig** *in person*; *25* **die Genialität** *genius*; *27*
blättertreibend *life-giving*

Warm die Lüfte

Warm die Lüfte,
es sprießt Gras auf sonnigen Wiesen.
Horch! —
Horch, es flötet die Nachtigall . . .
5 *Ich will singen:*

185

Droben hoch im düstern Bergforst,
es schmilzt und glitzert kalter Schnee,
ein Mädchen in grauem Kleide
lehnt an feuchtem Eichstamm,
10 *krank sind ihre zarten Wangen,*
die grauen Augen fiebern
durch Düsterriesenstämme.
'Er kommt noch nicht. Er läßt mich warten' ...

Stirb!
15 *Der Eine stirbt, daneben der Andere lebt:*
Das macht die Welt so tiefschön.

Alfred Mombert, 1872–1942, from his collection
Der Glühende (1896)

Song for voice and piano by Alban Berg, 1910

6 **droben hoch** *high up*; 7 **glitzern** *to glisten*; 11 **fiebern** *to be feverish*;
12 **Düsterriesenstämme** *dark gigantic trunks*; 15 **daneben** *whereas, while*

Das Heiligenstädter Testament

In this letter, which is really a *cri de coeur*, Beethoven writes about his deafness. It has become known as 'Das Heiligenstädter Testament', after the suburb in Vienna in which Beethoven was living at that time. The letter is dated 6 October 1802 but was never sent.

Für meine Brüder Karl und Johann van Beethoven!
O ihr Menschen, die ihr mich für feindselig, störrisch oder misanthropisch haltet oder erkläret, wie unrecht tut ihr mir! Ihr wißt nicht die geheime Ursache von dem, was
5 euch so scheinet. Mein Herz und mein Sinn waren von Kindheit an für das zarte Gefühl des Wohlwollens; selbst große Handlungen zu verrichten, dazu war ich immer aufgelegt, aber bedenkt nur, daß seit sechs Jahren ein heilloser Zustand mich befallen, durch unvernünftige
10 Ärzte verschlimmert. Von Jahr zu Jahr in der Hoffnung, gebessert zu werden, betrogen, endlich zu dem Überblick eines dauernden Übels (dessen Heilung vielleicht Jahre

Ludwig van Beethoven, 1770–1827
(Engraving by Blasius Höfel, 1814, after a pencil drawing by Louis Letronne but touched up from the life.)

dauern wird oder gar unmöglich ist) gezwungen, mit
einem feurigen, lebhaften Temperamente geboren, selbst
15 empfänglich für die Zerstreuungen der Gesellschaft,
mußte ich früh mich absondern, einsam mein Leben
zubringen. Wollte ich auch zuweilen mich einmal über
alles das hinaussetzen, o wie hart wurde ich durch die
verdoppelte traurige Erfahrung meines schlechten Gehörs
20 dann zurückgestoßen, und doch war's mir noch nicht
möglich, den Menschen zu sagen: 'Sprecht lauter, schreit,
denn ich bin taub.'
     Ganz allein, fast nur soviel, als es die höchste

Notwendigkeit fordert, darf ich mich in Gesellschaft
25 einlassen. Wie ein Verbannter muß ich leben; nahe ich
mich einer Gesellschaft, so überfällt mich eine heiße
Ängstlichkeit, indem ich befürchte, in Gefahr gesetzt zu
werden, meinen Zustand merken zu lassen. Aber welche
Demütigung wenn jemand neben mir stand und von
30 weitem eine Flöte hörte und ich nichts hörte oder jemand
den Hirten singen hörte und ich auch nichts hörte! Solche
Ereignisse brachten mich nahe an Verzweiflung, es fehlte
wenig, und ich endigte selbst mein Leben. — Nur sie, die
Kunst, sie hielt mich zurück.

Ludwig van Beethoven, 1770–1827

Mignon Lieder

The four Mignon songs appear in the novel *Wilhelm Meisters
Lehrjahre* (1795–6) by Goethe. Mignon is an enchanting young girl of
Italian origin, whom Wilhelm has rescued from a group of travelling
acrobats. She is the essence of Romanticism, a creature permeated
with a deep sense of longing, which she expresses in her songs.

Kennst du das Land

Sie fing jeden Vers feierlich und prächtig an, als ob sie auf
etwas Sonderbares aufmerksam machen, als ob sie etwas
Wichtiges vortragen wollte.

Kennst du das Land, wo die Zitronen blühn,
5 *Im dunkeln Laub die Gold-Orangen glühn,*
Ein sanfter Wind vom blauen Himmel weht,

Die Myrte still und hoch der Lorbeer steht?
Kennst du es wohl?
Dahin! dahin
10 *Möcht ich mit dir, O mein Geliebter, ziehn.*

Kennst du das Haus? Auf Säulen ruht sein Dach.
Es glänzt der Saal, es schimmert das Gemach,
Und Marmorbilder stehn und sehn mich an:
Was hat man dir, du armes Kind, getan?
15 *Kennst du es wohl?*
Dahin! dahin
Möcht ich mit dir, O mein Beschützer ziehn.

Kennst du den Berg und seinen Wolkensteg?
Das Maultier sucht im Nebel seinen Weg;
20 *In Höhlen wohnt der Drachen alte Brut;*
Es stürzt der Fels und über ihn die Flut!
Kennst du ihn wohl?
Dahin! dahin
Geht unser Weg! O Vater, laß uns ziehn!

25 Nachdem sie das Lied zum zweitenmal geendigt hatte,
hielt sie einen Augenblick inne, sah Wilhelmen scharf an
und fragte: 'Kennst du das Land?' — 'Es muß wohl Italien
gemeint sein', versetzte Wilhelm, 'Woher hast du das
Liedchen?' — 'Italien!' sagte Mignon bedeutend, 'Gehst
30 du nach Italien, so nimm mich mit, es friert mich hier.' —
'Bist du schon dort gewesen, liebe Kleine?' fragte
Wilhelm. Das Kind war still und nichts weiter aus ihm zu
bringen.

Johann Wolfgang Goethe, 1749–1832, *Wilhelm Meisters
Lehrjahre* (1795–6), 3. Buch, 1. Kapitel

Songs for voice and piano by Ludwig van Beethoven, 1809;
Franz Schubert, 1815; Franz Liszt, 1842; Robert Schumann,
1849; Hugo Wolf, 1888

1/2 **aufmerksam machen auf** *to draw attention to*; *9* **dahin** *thither*; *10* **ziehn**
to go (contraction of **ziehen**); *13* **das Marmorbild** *marble statue*; *18* **der
Wolkensteg** *misty path*; *19* **das Maultier** *mule*; *20* **der Drachen** *of dragons*
(genitive plural); *21* **stürzen** *to fall steeply*; *26* **inne halten** *to pause*;
28/9 **Woher hast du das Liedchen?** *Where did you learn that little song?*

Nur wer die Sehnsucht kennt

Er [Wilhelm] verfiel in eine träumende Sehnsucht, und wie einstimmend mit seinen Empfindungen war das Lied, das eben in dieser Stunde Mignon und der Harfner als ein unregelmäßiges

5 Duett mit dem herzlichsten Ausdrucke sangen:

Nur wer die Sehnsucht kennt,
Weiß, was ich leide!
Allein und abgetrennt
Von aller Freude,
10 *Seh ich ans Firmament*
Nach jener Seite.
Ach! der mich liebt und kennt
Ist in der Weite.
Es schwindelt mir, es brennt
15 *Mein Eingeweide.*
Nur wer die Sehnsucht kennt,
Weiß, was ich leide!

4. Buch, 11. Kapitel

Songs for voice and piano by Ludwig van Beethoven, 1807–8; Franz Schubert, 1815, 1816, 1826; Robert Schumann, 1849; Hugo Wolf, 1888

1 **verfallen in** *to sink into*; *2* **wie einstimmend** *as if in harmony*; *8* **abgetrennt** *separated*; *12* **der** *he who*; *14* **es schwindelt mir** *I am dizzy*

Heiß mich nicht reden

Mignon is oppressed by a secret which she may not confide: her lips are sealed by an oath.

Heiß mich nicht reden, heiß mich schweigen!
Denn mein Geheimnis ist mir Pflicht;
Ich möchte dir mein ganzes Innre zeigen,
Allein das Schicksal will es nicht.

5 *Zur rechten Zeit vertreibt der Sonne Lauf*
Die finstre Nacht, und sie muß sich erhellen;

Der harte Fels schließt seinen Busen auf,
Mißgönnt der Erde nicht die tiefverborgnen Quellen.

Ein jeder sucht im Arm des Freundes Ruh,
10 *Dort kann die Brust in Klagen sich ergießen;*
Allein ein Schwur drückt mir die Lippen zu.
Und nur ein Gott vermag sie aufzuschließen.

5. Buch, 16. Kapitel

Songs for voice and piano by Franz Schubert, 1826; Robert Schumann, 1849; Hugo Wolf, 1888

1 **heißen** *to bid*; *3* **mein ganzes Innre** *my innermost self*; *4* **allein** *but*; *5* **der Sonne Lauf** *the course of the sun*; *7* **aufschließen** *to open up*; *8* **mißgönnen** *to begrudge*; *9* **ein jeder** *everyone*; *10* **sich ergießen** *to pour out*; *12* **vermögen** *to be able*

So laßt mich scheinen

There is a birthday to celebrate, and Mignon is dressed up as an angel to present the gifts. Clad in these angelic garments she sings of her longing to be in heaven.

Es fand sich eben, daß der Geburtstag von Zwillingsschwestern, die sich immer sehr gut betragen hatten, nahe war; ich versprach, daß ihnen diesmal ein Engel die kleinen Geschenke bringen sollte, die sie wohl
5 verdient hätten. Sie waren äußerst gespannt auf diese Erscheinung. Ich hatte mir Mignon zu dieser Rolle ausgesucht, und sie ward an dem bestimmten Tage in ein langes, leichtes, weißes Gewand anständig gekleidet. Es fehlte nicht an einem goldenen Gürtel um die Brust und
10 an einem gleichen Diadem in den Haaren. Anfangs wollte ich die Flügel weglassen, doch bestanden die Frauenzimmer, die sie anputzten, auf ein Paar großer goldner Schwingen, an denen sie recht ihre Kunst zeigen wollten. So trat, mit einer Lilie in der einen Hand und mit
15 einem Körbchen in der anderen, die wundersame Erscheinung in die Mitte der Mädchen und überraschte mich selbst. 'Da kommt der Engel', sagte ich. Die Kinder traten alle wie zurück; endlich riefen sie aus: 'Es ist Mignon!' und getrauten sich doch nicht, dem

20 wundersamen Bilde näher zu treten. 'Hier sind eure
Gaben', sagte sie und reichte das Körbchen hin. Man
versammelte sich um sie, man betrachtete, man befühlte,
man befragte sie. 'Bist du ein Engel?' fragte das eine Kind.
'Ich wollte, ich wär' es', versetzte Mignon.
25   'Warum trägst du eine Lilie?'
'So rein und offen sollte mein Herz sein, dann wär' ich
glücklich.'
'Wie ist's mit den Flügeln? laß sie sehen!'
'Sie stellen schönere vor, die noch nicht entfaltet sind.'
30 Und so antwortete sie bedeutend auf jede unschuldige,
leichte Frage. Als die Neugierde der kleinen Gesellschaft
befriedigt war und der Eindruck dieser Erscheinung
stumpf zu werden anfing, wollte man sie wieder
auskleiden. Sie verwehrte es, nahm ihre Zither, setzte
35 sich hier auf diesen hohen Schreibtisch hinauf und sang
ein Lied mit unglaublicher Anmut.

So laßt mich scheinen, bis ich werde;
Zieht mir das weiße Kleid nicht aus!
Ich eile von der schönen Erde
40 *Hinab in jenes feste Haus.*

Dort ruh ich eine kleine Stille,
Dann öffnet sich der frische Blick;
Ich lasse dann die reine Hülle,
Den Gürtel und den Kranz zurück.

45 *Und jene himmlischen Gestalten,*
Sie fragen nicht nach Mann und Weib,
Und keine Kleider, keine Falten
Umgeben den verklärten Leib.

Zwar lebt ich ohne Sorg und Mühe,
50 *Doch fühlt ich tiefen Schmerz genung;*
Vor Kummer altert ich zu frühe,
Macht mich auf ewig wieder jung!

8. Buch, 2. Kapitel
Songs for voice and piano by Franz Schubert, 1826; Robert
Schumann, 1849; Hugo Wolf, 1888

1 es fand sich eben *it came about*; *2* sich betragen *to behave*; *7/8* ward gekleidet *was dressed* (ward is an archaic form of wurde); *10* gleich *same*; *11* weglassen *not to use*; *11/12* bestehen auf *to insist on*; *12* anputzen *to dress*; *19* sich getrauen *to dare*; *29* sie stellen schönere vor *they represent more beautiful ones*; *31* die Neugierde *curiosity*; *37* so *thus* (as an angel); *40* hinab *down*; *41* eine kleine Stille *a short while*; *42* der Blick *sight*; *43* die Hülle *robe*; *46* fragen nach *to be concerned about*; *48* verklärt *transfigured*; *49* zwar *though*; *50* genung *enough* (archaic form of genug)

Brief Hofmannsthals an Richard Strauss

Hofmannsthal discusses the significance of sixteenth-century Nürnberg as the setting for Wagner's opera *Die Meistersinger*.

Rodaun, 1.VII.27

Lieber Dr Strauss

Worauf der große Reiz und die große Kraft der *Meistersinger* (rein als Dichtung genommen) beruhen,
5 wodurch sich dieses Werk noch über alle anderen Werke dieses einzigartigen Mannes heraus hebt, das ist nicht so schwer zu erkennen. Es mischen sich da freilich mehrere Elemente, und auch ein selbstbiographisches ist darunter, aber das eigentlich entscheidende Element, das alle
10 anderen trägt, ist Nürnberg. Dieses Stadtganze, wie es in den dreißiger Jahren noch unverderbt dastand, die deutsche bürgerliche Geistes-, Gemüts- und Lebenswelt von 1500 nicht bloß wiederspiegelnd, sondern wahrhaft vergegenwärtigend, das war eines der großen
15 entscheidenden Erlebnisse der Romantik. Wie sehr es Nürnberg war, das Gewahrwerden deutschen Lebens und Wandels in diesem Stadtgebilde, das den Keim zu den *Meistersingern* in Wagners Seele legte, das erzählt er ja in der Selbstbiographie ganz genau und unvergeßlich.
20 Sogar die nächtliche Prügelei und der Nachtwächter, der zur Ruhe überleitet, kommen in diesem wahrhaft dichterischen Erlebnis vor. Das nun gibt dieser Oper ihre unzerstörbare Wirklichkeit: daß sie eine echte

geschlossene Welt wieder lebendig macht, die einmal da
25 war, — nicht wie *Lohengrin* und *Tannhäuser* oder gar der
Ring (der *Tristan* ist eine Sache für sich) erträumte oder
erklügelte Welten, die niemals nirgends da waren.

Hugo von Hofmannsthal, 1874–1929

4 **rein** *purely*; **beruhen** *to depend*; *5/6* **sich heraus heben** *to be distinguished*; *8* **darunter** *amongst them*; *10* **trägt** *governs*; *10/11* **in den dreißiger Jahren** *in the 1830s*; *11* **dastehen** *to exist*; *14* **vergegenwärtigen** *to bring to life*; *15* **entscheidend** *significant*; *16* **das Gewahrwerden** *perception*; *17* **der Wandel** *custom*; *17/18* **den Keim legen** *to sow the seed*; *20* **die Prügelei** *brawl*; *21/2* **vorkommen** *to occur*; *24* **geschlossen** *self-contained*; *26* **erträumt** *imagined*; *27* **erklügelt** *contrived*

Die Meistersinger von Nürnberg
The stage set for Act 2 of Wagner's opera, in the first production in
Munich, 1868. On the right of the street is the house of the goldsmith,
Veit Pogner, on the left the house and workshop of the shoemaker, Hans
Sachs. (Engraving by Theodor Pixis.)

Des Knaben Wunderhorn

The collection of folk poems *Des Knaben Wunderhorn* was compiled and edited by Achim von Arnim and Clemens Brentano and published in three volumes between 1805 and 1808. The anthology was dedicated to Goethe, who wrote this review in 1806.

Von Rechts wegen sollte dieses Büchlein in jedem Hause, wo frische Menschen wohnen, am Fenster, unterm Spiegel, oder wo sonst Gesang- und Kochbücher zu liegen pflegen, zu finden sein, um aufgeschlagen zu werden in
5 jedem Augenblick der Stimmung oder Unstimmung, wo man denn immer etwas Gleichtönendes oder Anregendes fände, wenn man auch allenfalls das Blatt ein paarmal umschlagen müßte.

Am besten aber läge doch dieser Band auf dem Klavier
10 des Liebhabers oder Meisters der Tonkunst, um den darin enthaltenen Liedern entweder mit bekannten, hergebrachten Melodien ganz ihr Recht widerfahren zu lassen oder ihnen schickliche Weisen anzuschmiegen, oder, wenn Gott wollte, neue bedeutende Melodien durch sie
15 hervorzulocken.

Würden dann diese Lieder nach und nach in ihrem eigenen Ton- und Klangelemente von Ohr zu Ohr, von Mund zu Mund getragen, kehrten sie allmählich belebt und verherrlicht zum Volke zurück, von dem sie zum Teil
20 gewissermaßen ausgegangen, so könnte man sagen, das Büchlein habe seine Bestimmung erfüllt und könne nun wieder als geschrieben und gedruckt verloren gehen, weil es in Leben und Bildung der Nation übergegangen.

Johann Wolfgang Goethe, 1749–1832

1 von **Rechts wegen** *by rights*; *3* **wo sonst** *wherever*; *3/4* **zu liegen pflegen** *are kept*; *5* **Stimmung oder Unstimmung** *good or bad spirits*; *6* **etwas Gleichtönendes oder Anregendes** *something in sympathetic or stimulating mood*; *7* **wenn auch** *even if*; *10* **der Liebhaber** *amateur*; *10/12* **um zu** *in order to* (with infinitive); *11/12* **hergebracht** *traditional*; *12* **ganz ihr Recht widerfahren lassen** *to do full justice to*; *13* **anschmiegen** *to attach*; *14* **wenn Gott wollte** *God willing*; *15* **hervorlocken** *to draw forth*; *16* **nach und nach** *gradually*; *16/17* **in ihrem eigenen Ton- und Klangelemente** *with their characteristic sound*; *21* **die Bestimmung** *purpose*; *22* **gedruckt** *printed*; *23* **die Bildung** *culture*; **übergegangen** *is absorbed*

Das Rheingold

The three Rhinemaidens, Woglinde, Wellgunde and Flosshilde, are swimming and singing in the waters of the Rhine. They delight in teasing Alberich, the ugly Nibelung dwarf, who chases and lusts after them. Suddenly the Rhinegold shines through the water and the Rhinemaidens revel in its golden light. Alberich learns that whoever renounces love and forges the gold into a ring becomes all powerful. He steals the gold, leaving the Rhinemaidens in darkness to bewail their loss.

1. Szene

Durch die Flut ist von oben her ein immer lichterer Schein gedrungen, der sich an einer hohen Stelle des mittelsten Riffes allmählich zu einem blendend hell strahlenden Goldglanze entzündet; ein zauberisch goldenes Licht bricht von hier durch das Wasser.

5 WOGLINDE: Lugt, Schwestern!
    Die Weckerin lacht in den Grund.

WELLGUNDE: Durch den grünen Schwall
    den wonnigen Schläfer sie grüßt.

FLOSSHILDE: Jetzt küßt sie sein Auge,
10   daß er es öffne.

WELLGUNDE: Schaut, es lächelt
    in lichtem Schein.

WOGLINDE: Durch die Fluten hin
    fließt sein strahlender Stern.

15 DIE 3 MÄDCHEN *[zusammen das Riff anmutig umschwimmend]*:
    Heiajaheia!
    Heiajaheia!
    Wallalallalala leiajahei!
    Rheingold!
20   Rheingold!
    Leuchtende Lust,
    wie lachst du so hell und hehr!
    Glühender Glanz
    entgleißet dir weihlich im Wag!
25   Heiajahei
    Heiajaheia!
    Wache, Freund,
    wache froh!
    Wonnige Spiele
30   spenden wir dir:

The Rhinemaidens
In the first performance of *Das Rheingold* in Bayreuth in 1876 the singers were Lilli Lehmann (Woglinde), Marie Lehmann (Wellgunde) and Minna Lammert (Flosshilde).

	flimmert der Fluß,
	flammet die Flut,
	umfließen wir tauchend,
	tanzend und singend,
35	im seligen Bade dein Bett.
	Rheingold!
	Rheingold!
	Heiajaheia!
	Wallalaleia heiajahei!
40	*[Mit immer ausgelassenerer Lust umschwimmen*
	die Mädchen das Riff. Die ganze Flut flimmert
	in hellem Goldglanze.]
ALBERICH	*[dessen Augen, mächtig vom Glanze angezogen,*
	starr an dem Golde haften]:
45	Was ist's ihr Glatten,
	das dort so glänzt und gleißt?

DIE 3 MÄDCHEN:	Wo bist du Rauher denn heim,
	daß vom Rheingold nie du gehört?
WELLGUNDE:	Nichts weiß der Alp
50	von des Goldes Auge,
	das wechselnd wacht und schläft?
WOGLINDE:	Von der Wassertiefe
	wonnigem Stern,
	der hehr die Wogen durchhellt?
55 DIE 3 MÄDCHEN:	Sieh, wie selig
	im Glanze wir gleiten!
	Willst du Banger
	in ihm dich baden,
	so schwimm und schwelge mit uns!
60	Wallalalala leialalei!
	Wallalalala leiajahei!
ALBERICH:	Eurem Taucherspiele
	nur taugte das Gold?
	Mir gält' es dann wenig!
65 WOGLINDE:	Des Goldes Schmuck
	schmähte er nicht,
	wüßte er all seine Wunder!
WELLGUNDE:	Der Welt Erbe
	gewänne zu eigen,
70	wer aus dem Rheingold
	schüfe den Ring,
	der maßlose Macht ihm verlieh'.
FLOSSHILDE:	Der Vater sagt' es,
	und uns befahl er,
75	klug zu hüten
	den klaren Hort,
	daß kein Falscher der Flut ihn
	entführe:
	drum schweigt, ihr schwatzendes
	Heer!
WELLGUNDE:	Du klügste Schwester,
80	verklagst du uns wohl?
	Weißt du denn nicht,
	wem nur allein
	das Gold zu schmieden vergönnt?
WOGLINDE:	Nur wer der Minne

85		Macht versagt,
		nur wer der Liebe
		Lust verjagt,
		nur der erzielt sich den Zauber,
		zum Reif zu zwingen das Gold.
90	WELLGUNDE:	Wohl sicher sind wir
		und sorgenfrei:
		denn was nur lebt, will lieben;
		meiden will keiner die Minne.
	WOGLINDE:	Am wenigsten er,
95		der lüsterne Alp:
		vor Liebesgier
		möcht er vergehn!
	FLOSSHILDE:	Nicht fürcht ich den,
		wie ich ihn erfand:
100		seiner Minne Brunst
		brannte fast mich.
	WELLGUNDE:	Ein Schwefelbrand
		in der Wogen Schwall:
		vor Zorn der Liebe
105		zischt er laut.
	DIE 3 MÄDCHEN:	Wallala! Wallaleialala!
		Lieblichster Albe,
		lachst du nicht auch?
		In des Goldes Schein
110		wie leuchtest du schön!
		O komm, Lieblicher, lache mit uns!
		Heijaheia! Heiajaheia!
		Wallalalala leiajahei!
		[Sie schwimmen lachend im Glanze auf und ab.]
115	ALBERICH	*[die Augen starr auf das Gold gerichtet, hat dem Geplauder der Schwestern wohl gelauscht]:*
		Der Welt Erbe
		gewänn' ich zu eigen durch dich?
		Erzwäng' ich nicht Liebe,
120		doch listig erzwäng' ich mir Lust?
		[furchtbar laut] Spottet nur zu!
		Der Niblung naht eurem Spiel!
		[Wütend springt er nach dem mittleren Riff hinüber und klettert in grausiger Hast nach dessen Spitze

125   *hinauf. Die Mädchen fahren kreischend auseinander*
         und tauchen nach verschiedenen Seiten hin auf.]

DIE 3 RHEINTÖCHTER: Heia! Heia! Heiajahei!
         Rettet euch!
         Es raset der Alp!
130   In den Wassern sprüht's,
         wohin er springt.
         die Minne macht ihn verrückt!
         [Sie lachen im tollsten Übermut.]

ALBERICH *[gelangt mit einem letzten Satze zur Spitze des Riffes]:*
135   Bangt euch noch nicht?
         So buhlt nun im Finstern,
         feuchtes Gezücht!
         [Er streckt die Hand nach dem Golde aus.]
         Das Licht lösch ich euch aus;
140   entreiße dem Riff das Gold,
         schmiede den rächenden Ring;
         denn hör es die Flut:
         so verfluch ich die Liebe!
         [Er reißt mit furchtbarer Gewalt das Gold aus dem
145   *Riffe und stürzt damit hastig in die Tiefe, wo er*
         schnell verschwindet. Dichte Nacht bricht plötzlich
         überall herein. Die Mädchen tauchen jach dem
         Räuber in die Tiefe nach.]

FLOSSHILDE: Haltet den Räuber!
150 WELLGUNDE: Rettet das Gold!
WOGLINDE,
WELLGUNDE: Hilfe! Hilfe!
DIE 3 MÄDCHEN: Weh! Weh!
         [Die Flut fällt mit ihnen nach der Tiefe hinab, aus
         dem untersten Grunde hört man Alberichs
155   *gellendes Hohngelächter. In dichtester Finsternis*
         verschwinden die Riffe; die ganze Bühne ist von der
         Höhe bis zur Tiefe von schwarzem Wassergewoge
         erfüllt, das eine Zeitlang immer noch abwärts zu
         sinken scheint.]

Libretto by Richard Wagner, 1813–83

Opera by Wagner, 1869, later incorporated into *Der Ring des Nibelungen* as the Prologue

1 dringen *to penetrate*; *5* lugen *to look*; *6* die Weckerin *she (the sun) who wakes*; *7* der Schwall *flood*; *8* der Schläfer *sleeping one (the gold)*; *24* entgleißet dir weihlich im Wag *shines blessed through the waters*; *30* spenden *to offer*; *40* ausgelassen *exuberant*; *43* angezogen *attracted*; *44* haften *to fix*; *45* die Glatten *smooth creatures*; *47* Rauher *ruffian*; *49* der Alp *demon*; *57* Banger *fearful one*; *59* schwelgen *to revel*; *62* das Taucherspiel *diving game*; *63* taugen *to be suited to*; *64* es gält' *it would be worth* (subjunctive); *66* schmähen *to despise*; *69* gewänne *would win* (subjunctive); *71* schüfe *would create* (subjunctive); *72* verlieh' *would bestow* (subjunctive); *78* ihr schwatzendes Heer *you prattling lot*; *83* vergönnt *is granted*; *84* die Minne *love*; *87* verjagen *to drive out*; *88* nur der *only he*; sich erzielen *to acquire*; *95* lüstern *lecherous*; *96* die Liebesgier *greed for love*; *100* die Brunst *passion*; *102* der Schwefelbrand *sulphurous fire*; *115* gerichtet *fixed*; *119* erzwäng' ich nicht Liebe *if I cannot force love*; *120* listig *with cunning*; *122* das Spiel *toy*; *133* der Übermut *high spirits*; *136* buhlen *to court*; *137* das Gezücht *brood*; *140* entreißen *to tear away*; *147* jach *straight away*; *153* hinabfallen *to subside*; *155* gellend *piercing*; das Hohngelächter *mocking laughter*

4 REFERENCE

Musical Vocabulary

The abbreviations *m* (masculine), *f* (feminine), *n* (neuter) and *pl* (plural) are used throughout to show the genders of nouns.

The ending **-in** is added to masculine nouns denoting occupations to make the feminine form: **der Flötist, die Flötistin; der Sänger, die Sängerin**. Only the masculine forms are given here.

General Terminology (German–English)

As German adjectives and adverbs are identical, only the adjectival meaning is given here; the adverbial meaning may be deduced: **anmutig** *graceful* [*gracefully*].

ab	from, down, off, exit
abdämpfen	to mute, dampen
Abgang *m*	exit (off stage)
abgestoßen	detached, staccato
abnehmen	to decrease
abnehmend	decreasing
absolutes Gehör	perfect pitch
abstimmen	to tune down
Abstrich *m*	down bow
Achtel *n*, **Achtelnote** *f*	quaver
Achtung!	attention! stand by!
Akkord *m*	chord
Akkordeon *n*	accordion
Akt *m*	act
Akzent *m*	accent
Aliquote *f*	mutation stop (organ)
allein	alone, only, but
allmählich	gradually
als	as, when, than
leiser als zuvor	quieter than before
Alt *m*	alto, countertenor
Altblockflöte *f*	treble recorder
Altflöte *f*	alto flute
Altistin *f*	contralto
Altschlüssel *m*	alto clef
an	on, at, to
andächtig	devoted
Anfang *m*	beginning
anfangen	to begin

205

angebunden	tied, slurred
Anmerkung *f*	note
Anmerkung für den Dirigenten	note for the conductor
anmutig	graceful
anreissen	to use strong pizzicato
Ansatz *m*	attack, touch, embouchure
Anschlag *m*	attack, touch
anschwellend	growing, increasing
Antwort *f*	answer, fugal answer
anwachsend	growing
Anweisung *f*	stage direction
Art *f*	way, manner
nach militärischer Art	in military style
Assistent *m*	assistant stage manager
Atem *m*	breath
Atempause *f*	very slight pause
auf	on, on to, up
Auffassung *f*	interpretation
aufführen	to perform, present
Aufführung *f*	performance
aufgeregt	excited, agitated
Auflage *f*	edition
auflösen	to resolve
Auflösungszeichen *n*	natural (sign)
Aufnahme *f*	recording
Aufstrich *m*	upbow
Auftakt *m*	upbeat
auftreten	to appear on stage, to enter
Auftritt *m*	scene, entrance (on stage)
Aufzug *m*	act
aus	out, out of
Ausbildung *f*	training
Ausdruck *m*	expression
ausdrucksvoll	expressively
Ausgabe *f*	edition
Ausgang *m*	exit (of building)
Aussprache *f*	pronunciation
Ausstattung *f*	design
ausverkauft	sold out
auswendig	from memory, by heart
Auszug *m*	arrangement, reduction
Klavierauszug *m*	piano reduction, piano score, vocal score
Balkon *m*	gallery
Ballett *n*	ballet
Band *m*	volume (book)
Band *n*	tape (recording)
Bariton *m*	baritone

Baß *m*	bass, bass singer
Baßbalken *m*	bass bar
Baßblockflöte *f*	bass recorder
Baßflöte *f*	bass flute
Baßgeige *f*	double bass
Baßist *m*	double bass player
Baßschlüssel *m*	bass clef
Bassetthorn *n*	basset-horn
Baumwollschlegel *m*	cotton stick (percussion)
Be *n*	flat (sign)
Doppelbe	double flat (sign)
bearbeiten	to arrange, adapt
Becken *n*	cymbal
bedächtig	deliberate, slow
bedeckt	covered, stopped
begeistert	enthusiastic
begleiten	to accompany
behaglich	comfortable, easy
beide	both
Beifall *m*	applause
beinahe	almost
belebt	lively, animated
Beleuchtung *f*	lighting
Beleuchtungschef *m*	lighting director
Beleuchtungsmeister *m*	lighting designer
beruhight	calm
beschleunigen	to get faster
besetzt	scored, cast
3 fach/dreifach besetzt	scored for three
Besetzung *f*	instrumentation, cast
betonen	to accent
Betonung *f*	accent, accentuation
beweglich	agile
bewegt	quick, with movement
Bewegung *f*	movement
beziffert	figured
bezifferter Baß	figured bass
Bibliothek *f*	library
bimmeln	to tinkle
Bindung *f*	slur, tie
bis	until
bittend	pleading, imploring
blasen	to blow
Blasinstrument *n*	wind instrument
Blasorchester *n*	wind band
Blatt *n*	sheet of music, page of book
vom Blatt spielen	to play at sight
vom Blatt singen	to sing at sight

207

Blech *n*	brass
Blechbläser *m*	brass player
Blechblasinstrument *n*	brass instrument
Blockflöte *f*	recorder
Bogen *m*	bow
Bohrung *f*	bore
Bratsche *f*	viola
Bratschist *m*	viola player
breit	broad
breit gestrichen	with broad bows
Brustwerk *n*	division of organ pipes immediately above the player
Bühne *f*	stage
Bühnenarbeiter *m*	stage-hand
Bühnenaussprache *f*	standard German pronunciation for actors and singers
Bühnenbild *n*	set
Bühnenbildner *m*	designer
Bühnenmeister *m*	stage manager
Bund *m*	fret
Celesta *f*	celesta
Cellist *m*	cellist
Cello *n*	cello
Cembalo *n*	harpsichord
Chor *m*	choir, chorus, set of strings
sechschörig	six-stringed
Chorsänger *m*	chorus member
Choral *m*	choral
Chorleiter *m*	choirmaster
Chromatik *f*	chromaticism
Collegium musicum *n*	choral society
dämpfen	to dampen, mute
Dämpfer *m*	mute
Dämpfer ab	mute off
Dämpfer auf	mute on
mit Dämpfer	with mute
ohne Dämpfer	without mute
Darstellung *f*	representation, presentation
dasselbe	the same
Daumen *m*	thumb
dazu	in addition
decken	to cover, 'drown'
deklamieren	to declame
demütig	humble
derb	coarse, robust
deutlich	clear
Dezime *f*	tenth (interval)

Dichter *m*	poet, writer, playwright
Dirigent *m*	conductor
dirigieren	to conduct
Diskant *m*	descant
Disposition *f*	specification (organ)
Dom *m*	cathedral
Dominante *f*	dominant
Donner *m*	thunder
doppel	double
Doppelbe *n*	double flat (sign)
Doppelganznote *f*	breve
Doppelgriff *m*	double stop
Doppelkreuz *n*	double sharp (sign)
Doppelschlag *m*	turn (ornament)
Doppelstrich *m*	double bar
Doppeltaktnote *f*	breve
drängend	pressing on, urgently
Drama *n*	drama
Drehbühne *f*	revolving stage
Drehleier *m*	hurdy-gurdy
Drehorgel *f*	barrel organ
Dreiklang *m*	triad
drucken	to print
Druckfehler *m*	printing error
drücken	to press
Dudelsack *m*	bagpipe
düster	gloomy, dark
dumpf	hollow, dull
Duole *f*	duplet
Dur	major
durch	through
durchaus	throughout, thoroughly
durchführen	to develop
Durchführung *f*	development, fugal entry
durchkomponiert	through-composed, continuous
Dynamik *f*	dynamics
eben	just
eben so leise	just as soft
Echoklavier *n*	echo manual
eilen	to hurry
eilend	hurrying on
nicht eilen	do not hurry
einfach	simple, single
einfaches Holz *n*	single woodwind
Eingang *m*	entrance (of building)
Einleitung *f*	introduction
einmal	once

auf einmal	at once, suddenly
Einsatz *m*	entry, cue (musical)
Einschnitt *m*	break, pause, caesura
Einsingzimmer *n*	warm-up room
Einspielraum *m*	warm-up room
einstimmig	in unison
einstudieren	to coach
Empfindung *f*	feeling, sentiment
energisch	energetic
Englischhorn *n*	cor anglais, English horn
Entfernung *f*	distance
entschieden	resolute, decisive
Entwurf *m*	sketch, draft
erhaben	lofty, exalted
erniedrigen	to lower
ernst	serious
erst	not until, only, first
Erstaufführung *f*	first performance
erster Rang *m*	dress circle
ersterbend	dying away
etwas	something, somewhat
etwas schneller	somewhat faster
Fach *n*	subject, category
Fachmann *m*	expert, professional
Fachpartie *f*	principal role
Fagott *n*	bassoon
Fagottist *m*	bassoonist
Farbe *f*	colour
Fassung *f*	setting, version
revidierte Fassung	revised version
feierlich	solemn, festive
Fell *n*	skin (of a drum)
Fermate *f*	pause
Ferne *f*	distance
wie aus weiter Ferne	as if from far away
Fernwerk *n*	echo organ
festlich	festive
feurig	fiery
Fidel *f*, **Fiedel** *f*	fiddle
Filz *m*	felt
Finger *m*	finger
Fingersatz *m*	fingering
finster	sombre, dark
Flageolett *n*	harmonic
künstliches Flageolett	artificial harmonic
Flatterzunge *f*	fluttering tonguing
flehend	pleading
fließend	flowing

210

Flöte *f*	flute
Flötist *m*	flautist
flott	buoyant, brisk, gay
flüchtig	fleeting
Flügel *m*	grand piano
Flügelhorn *n*	flugelhorn
flüstern	to whisper
Forschung *f*	research
frei	free
freihängend	free-hanging
freudig	joyful
frisch	brisk, fresh
froh, fröhlich	happy, joyful
fromm	pious
Frosch *m*	frog, heel (of a bow)
am Frosch	at the heel
früh	early
Fuge *f*	fugue
Gage *f*	fee
Gallerie *f*	gallery
Gambe *f*	viol, viola da gamba
ganz	whole, quite
ganze Note *f*	semibreve
ganze Pause *f*	semibreve rest
Garderobe *f*	wardrobe, dressing-room
gastieren	to tour
Gastspiel *n*	guest performance
Gebläse *n*	wind supply (organ)
gebrochen	divided, divisi, broken
gebrochener Akkord *m*	broken chord
gebunden	tied, legato, fretted
gedämpft	muted (string instrument)
gedeckt	covered, muted, stopped
gedehnt	sustained
gegen	against
gehalten	held, sustained
geheimnisvoll	mysterious
gehend	andante
Gehör *n*	hearing
Gehörbildung *f*	aural training
Geige *f*	violin, fiddle
Geiger *m*	violinist, fiddler
Geigenbauer *m*	violin maker
geistlich	sacred, spiritual
Geläute *n*	peal of bells
gelassen	calm, tranquil
gemächlich	leisurely
gemäßigt	moderate

211

gemessen	measured, moderate
gemischt	mixed
gemischter Chor	choir of mixed voices
Gemshorn *n*	type of medieval flute, soft organ stop
Generalbaß *m*	continuo
Generalpause *f*	tacit, pause in all parts
Generalprobe *f*	final dress-rehearsal
Generalsetzerkombination *f*	general setter piston (organ)
Geräusch *n*	sound, noise
gering	little
Gesamtausgabe *f*	complete edition
Gesamtkunstwerk *n*	total art work
Gesang *m*	singing, song
Gesangverein *m*	choral society
gesangvoll	melodious
geschlagen	hit, struck
geschwind	swift, quick
gestimmt	tuned
gestopft	muted (brass instrument)
gestoßen	detached
gestrichen	bowed
geteilt	divided
getragen	sustained
Gewalt *f*	power, force
gewaltig	powerful, forceful
Gewandmeisterin *f*	wardrobe mistress
gewirbelt	rolled
gezogen	sustained, portamento
Gitarre *f*	guitar
Gitarrenspieler *m*	guitarist
gleich	same, immediately
gleich abdämpfen	dampen immediately
gleichmäßig	even, equal
gleichzeitig	simultaneous
Glocke *f*	bell
Glocken *pl*	tubular bells
Glockengeläute *n*	bell sounds
Glockenspiel *n*	glockenspiel
Glöckchen *n*	little bell
Gong *m*	gong
graziös	gracious
grell	shrill
Griffbrett *n*	fingerboard
am Griffbrett	on the fingerboard
Griffloch *n*	finger-hole
groß	big, major
große Trommel *f*	bass drum

großer Dreiklang *m*	major triad
Grundton *m*	tonic, keynote
Gummischlegel *m*	rubber stick
gut	good
Hackbrett *n*	dulcimer
halb	half
Halbe *f*, halbe Note *f*	semibreve
halbe Pause *f*	semibreve rest
Halbschluß *m*	imperfect cadence
Halbton *m*	semitone
Hals *m*	neck
Halt!	Stop!
Haltbogen *m*	tie
Hand *f*	hand
Handlung *f*	action, plot
Handzug *m*	hand stop (organ)
Harfe *f*	harp
Harfenist *m*	harpist
Harmonie *f*	harmony, wind band
Harmoniemusik *f*	music for wind instruments
Harmoniestück *n*	piece for wind instruments
Harmonik *f*	harmony
hart	hard, severe, rough
Hast *f*	haste
ohne Hast	without haste
haupt	main
Hauptprobe *f*	dress-rehearsal
Hauptrolle *f*	principal role
Hauptwerk *n*	great organ
heftig	strong, heavy
heilig	holy
heiter	cheerful
Held *m*	hero
Heldentenor *m*	Heldentenor (tenor of powerful voice and wide range)
hell	clear, bright
Herausgeber *m*	publisher
hervor	forward, brought out
hervortretend	prominent
herzlich	heartfelt
Heuler *m*	cipher (organ)
Hilfslinie *f*	leger line
hinter der Bühne *f*	backstage
hoch	high
zu hoch	sharp
Höhe *f*	height
Schalltrichter in die Höhe	bells up
Hohepunkt *m*	climax

213

hörbar	audible
hören	to hear, listen to
Hörerziehung *f*	aural training
Hof *m*	court
hohl	hollow, dull
Holz *n*	wood
Holzblasinstrument *n*	woodwind instrument
Holzblock *m*	woodblock
Holzharmonie *f*	woodwind band
Holzschlegel *m*	wooden stick
Honorar *n*	fee
Horn *n*	French horn
Hornist *m*	French horn player
Humor *m*	humour
mit Humor	with humour
humorvoll	humorously
Hymne *f*	hymn
immer	always, still
immer gedämpft	still muted
immer schneller	faster and faster
in	in
Inhalt *m*	contents
innig	fervent, intimate
Inspizient *m*	stage manager
Inspiziententisch *m*	prompt desk
Instrument *n*	instrument
Instrumentierung *f*	instrumentation
Inszenierung *f*	production
Intendant *m*	general manager of theatre
Intervall *n*	interval
Jagdhorn *n*	hunting horn
Jalousie *f*	swell shutter (organ)
Jalousieschweller *m*	swell box (organ)
jauchzen	to exult, be joyful
Jazz *m*	jazz
jodeln	to yodel
jubeln	to rejoice
Jugend *f*	youth
Jugendorchester *n*	youth orchestra
Kadenz *f*	cadence
Kadenz mit Halbschluß *m*	imperfect cadence
Kadenz mit Plagalschluß *m*	plagal cadence
Kadenz mit Trugschluß *m*	interrupted cadence
vollständige Kadenz	perfect cadence
Kammerkonzert *n*	chamber concerto, chamber concert
Kammermusik *f*	chamber music

Kammerorchester n	chamber orchestra
Kammersänger m	honorary title for distinguished singer
Kammerton m	concert pitch
Kammervirtuose m	honorary title for distinguished instrumentalist
Kanon m	canon
Kantate f	cantata
Kantor m	church choirmaster
Kantorei f	instrumental/choral ensemble
Kapelle f	chapel, church choir, court orchestra
Kapellmeister m	conductor, director of music
Karte f	ticket
Kastagnetten pl	castanets
keck	bold, pert
Kesselpauke f	kettledrum
Kielflügel m	harpsichord
Kinnstütze f	chin rest
Kirche f	church
Klage f	lament
klagend	plaintive, lamenting
Klang m	sound, tone, timbre
klangvoll	sonorous
Klappe f	key (wind instrument)
Klarinette f	clarinet
Klarinettist m	clarinettist
Klavier n	piano (upright), keyboard instrument
Klavierauszug m	piano reduction, piano score, vocal score
Klavierhauptprobe f	technical rehearsal with piano
Klavichord n	clavichord
klein	small, minor
kleiner Terz f	minor third
kleine Trommel f	side drum, snare drum
klingen	to sound, ring
Knabenchor m	boys' choir
Komödie f	comedy
komponieren	to compose
Komponist m	composer
konsequent	strict, rigorous
Konservatorium n	conservatory
Kontrabaß m	double bass
Kontrafagott n	double bassoon
Kontrapunkt m	counterpoint
Konzert n	concerto, concert, recital
Konzertmeister m	leader of an orchestra

215

Koppel *f*	coupler
Kornett *n*	cornet
Korrepetitor *m*	répétiteur
Kostüm *n*	costume
Kostümbildner *m*	costume designer
kräftig	strong, forceful
Kreis *m*	cycle, circle
Liederkreis *m*	song cycle
Kreuz *n*	sharp (sign)
Doppelkreuz	double sharp (sign)
Krummhorn *n*	crumhorn
Künstler *m*	artist
Künstlergarderobe *f*	dressing-room
Kuhglocke *f*	cowbell
Kulissen *pl*	scenery, wings
Kunst *f*	art
Kunstwerk *n*	work of art
kurz	short
Ländler *m*	ländler (rustic waltz)
läuten	to chime, ring
Lage *f*	position
Laie *m*	amateur
Lampenfieber *n*	butterflies, stage-fright
langsam	slow
laut	loud
Laut *m*	sound
Laute *f*	lute
Lautenist *m*	lutenist
Lautenmacher *m*	lute maker
Lautstärke *f*	dynamic
lebendig	lively, vivacious
lebhaft	lively
leer	empty
leere Saite *f*	open string
leicht	gentle, light
Leid *n*	sorrow
leidenschaftlich	passionate
Leierkasten *m*	barrel organ
leise	quiet, soft
leiten	to direct, conduct
Leiter *m*	director, conductor
technischer Leiter	stage director
Leitmotiv *n*	representational theme, leitmotiv
Leitton *m*	leading note
Leitung *f*	direction
lieblich	sweet
Lied *n*	song
Lieder *pl*	songs

Liederkreis *m*	song cycle
Liniensystem *n*	stave
links	left, stage left
loben	to praise
Loge *f*	box (theatre)
Los!	Go!
Luftpause *f*	pause for breath, short pause
lustig	jolly, merry
Lustspiel *n*	comedy
mächtig	powerful
Mal *n*	time
2 mal/zweimal	twice
Manieren *pl*	ornaments
Manual *n*	manual
Manualkoppel *f*	manual coupler (organ)
Marimbaphon *n*	marimba
markiert	clearly accented
markig	emphatic
Marsch *m*	march
Maskenbildner *m*	make-up man
mäßig	moderate, in the style of
marschmäßig	in the style of a march
Mediante *f*	mediant
mehr	more
Meister *m*	master
Meistersinger *m*	mastersinger
Meisterwerk *n*	masterpiece
Melodie *f*	melody
Mensuration *f*	scale (of organ pipe)
merklich	noticeable, perceptible
Messe *f*	mass
Metallstab *m*	metal rod
Metronom *n*	metronome
Militärtrommel *f*	side drum
Minnelied *n*	love-song
Minnesinger *m*	troubadour
mitteltönig	mean-tone (tuning)
Mixtur *f*	mixture stop (organ)
modulieren	to modulate
möglich	possible
so schnell wie möglich	as quickly as possible
möglichst schnell	as quickly as possible
Moll	minor
Mordent *m*	lower mordent
Mundharmonika *f*	harmonica
Mundstück *n*	mouthpiece
munter	cheerful
Musik *f*	music

musikalisch	musical
Musikant *n*	minstrel
Musiker *m*	musician
Musikerziehung *f*	music education
Musikhochschule *f*	music college
Musiklehre *f*	music theory
Musiksendung *f*	music broadcast
Musikstunde *f*	music lesson
Musikverlag *m*	music publishing house
Musikwissenschaft *f*	musicology
musizieren	to make music
nach	after, to, in the manner of
C nach Des	(tune) C to D flat
nach hinten	upstage
nach und nach	gradually
nach vorn	downstage
nachdenklich	reflective, contemplative
Nachschlag *m*	turn (ornament)
Nachspiel *n*	postlude
Nachtstück *n*	nocturne
Nationalhymne *f*	national anthem
Naturton *m*	natural, open note
Naturtrompete *f*	valveless trumpet
neben	adjacent, next, beside
Nebennote *f*	subsidiary, auxiliary note
neu	new
neue Musik *f*	new music
Niederschlag *m*	downbeat
Niederstrich *m*	downbow
noch	still, yet
noch einmal	once more
noch zweimal	twice more
noch langsamer	slower still
None *f*	ninth (interval)
Notation *f*	notation
Note *f*	note
Noten *pl*	written music, copy, part
Notenschrift *f*	notation
Notenständer *m*	music stand
notieren	to notate
oben	above
Oberton *m*	harmonic
Oberwerk *n*	division of pipes high in the case
Oboe *f*	oboe
Oboist *m*	oboist
oder	or
offen	open, unmuted

offene Saite f	open string
ohne	without
Oktave f	octave
Oktett n	octet
Oper f	opera, opera company
Opernhaus n	opera house
Opuszahl f	opus number
Oratorium n	oratorio
Orchester n	orchestra
Orchesterbesetzung f	orchestration, orchestral forces
Orchestergraben m	orchestra pit
Organist m	organist
Orgel f	organ
Orgelbauer m	organ builder
Ostern n	Easter
parallel	relative (key)
Parkett n	stalls
Particell n	short score
Partie f	role
Partitur f	full score
Passion f	Passion music
Pauke f	kettledrum
Pauken pl	kettledrums, timpani
Pauker m	timpanist
Pause f	pause, interval (theatre)
Pausenzeichen n	pause sign
Pedal n	pedal
Pedalkoppel f	pedal coupler (organ)
Pedalwerk n	pedal organ
Peitsche f	whip
Pfeife f	fife, whistle
Phrase f	phrase
Pianist m	pianist
Pikkolo m	piccolo
Plagalschluß m	plagal cadence
Platte f	record
Plektrum m	plectrum
plötzlich	suddenly
Polka f	polka
pompös	pompous
Posaune f	trombone
Posaunist m,	trombonist
Positiv n	positive organ (choir organ, nearest equivalent)
prachtvoll	splendid, magnificent
prächtig	splendid
Praller m, Pralltriller m,	upper mordent

Première *f*	first night
Prinzipal *m*	principal (diapason, nearest equivalent)
Probe *f*	rehearsal
eine Probe abhalten	to rehearse
eine Probe machen	to rehearse
proben	to rehearse
Probespiel *n*	audition
probieren	to rehearse
Prospekt *m*	case design (organ), back-cloth
Psalm *f*	psalm
Publikum *n*	public, audience
Pult *n*	desk, orchestral desk, music stand
Punkt *m*	dot
punktiert	dotted
Quarte *f*	fourth (interval)
Quartett *n*	quartet
Quelle *f*	source
Querflöte *f*	transverse flute
Quinte *f*	fifth (interval)
leere Quinte	open fifth, bare fifth
Quintett *n*	quintet
Rackett *n*	racket
Rampe *f*	footlights, stage front
Rand *m*	edge
Rang *m*	rank, order
erster Rang	dress circle
zweiter Rang	upper circle
rasch	quick, swift
Ratsche *f*	rattle
rauh	rough
rauschen	to murmur, rustle
recht	right
rechts	right, stage right
regelmäßig	regular
Regie *f*	production
Regisseur *m*	producer, director
Register *n*	organ stop
Registertraktur *f*	stop action (organ)
Registerzug *m*	organ stop
Reigen *m*	round dance
Reihe *f*	row
Reim *m*	rhyme
rein	perfect, pure, clean
Repetitor *m*	répétiteur
Reprise *f*	repeat of theme, recapitulation
Requisit *n*	prop

Resonanz f	resonance
Resonanztisch m	soundboard
revidiert	revised
Rezitativ n	recitative
Rhythmus m, **Rhythmik** f	rhythm
Rohr n	reed
Rohrwerk n	reed division (organ)
Rolle f	role
Rollschweller	general crescendo pedal to bring out all stops
Romantik f	Romanticism
ruckweise	jerky
Rückpositiv n	positive organ with pipes behind the player
Rücksicht f	respect, regard
Rührtrommel f	tenor drum
Ruhe f	peace, silence, quiet
ruhelos	restless
ruhevoll, ruhig	peaceful, calm
Rundfunk m	broadcast, radio
Rute f	switch
Säge f	saw
Sänger m	singer
Saite f	string
Darmsaite	gut string
leere Saite	open string
Metallsaite	metal string
Saitenhalter m	tailpiece
Sammlung f	collection
sanft	gentle, soft
Satz m	movement, setting
Schall m	sound, peal, ring
schalldicht	soundproof
schallen	to sound, peal, ring
Schallplatte f	record
Schalltrichter m	bell (of a wind instrument)
Schalltrichter in die Höhe	bells up
Schalmei f	shawm
scharf	harsh, rigorous, exact, projected
Schauspiel n	play
Scheinwerfer m	spotlight
Schelle f	bell
Schellen pl	jingle bells, sleighbells
Schellentrommel f	tambourine
scherzend	joking
Schlägel m	drumstick
Schlag m	stroke, beat, blow
Viertelschlag m	crotchet beat

schlagen	to hit
Schlager *m*	pop song
Schlaginstrument *n*	percussion instrument
Schlagzeug *n*	percussion, drums (jazz)
Schlagzeuger *m*	percussionist
Schlegel *m*	drumstick, percussion stick
Schleifer *m*	slide (ornament)
schleppen	to drag
nicht schleppen	do not drag
schleppend	dragging
Schlüssel *m*	clef
Schluß *m*	ending, cadence
schmetternd	blaring, shattering, blazing
Schminke *f*	make-up
sich schminken	to make-up
Schnarrsaite *f*	snare
Schnecke *f*	scroll
schnell	quick
schön	beautiful
Schräge *f*	rake (sloping stage)
schütteln	to shake
schwach	weak, faint
Schwammschlegel *m*	soft sponge stick
schwebend	floating
Schwebung *f*	fluctuation, beats between notes not quite in tune
schweigen	to be silent
Schwelltritt *m*	swell pedal (organ)
Schwellwerk *n*	swell organ
schwer	heavy
schwerfällig	heavy, deliberate
schwermütig	melancholy, heavy-hearted
Schwung *m*	swing
mit Schwung	with movement
Sechzehntel *n*, Sechzehntelnote *f*	semiquaver
Seele *f*	soul, sound-post (of a string instrument)
sehnsuchtsvoll	longingly, ardently
sehr	very
Seitenbühne *f*	wings
Sekunde *f*	second
Septett *n*	septet
Septime *f*	seventh (interval)
Setzerkombination *f*	setter piston (organ)
seufzen	to sigh
Sexte *f*	sixth (interval)
Sextett *n*	sextet
Signallampe *f*	cue light

Sinfonie *f*	symphony
sinfonische **Dichtung** *f*	symphonic poem
singen	to sing
Singspiel *n*	singspiel (opera with spoken dialogue)
Sitzprobe *f*	rehearsal for singers with orchestra
Skizze *f*	sketch
sofort	immediately
Solist *m*	soloist
Sopranblockflöte *f*	descant recorder
sordiniert	muted
Souffleur *m*	prompter
Souffleurkasten *m*	prompt box
soufflieren	to prompt
spielen	to play, to act
Spieloper *f*	comic opera
Spielmann *m*	minstrel
Spieltisch *m*	console
Spinett *n*	spinet
Sprechgesang *m*	spoken song
Sprechstimme *f*	vocal style, more spoken than sung
springend	jumping
springender **Bogen** *m*	spiccato
Spitze *f*	point
an der Spitze	at the point
Stachel *m*	spike
Ständchen *n*	serenade
Stange *f*	stick (of bow)
stark	strong
Steg *m*	bridge (of a string instrument)
am Steg	near the bridge
auf dem Steg	on the bridge
steigern	to intensify
steigernd	increasing
Steigerung *f*	intensification
Stellwerk *n*	lighting control box (theatre)
sterbend	dying away
stets	always
Stichwort *n*	cue (spoken)
Stierhorn *n*	stierhorn (Wagnerian instrument; the part is often played by trombones)
Stil *m*	style
still	still, calm
Stimme *f*	voice
stimmen	to tune
Stimmführung *f*	part-writing
Stimmgabel *f*	tuning-fork

stimmig	voiced
dreistimmig	three-part
Stimmung *f*	atmosphere, mood, pitch
Stimmzimmer *n*	band-room
straff	strict
ein straffes Tempo *n*	strict time
streichen	to bow, stroke
Streicher *pl*	strings
Streichinstrument *n*	string instrument
streng	strict
Strich *m*	stroke
Strich für Strich	separate bows
Strichart *f*	bowing
Stück *n*	piece
stürmisch	stormy
stumm	silent, dumb
Subdominantparallele *f*	submediant
süß	sweet
summen	to hum
Synkope *f*	syncopation
System *n*	stave
Szene *f*	scene
Tabulatur *f*	tablature
täppisch	awkward, clumsy
Tafelmusik *f*	music to be played during or after meals
Takt *m*	bar, beat, time
ein Takt wie vorher zwei	one bar in the time of two previous bars
im Takt	in time
taktmäßig	in time
Taktmesser *m*	metronome
Taktschlag *m*	beat
Taktstock *m*	baton
Taktstrich *m*	bar-line
Taktzeichen *n*	time signature
Tambour *m*	military drummer
Tamburin *n*	tambourine
Tamtam *m*	tam-tam
Tanz *m*	dance
Tastatur *f*	keyboard
Taste *f*	key (keyboard instrument)
Tasteninstrument *n*	keyboard instrument
technischer Direktor *m*	technical director
Teil *m*	part, division (organ)
Teilgehäuse *n*	division case (organ)
Teller *m*	cymbal plate
Tenor *m*	tenor

Tenorschlüssel *m*	tenor clef
Terz *f*	third (interval)
Theater *n*	theatre
Theaterkasse *f*	box office
Theaterstück *n*	play
Thema *n*	theme, subject
Theorbe *f*	theorbo
tief	low, deep
zu tief	flat
Ton *m*	note, tone, timbre, whole tone, music
Tonalität *f*	tonality
Tonart *f*	key
Tonband *n*	tape
Tonbandaufnahme *f*	tape recording
Tondichtung *f*	symphonic poem, tone poem
Tonfall *m*	inflection of voice in speech
Tonkunst *f*	composition
Tonleiter *f*	scale
Tonreihe *f*	note row
Tragödie *f*	tragedy
Traktur *f*	action (organ)
elektrische Traktur	electric action
mechanische Traktur	mechanical action, tracker action
transponieren	to transpose
Trauermarsch *m*	funeral march
Trauermusik *f*	funeral music
Trauerspiel *n*	tragedy
traurig	sad
Traversflöte *f*	flute (before 1750)
treibend	pressing on
Tremulant *m*	tremulant (organ stop)
Triller *m*	trill
Triller mit Nachschlag *m*	trill with turn
Triller ohne Nachschlag *m*	trill without turn
Triole *f*	triplet
Trommel *f*	drum
große Trommel *f*	bass drum
kleine Trommel *f*	side drum, snare drum
Rührtrommel *f*	tenor drum
Trompete *f*	trumpet
Trompeter *m*	trumpeter
trübe	gloomy, sad
Trugschluß *m*	interrupted cadence
Tuba *f*	tuba
Tubist *m*, **Tubaspieler** *m*	tuba player
üben	to practise

über	over, above
Übergang *m*	transition
übermäßig	augmented
übermäßiger Dreiklang *m*	augmented triad
übermütig	high-spirited
übersetzen	to translate
Übung *f*	exercise
Umkehrung *f*	inversion
umstimmen	to change the usual tuning
unbestimmt	indefinite
ungeduldig	impatient
ungefähr	approximate
unhörbar	inaudible
unmerklich	imperceptible
unmerklich schneller	imperceptibly faster
unruhig	restless
unten	below, underneath
unter	under, lower
Unterdominante *f*	subdominant
Untermediante *f*	submediant
Unterricht *f*	lesson, teaching, instruction
Untertitel *m*	subtitle
Uraufführung *f*	world première
ursprünglich	original
Urtext *m*	original version
Variante *f*	variation
Ventil *n*	valve, pallet
sich verbeugen	to bow
verdoppeln	to double
Verein *m*	society
Verfolger *m*	follow spot
verhallen	to die away
verkleinert	diminished
verklingen, verlöschen	to die away
vermindert	diminished
verminderter Dreiklang *m*	diminished triad
Verschiebung *f*	shift, soft pedal
mit Verschiebung	with soft pedal, una corda, with rubato
verschwinden	to disappear
Versenkung *f*	trap (theatrical)
versetzen	to transpose
Versetzungszeichen *n*	accidental (sign)
verstimmt	out of tune
vertonen	to set to music
Vertrag *m*	contract
Verzeichnis *n*	catalogue
Verzierung *f*	ornament

viel	much, many
vierhändig	for four hands
Viertel n, **Viertelnote** f	crotchet
Viola f	viola
Violine f	violin
Violinschlüssel m	treble clef
Volk n	folk, people
Volkslied n	folksong
volkstümlich	folk-like
Volksweise f	folktune
voll	full
volles **Werk** n	full organ
vollständig	complete
vollständige **Kadenz** f	perfect cadence
von	from
vor	before, in front of, ago
Vorbühne f	apron stage
Vorhalt m	suspension
Vorhang m	curtain
eiserner **Vorhang**	safety curtain
Vorhang nehmen	to take a curtain call
vorhin	previously
vorige	previous
Vorschlag m	appoggiatura
vorsingen	to sing in front of someone
Vorsingen n	audition (of singers)
Vorspiel n	prelude
vorspielen	to play in front of someone
Vorspielen n	audition (of players)
Vorstellung f	performance
vorwärts	onwards
Wachtelpfeife f	quail pipe
Wärme f	warmth
Waldhorn n	hunting horn, natural horn
Walze f	crescendo pedal (organ)
Walzer m	waltz
Walzer tanzen	to waltz
wechseln	to change
weg	away, off
wehmütig	sorrowful
weich	soft, gentle
Weihnachtslied n	Christmas carol
weinend	weeping
Weise f	way, manner, melody
weltlich	secular
wenig	little, few
werdend	becoming
stärker werdend	becoming louder

227

Werk *n*	work
Werkprinzip *n*	organ design
widerhallen	to resound
wie	as, how, as if
wie vorhin, wie zuvor	as before
wieder	again
wiederholen	to repeat
wiegen	to rock
Wiegenlied *n*	lullaby
wild	wild
Windlade *f*	wind-chest
Wirbel *m*	drum-roll, tuning-peg
wohltemperiert	well-tempered, equal-tempered
wuchtig	vigorous, powerful
wütend	furious
Wunsch *m*	wish
nach Wunsch	ad lib., according to one's wish
Wut *f*	temper, fury
Xylophon *n*	xylophone
zählen	to count
Zäsur *f*	break, pause
zart	tender, delicate
Zeichen *n*	sign
Zeit *f*	time
sich Zeit lassen	to take time
zeitgenössisch	contemporary
Zeitmaß *n*	tempo, speed
Zeitschrift *f*	magazine, journal
Ziehharmonika *f*	accordion
ziemlich	fairly, rather
zierlich	elegant, graceful
Zimbelstern *m*	cymbelstern (rotating star of bells on top of organ pipes)
Zither *f*	zither
zitternd	trembling
zögernd	hesitating, hesitant, delaying
zu	too, to, closed
zu 2/zwei	second instrument to play the same part
Züge *pl*	flies (theatrical)
zufällig	by chance
Zug *m*	organ stop, slide (trombone)
Zugposaune *f*	slide trombone
Zugtrompete *f*	slide trumpet
Zuhörer *m*	listener, audience
zunehmend	increasing
Zunge *f*	tongue, reed (organ)

Zungenstimmen *pl*	reeds (organ)
zupfen	to pluck
Zupfinstrument *n*	plucked instrument
zurückhalten	to hold back
zusammen	together
Zuschauer *pl*	audience
Zuschauerraum *m*	auditorium
Zweiunddreißigstel *n*, **Zweiunddreißigstelnote** *f*	demisemiquaver
zwischen	between
Zwischenspiel *n*	interlude, episode in a fugue
Zwölftonmusik *f*	twelve-note music

Organ Terminology (German–English)

Aliquote *f*	mutation stop
Brustwerk *n*	division of pipes immediately above the player
Disposition *f*	specification
Fernwerk *n*	echo organ
Flöte *f*	flute
Gebläse *n*	wind supply
Generalsetzerkombination *f*	general setter piston
Handzug *m*	hand stop
Hauptwerk *n*	great organ (nearest equivalent)
Heuler *m*	cipher
Intonation *f*	voicing
Jalousie *f*	swell shutter
Jalousieschweller *m*	swell box
Koppel *f*	coupler
Manual *n*	manual
Manualkoppel *f*	manual coupler
Mensuration *f*	scale (of pipe)
Mixtur *f*	mixture stop
Oberwerk *n*	division of pipes high in the case
Orgel *f*	organ
Orgelbauer *m*	organ builder
Pedal *n*	pedal
Pedalkoppel *f*	pedal coupler
Pedalwerk *n*	pedal organ
Pfeife *f*	pipe
Positiv *n*	positive organ, (choir organ, nearest equivalent)
Prinzipal *m*	principal (diapason, nearest equivalent)
Prospekt *m*	case design

Register *n*	stop
Registertraktur *f*	stop action
Registerzug *m*	organ stop
Rohr *n*	reed
Rohrwerk *n*	reeds
Rollschweller *m*	general crescendo pedal to bring out all the stops
Rückpositiv *n*	positive organ with pipes behind the player
Schwelltritt *m*	swell pedal
Schwellwerk *n*	swell organ
Setzerkombination *f*	setter piston
Spieltisch *m*	console
Streicher *pl*	strings
Teil *m*	division
Teilgehäuse *n*	division case
Traktur *f*	action
elektrische Traktur	electric action
mechanische Traktur	mechanical action
	tracker action
Tremulant *m*	tremulant
Ventil *n*	pallet, valve
volles Werk *n*	full organ
Walze *f*	crescendo pedal
Werkprinzip *n*	organ design
Windlade *f*	wind-chest
Zimbelstern *m*	cymbelstern (rotating star of bells on top of pipes)
Zug *m*	organ stop
Zunge *f*	reed
Zungenstimmen *pl*	reeds

Abbreviations

Abb.	Abbildung	*illustration*
Abk.	Abkürzung	*abridgment, abbreviation, reduction*
Abs.	Absender	*sender, dispatcher*
allg.	allgemein	*general*
Anm.	Anmerkung	*note*
Art.	Artikel	*article*
Aufl.	Auflage	*edition*
Ausg.	Ausgabe	*edition*
Bd(e)	Band (⁻e)	*volume(s)*
bearb.	bearbeitet	*revised*
bes.	besonders	*especially*
best.	bestimmt	*definitely*
betr.	betrifft	*concerning*

230

BRD Bundesrepublik Deutschland	*Federal Republic of Germany*
b.w. bitte wenden	*please turn over, p.t.o.*
BWV Bach-Werke-Verzeichnis	*prefix to the numbering system of the works of Johann Sebastian Bach in the catalogue by Wolfgang Schmieder*
ca. circa	*about, circa*
D Deutsch	*prefix to the numbering system of the works of Franz Schubert in the catalogue by Otto Deutsch*
DDR Deutsche Demokratische Republik	*German Democratic Republic*
desgl. desgleich	*likewise*
dgl. dergleichen	*likewise*
d. Gr. der Große	*the Great*
d.h. das heißt	*that is, i.e.*
d.i. das ist	*that is, i.e.*
DM Deutsche Mark	*German Mark*
do. ditto	*ditto*
dt., dtsch. deutsch	*German*
d. Vf. der Verfasser	*author*
ebd. ebenda	*in the same place*
ev. evangelisch	*Protestant*
evtl. eventuell	*possibly*
Ez. Einzahl	*singular*
f. folgende (Seite)	*following (page)*
ff. folgende (Seiten)	*following (pages)*
Forts. Fortsetzung	*continuation*
frz. französisch	*French*
geb. geboren	*born*
gen. gennant	*mentioned, called*
gebr. gebräuchlich	*customary*
gesch. geschieden	*divorced*
Gesch. Geschichte	*history*
gest. gestorben	*died*
get. geteilt	*divided*
gez. gezeichnet	*signed*
G.m.b.H. Gesellschaft mit beschränkter Haftung	*limited company*
hl. heilig	*holy*
Hob. Hoboken	*prefix to the numbering system of the works of Joseph Haydn in the catalogue by Anthony van Hoboken*

231

hpt haupt	*main*
hrsg. herausgegeben	*edited*
i. im, in	*in*
inkl. inklusiv	*inclusive*
Jb. Jahrbuch	*annual*
Jh. Jahrhundert	*century*
K Köchel	*prefix to the numbering system of the works of Wolfgang Amadeus Mozart in the catalogue by Ludwig von Köchel*
Kap. Kapitel	*chapter*
kath. Katholisch	*Catholic*
kgl. königlich	*royal*
Kpll. Kapellmeister	*conductor, director of music*
l. links	*left*
lat. lateinisch	*Latin*
lfd. laufend	*current*
Lit. Literatur	*literature*
Ltg. Leitung	*direction*
luth. lutherisch	*Lutheran*
med. medizinisch	*medical*
Mz. Mehrzahl	*plural*
n. Chr. nach Christus	*A.D.*
N.N. nomen nescio	*unknown*
Nr. Nummer	*number*
o. ohne	*without*
o.ä. oder ähnliche	*or similar*
od. oder	*or*
offiz. offiziell	*official*
Orch. Orchester	*orchestra*
Öst. Österreich	*Austria*
Pf Pfennig	*Pfennig (German penny)*
Pfd. Pfund	*pound*
P.H. Pädagogische Hochschule	*College of Education*
Pkt. Punkt	*point, stop*
P.S. Postskriptum	*postscript*
r. rechts	*right*
S. Seite	*page*
s. siehe	*see*
s.o. siehe oben	*see above*
sog. sogenannt	*so-called*
St. Sankt	*saint*
Str. Straße	*street, road*
s.u. siehe unten	*see below*

Taf. Tafel	*plate (illustration)*
u. und	*and*
u.a. unter anderen	*among other things*
u.ä. und ähnliche	*and similar*
urspr. ursprünglich	*originally*
usf und so fort	*and so on*
usw und so weiter	*etc.*
u.v.a. und viel andere	*and many others*
v. Chr. vor Christus	*B.C.*
vgl. vergleiche	*compare, cf.*
wiss. wissenschaftlich	*academic, scientific*
WoO Werke ohne Opuszahl	*works without opus number*
Wq Wotquenne	*prefix to the numbering system of the works of C.P.E.Bach in the catalogue by Alfred Wotquenne*
z. zu	*to, at*
z.B. zum Beispiel	*for example*
z.T. zum Teil	*partly*
zus. zusammen	*together*
z.Z. zur Zeit	*at the time*

Vocal Categories of Operatic Roles

It is customary in German opera houses for operatic roles to be classified in vocal categories, into one or more of which a singer is cast, according to the characteristics of his or her voice. A principal singer expects to sing the roles in these categories as they arise in the repertory. As can be seen from the list of selected roles below, there is some overlap: Carmen may be cast as **Charaktersopran**, **dramatischer Mezzosopran** or **dramatischer Alt**.

Soubrette
Papagena (Mozart, *Die Zauberflöte*)
Marzelline (Beethoven, *Fidelio*)
Ännchen (Weber, *Der Freischütz*)

Lyrischer Koloratur Sopran / Koloratursoubrette
Susanna (Mozart, *Le nozze di Figaro*)
Woglinde (Wagner, *Das Rheingold*)
Marzelline (Beethoven, *Fidelio*)

Lyrischer Sopran
Pamina (Mozart, *Die Zauberflöte*)
Wellgunde (Wagner, *Das Rheingold*)
Mimì (Puccini, *La bohème*)

Jugendlich-dramatischer Sopran
Desdemona (Verdi, *Otello*)
Eva (Wagner, *Die Meistersinger von Nürnberg*)
Tatiana (Tchaikovsky, *Eugene Onegin*)

Dramatischer Koloratursopran
Königin der Nacht (Mozart, *Die Zauberflöte*)
Donna Anna (Mozart, *Don Giovanni*)
Violetta (Verdi, *La traviata*)

Dramatischer Sopran
Leonore (Beethoven, *Fidelio*)
1. Dame (Mozart, *Die Zauberflöte*)
Aida (Verdi, *Aida*)

Charaktersopran
Carmen (Bizet, *Carmen*)
Mimi (Puccini, *La bohème*)
Marie (Berg, *Wozzeck*)

Hochdramatischer Sopran
Alceste (Gluck, *Alceste*)
Isolde (Wagner, *Tristan und Isolde*)
Brünnhilde (Wagner, *Der Ring des Nibelungen*)

Dramatischer Mezzosopran
Carmen (Bizet, *Carmen*)
2. Dame (Mozart, *Die Zauberflöte*)
Amneris (Verdi, *Aida*)

Lyrischer Mezzosopran / Spielalt
Marcellina (Mozart, *Le nozze di Figaro*)
Hänsel (Humperdinck, *Hänsel und Gretel*)
Floßhilde (Wagner, *Das Rheingold*)

Dramatischer Alt
Dalila (Saint-Saëns, *Samson*)
Carmen (Bizet, *Carmen*)
Amneris (Verdi, *Aida*)

Tiefer Alt
Mistress Quickly (Verdi, *Falstaff*)
Erda (Wagner, *Siegfried*)
3. Dame (Mozart, *Die Zauberflöte*)

Spieltenor / Tenorbuffo
Jaquino (Beethoven, *Fidelio*)
Monostatos (Mozart, *Die Zauberflöte*)
Mime (Wagner, *Das Rheingold*)

Lyrischer Tenor
Tamino (Mozart, *Die Zauberflöte*)
Alfredo (Verdi, *La traviata*)
Albert Herring (Britten, *Albert Herring*)

Jugendlicher Heldentenor
Florestan (Beethoven, *Fidelio*)
Don José (Bizet, *Carmen*)
Radames (Verdi, *Aida*)

Charaktertenor
Herodes (Strauss, *Salome*)
Dr Caius (Verdi, *Falstaff*)
Loge (Wagner, *Das Rheingold*)

Heldentenor
Otello (Verdi, *Otello*)
Tristan (Wagner, *Tristan und Isolde*)
Peter Grimes (Britten, *Peter Grimes*)

Lyrischer Bariton
Papageno (Mozart, *Die Zauberflöte*)
Figaro (Rossini, *Il barbiere di Siviglia*)
Wolfram (Wagner, *Tannhäuser*)

Kavalierbariton
Don Giovanni (Mozart, *Don Giovanni*)
Scarpia (Puccini, *Tosca*)
Wolfram (Wagner, *Tannhäuser*)

Charakterbariton
Pizarro (Beethoven, *Fidelio*)
Figaro (Mozart, *Le nozze di Figaro*)
Wozzeck (Berg, *Wozzeck*)

Heldenbariton / Hoher Baß
Scarpia (Puccini, *Tosca*)
Falstaff (Verdi, *Falstaff*)
Wotan (Wagner, *Der Ring des Nibelungen*)

Spielbaß / Baßbuffo
Leporello (Mozart, *Don Giovanni*)
Dr Bartolo (Rossini, *Il barbiere di Siviglia*)
Beckmesser (Wagner, *Die Meistersinger von Nürnberg*)

Schwerer Spielbaß / Schwerer Baßbuffo
Osmin (Mozart, *Die Entführung aus dem Serail*)
Basilio (Rossini, *Il barbiere di Siviglia*)
Ochs (Strauss, *Der Rosenkavalier*)

Charakterbaß / Baß-Bariton
Don Alfonso (Mozart, *Così fan tutte*)
Don Fernando (Beethoven, *Fidelio*)
Hunding (Wagner, *Die Walküre*)

Seriöser Baß
Sarastro (Mozart, *Die Zauberflöte*)
Ramphis (Verdi, *Aida*)
Pogner (Wagner, *Die Meistersinger von Nürnberg*)

Musical Signs

Note names

♮	♯	𝄪	♭	𝄫
A	Ais	Aisis	As	Ases
H	His	Hisis	B	Bes
C	Cis	Cisis	Ces	Ceses
D	Dis	Disis	Des	Deses
E	Eis	Eisis	Es	Eses
F	Fis	Fisis	Fes	Feses
G	Gis	Gisis	Ges	Geses

The stave

1   2   3   4   5   6   7   8   9   10   11   12   13   14

1 **Violinschlüssel** *m*
2 **Altschlüssel** *m*
3 **Tenorschlüssel** *m*
4 **Baßschlüssel** *m*
5 **Kreuz** *n*
6 **Doppelkreuz** *n*
7 **Be** *n*

8 **Doppelbe** *n*
9 **Auflösungszeichen** *n*
10 **Taktstrich** *m*
11 **Takt** *m*
12 **Doppeltaktstrich** *m*
13 **Wiederholungszeichen** *n*
14 **Pausenzeichen** *n*

Note values

🏵	**Doppeltaktnote** *f*	
○	**ganze Note** *f*	
𝅗𝅥	**Halbe** *f*	
𝅘𝅥	**Viertel** *n*	
𝅘𝅥𝅮	**Achtel** *n*	
𝅘𝅥𝅯	**Sechzehntel** *n*	
𝅘𝅥𝅰	**Zweiunddreißigstel** *n*	
𝅘𝅥𝅱	**Vierundsechzigstel** *n*	

Rests

⅄	**Doppeltaktpause** *f*
▬	**ganze Pause** *f*
▬	**halbe Pause** *f*
𝄽	**Viertelpause** *f*
𝄾	**Achtelpause** *f*
𝄿	**Sechzehntelpause** *f*
𝅀	**Zweiunddreißgstelpause** *f*
𝅁	**Vierundsechzigstelpause** *f*

Time signatures

$\frac{2}{2}$	**Zweihalbetakt** *m*	$\frac{4}{4}$	**Viervierteltakt** *m*
$\frac{2}{4}$	**Zweivierteltakt** *m*	$\frac{6}{8}$	**Sechsachteltakt** *m*
$\frac{3}{4}$	**Dreivierteltakt** *m*	$\frac{9}{8}$	**Neunachteltakt** *m*
$\frac{3}{8}$	**Dreiachteltakt** *m*	$\frac{12}{16}$	**Zwölfsechzehnteltakt** *m*

Instruments (English–German)

accordion	Akkordeon *n*, Ziehharmonika *f*
alto flute	Altflöte *f*
bagpipe	Dudelsack *m*
barrel organ	Drehorgel *f*, Leierkasten *m*
bass drum	große Trommel *f*
basset-horn	Bassetthorn *n*
bass flute	Baßflöte *f*
bassoon	Fagott *n*
bass recorder	Baßblockflöte *f*
baton	Taktstock *m*
bell	Glocke *f*
tubular bells	Glocken *pl*
jingle bells, sleighbells	Schellen *pl*
bow	Bogen *m*
brass instrument	Blechblasinstrument *n*

237

bridge	Steg *m*
near the bridge	am Steg
on the bridge	auf dem Steg
castanets	Kastagnetten *pl*
celesta	Celesta *f*
cello	Cello *n*
chamber orchestra	Kammerorchester *n*
clarinet	Klarinette *f*
clavichord	Klavichord *n*
cor anglais	Englischhorn *n*
cornet	Kornett *n*
cowbell	Kuhglocke *f*
crumhorn	Krummhorn *n*
cymbal	Becken *n*
free-hanging cymbal	freihängendes Becken
descant recorder	Sopranblockflöte *f*
drum	Trommel *f*
bass drum	große Trommel *f*
kettledrum	Pauke *f*
military drum	Militärtrommel *f*
side drum, snare drum	kleine Trommel *f*
tenor drum	Rührtrommel *f*
timpani	Pauken *pl*
drum-roll	Wirbel *m*
drumstick	Schlägel *m*, Schlegel *m*
double bass	Kontrabaß *m*
double bassoon	Kontrafagott *n*
dulcimer	Hackbrett *n*
English horn	Englischhorn *n*
fiddle	Geige *f*, Fidel *f*, Fiedel *f*
fingerboard	Griffbrett *n*
flugelhorn	Flügelhorn *m*
flute	Flöte *f*
alto flute	Altflöte *f*
bass flute	Baßflöte *f*
transverse flute	Querflöte *f*
glockenspiel	Glockenspiel *n*
gong	Gong *m*
guitar	Gitarre *f*
harmonika	Mundharmonika *f*
harp	Harfe *f*
harpsichord	Cembalo *n*, Kielflügel *m*,
heel (of a bow)	Frosch *m*
at the heel	am Frosch
horn (French)	Horn *n*

hunting horn	Jagdhorn *n*, Waldhorn *n*
hurdy-gurdy	Drehleier *m*
instrument	Instrument *n*
kettledrum	Pauke *f*
key (keyboard instrument)	Taste *f*
key (wind instrument)	Klappe *f*
keyboard	Tastatur *f*
keyboard instrument	Tasteninstrument *n*
lute	Laute *f*
marimba	Marimbaphon *n*
mouthpiece	Mundstück *n*
mute	Dämpfer *m*
mute on	Dämpfer auf
mute off	Dämpfer ab
muted (brass instrument)	gestopft
muted (string instrument)	gedämpft
oboe	Oboe *f*
open (unmuted)	offen
open string	leere Saite *f*, offene Saite *f*
orchestra	Orchester *n*
organ	Orgel *f*
percussion	Schlagzeug *n*
percussion instrument	Schlaginstrument *n*
percussion stick	Schlegel *m*
piano	Klavier *n*
grand piano	Flügel *m*
piccolo	Pikkolo *m*
plucked instrument	Zupfinstrument *n*
racket	Rackett *n*
rattle	Ratsche *f*
recorder	Blockflöte *f*
descant recorder	Sopranblockflöte *f*
treble recorder	Altblockflöte *f*
bass recorder	Baßblockflöte *f*
reed	Rohr *n*
saw	Säge *f*
shawm	Schalmei *f*
side drum	kleine Trommel *f*
slide	Zug *m*
snare	Schnarrsaite *f*
snare drum	kleine Trommel *f*
spinet	Spinett *n*
string	Saite *f*
string instrument	Streichinstrument *n*

239

strings	Streicher *pl*
switch	Rute *f*
tailpiece	Saitenhalter *m*
tambourine	Tamburin *n*, Schellentrommel *f*
tam-tam	Tamtam *m*
tenor drum	Rührtrommel *f*
theorbo	Theorbe *f*
timpani	Pauken *pl*
transverse flute	Querflöte *f*
treble recorder	Altblockflöte *f*
trombone	Posaune *f*
trumpet	Trompete *f*
valveless trumpet	Naturtrompete *f*
tuba	Tuba *f*
tubular bells	Glocken *pl*
tuning-peg	Wirbel *m*
valve	Ventil *n*
viol	Gambe *f*
viola	Bratsche *f*
viola da gamba	Gambe *f*
violin	Geige *f*, Violine *f*
whip	Peitsche *f*
wind band	Blasorchester *n*, Harmonie *f*
wind instrument	Blasinstrument *n*
woodblock	Holzblock *m*
wooden stick	Holzschlegel *m*
woodwind instrument	Holzblasinstrument *n*
xylophone	Xylophon *n*
youth orchestra	Jugendorchester *n*
zither	Zither *f*

Theatre Terminology (English–German)

act	Akt *m*, Aufzug *m*
to act	spielen
to appear on stage	auftreten
applause	Beifall *m*
apron stage	Vorbühne *f*
assistant stage manager	Assistent *m*
audience	Publikum *n*, Zuschauer *pl*
audition	Vorsingen *n*, Vorspielen *n*
auditorium	Zuschauerraum *m*
back-cloth	Prospekt *m*

backstage	hinter der Bühne *f*
ballet	Ballett *n*
band-room	Stimmzimmer *n*
Beginners please	Achtung anfangen
blackout	Blackout *m*, *n*
to bow	sich verbeugen
box	Loge *f*
box office	Theaterkasse *f*
cast	Besetzung *f*
chorus	Chor *m*
chorus member	Chorsänger *m*
to coach	einstudieren
comedy	Lustspiel *n*, Komödie *f*
comic opera	Spieloper *f*
conductor	Dirigent *m*, Leiter *m*
contract	Vertrag *m*
costume	Kostüm *n*
costume designer	Kostümbildner *m*
cue (musical)	Einsatz *m*
cue (spoken)	Stichwort *m*
cue light	Signallampe *f*
curtain	Vorhang *m*
to take a curtain call	Vorhang nehmen
design	Ausstattung *f*
designer	Bühnenbildner *m*
director	Regisseur *m*
downstage	nach vorn
dress circle	erster Rang *m*
dressing room	Garderobe *f*, Künstlergarderobe *f*
dress-rehearsal	Hauptprobe *f*
final dress-rehearsal	Generalprobe *f*
to enter	auftreten
entrance (of building)	Eingang *m*
entrance (on stage)	Auftritt *m*
exit (of building)	Ausgang *m*
exit (off stage)	Abgang *m*
fee	Gage *f*, Honorar *n*
first night	Première *f*
first performance	Erstaufführung
flies	Züge *pl*
follow spot	Verfolger *m*
footlights	Rampe *f*
gallery	Balkon *m*, Gallerie *f*
Go!	Los!
guest performance	Gastspiel *n*
interval	Pause *f*

left	links
lighting	Beleuchtung *f*
lighting control box	Stellwerk *n*
lighting designer	Beleuchtungsmeister *m*
lighting director	Beleuchtungschef *m*
make-up	Schminke *f*
to make up	sich schminken
make-up man	Maskenbildner *m*
manager, general	Intendant *m*
opera, opera company	Oper *f*
opera house	Opernhaus *n*
orchestra pit	Orchestergraben *m*
to perform	aufführen
performance	Aufführung *f*
first performance	Erstaufführung *f*
piano technical rehearsal	Klavierhauptprobe *f*
pit, orchestra	Orchestergraben *m*
play	Theaterstück *n*, Schauspiel *n*
première	Première *f*
world première	Uraufführung *f*
principal role	Hauptrolle *f*, Fachpartie *f*
producer	Regisseur *m*
production	Regie *f*, Inszenierung *f*
to prompt	soufflieren
prompt box	Souffleurkasten *m*
prompt desk	Inspiziententisch *m*
prompter	Souffleur *m*
prop	Requisit *n*
rake (sloping stage)	Schräge *f*
rehearsal	Probe *f*
répétiteur	Korrepetitor *m*, Repetitor *m*
revolving stage	Drehbühne *f*
right	rechts
role	Rolle *f*, Partie *f*
safety curtain	eisener Vorhang *m*
scene	Auftritt *m*, Szene *f*
scenery	Kulissen *pl*
set	Bühnenbild *n*
Sitzprobe (rehearsal for singers with orchestra)	Sitzprobe *f*
spotlight	Scheinwerfer *m*
stage	Bühne *f*
stage direction	Anweisung *f*
stage director	technischer Leiter *m*
stage-hand	Bühnenarbeiter *m*

242

stage left (prompt side)	links
stage right (opposite prompt)	rechts
stage manager	Bühnenmeister *m*, Inspizient *m*
stalls	Parkett *n*
Stand by	Achtung!
Stop!	Halt!
technical director	technischer Direktor *m*
theatre	Theater *n*
thunder	Donner *m*
to tour	gastieren
tragedy	Tragödie *f*, Trauerspiel *n*
trap	Versenkung *f*
upper circle	zweiter Rang *m*
upstage	nach hinten
vocal score	Klavierauszug *m*
wardrobe	Garderobe *f*
wardrobe mistress	Gewandmeisterin *f*
warm-up room	Einsingzimmer *n*
wings	Seitenbühne *f*

Specimen Contract for an Opera Singer

VERTRAGLICHE VEREINBARUNG

zwischen der Direktion des Opernhauses H—— und
Frau Katharina Reich

Das Opernhaus verpflichtet Frau Katharina Reich für
die Zeit 3. Mai–29. Juni 19—

Werk: Die Zauberflöte
   Partie: Pamina

Daten:
   Proben: 3.–5. Mai 19— Proben in H——
                          6. Mai 19— Reise und Probe in W——
                          28. Juni 19— Probe in K——
   Vorstellungen: 7. Mai 19— Vorstellung in W——
                          16. Juni 19— Vorstellung in H——
                          23. Juni 19— Vorstellung in H——
                          29. Juni 19— Vorstellung in K——

   Ä n d e r u n g e n   v o r b e h a l t e n !

Gage:
   Proben: Pro Probentag ¹/₁₂ (einen Zwölften) brutto des
      Vorstellungshonorars.
   Vorstellungen: Vorstellungshonorar von DM——
      brutto.
   Tagesspesen: DM——.
   Reiseentschädigung: Ersatz der anfallenden Flugreisen.
Damit sind sämtliche finanzielle Verpflichtungen
abgegolten.

Frau Katharina Reich garantiert, daß sie bei eventuellen
Gastspielen der Oper mit der Zauberflöte zur Verfügung
steht, wenn diese Gastspiele neun Monate vorher
verbindlich zugesagt werden.

Unterschrift: ————————————— Katharina Reich
Name laut Paß:
Geburtsdatum:
Nationalität:
Ständige Adresse: Telefon:

1 **vertragliche Vereinbarung** *contractual agreement*; *4* **verpflichten** *to engage*; *16* **Änderungen vorbehalten** *subject to alteration*; *17* **die Gage** *fee*; *18* **brutto** *gross*; *19* **das Honorar** *fee*; *22* **Tagesspesen** *daily allowance*; *23* **Reiseentschädigung** *travel expenses*; **der Ersatz** *reimbursement*; *24* **die Verpflichtung** *obligation*; *25* **abgegolten** *fulfilled*; *26* **eventuell** *possible*; *27* **das Gastspiel** *performance on tour*; *27/8* **zur Verfügung stehen** *to be available*; *29* **verbindlich zusagen** *to accept definitely*; *31* **laut** *according to*; **der Paß** *passport*

Specimen Letter of Application

Norddeutscher Rundfunk   London, den 10. Februar 19—
Funkhaus Hamburg
Orchesterbüro

Sehr geehrter Herr,

Ich möchte mich um die Stelle als erster Geiger in Ihrem Orchester bewerben. Könnten Sie mir bitte das Anmeldungsformular übersenden und mir mitteilen, welche Pflichtstücke für das Probespiel erforderlich sind?

Hochachtungsvoll

der Rundfunk *radio*; **das Funkhaus** *broadcasting house*; **sich bewerben um** *to apply for*; **das Anmeldungsformular** *application form*; **das Probespiel** *audition*

245

The Gothic Alphabet

𝔄 𝔅 ℭ 𝔇 𝔈 𝔉 𝔊 ℌ 𝔍 𝔍 𝔎 𝔏 𝔐
a b c d e f g h i j k l m

𝔑 𝔒 𝔓 𝔔 𝔕 𝔖 𝔗 𝔘 𝔙 𝔚 𝔛 𝔜 ℨ
n o p q r sſ t u v w x y z

Gesellschaft der Musikfreunde in Wien
Bösendorferstraße 12
A 1010 Wien

Gothic type (Fraktur) was used for the setting of printed books from the sixteenth century until World War 1 (it is used for the passage on pp. 164-5). Roman type was then introduced and by 1945 it had replaced the old style. Gothic lettering can still be found on old street signs and it is now used for ornamental effect on posters, inn signs and letter headings.

Notes on Authors

Peter Altenberg, 1859–1919. Pseudonym of Richard Engländer. Austrian poet. Altenberg spent his whole life in Vienna and was well known in literary and artistic circles. He was a friend of Alban Berg, whose *Fünf Orchesterlieder nach Ansichtskarten* are settings of five of his short prose poems.

Carl Philipp Emanuel Bach, 1714–88. German composer, the third son of J.S.Bach. From 1738 until 1767 he was cembalist at the court of Frederick the Great in Berlin. He then succeeded Telemann as director of church music in Hamburg. In addition to his many musical compositions, Bach wrote a celebrated treatise on keyboard playing, *Versuch über die wahre Art das Clavier zu spielen* (1753).

Bertolt Brecht, 1898–1956. German poet, dramatist and theatrical producer. Brecht was politically motivated throughout his life and became a Marxist. In addition to his political poems and experimental plays, he collaborated with the composer Kurt Weill in writing *Die Dreigroschenoper*, *Aufstieg und Fall der Stadt Mahagonny*, the school opera *Der Jasager* and *Happy End*. Blacklisted by the Nazi party, he left Berlin in 1933 for Switzerland, and then California, where he lived and worked during the war. In 1949 he returned to East Berlin and founded the famous theatre company the Berliner Ensemble.

Georg Büchner, 1813–37. German dramatist. He was an active revolutionary in Hesse in Germany until 1835, when he escaped first to Strasbourg and then Zürich as a political refugee. He had studied medicine and became a university teacher in Zürich. His literary reputation rests on three plays, *Dantons Tod*, *Woyzeck* and *Leonce und Lena*, and the prose fragment *Lenz*. Only *Dantons Tod* was published in his lifetime; it was made into an opera by the Austrian composer Gottfried von Einem in 1949. Alban Berg's opera *Wozzeck*, based on the second of Büchner's plays, was first performed in 1925. Büchner died of typhoid at the age of 23.

Matthias Claudius, 1740–1815. German poet and journalist. The son of a Lutheran pastor, he studied law and theology. He became editor of the popular newspaper the *Wandsbecker Bote* and was its chief contributor under the pseudonym Asmus. His poetry is devout and simple but powerful. He created the character Freund Hain, the personification of death, who is depicted in an engraving in Matthias's books as a skeleton holding a scythe.

Carl Czerny, 1791–1857. Austrian pianist, teacher and composer. Czerny was a pupil of Beethoven between 1800 and 1803 and himself became a celebrated teacher; Liszt was one of his pupils. He wrote over a thousand musical compositions, but is best known for his piano studies and exercises.

Richard Dehmel, 1863–1920. German lyric poet. He was one of the main writers of the Jugendstil in Berlin around 1900. He wrote plays, poetry, and an autobiography, *Mein Leben*, which was published posthumously. The poem *Verklärte Nacht*, from the collection *Weib und Welt*, was the inspiration for Schoenberg's eponymous string sextet. It shows compassion and the poet's desire to spiritualize sexuality.

Joseph von Eichendorff, 1788–1857. German poet and novelist. A respected soldier and then a government official, Eichendorff was one of the greatest German Romantic poets. As a young man he met other poets of the Romantic movement, including Arnim, Brentano, Kleist and Schlegel, and his poetry attracted the great song composers Schumann, Mendelssohn, Strauss and Wolf. His best-known prose work is *Aus dem Leben eines Taugenichts*, a light-hearted story of the adventures of a good-for-nothing.

Paul Gerhardt, 1607–76. German poet, Lutheran pastor and Protestant hymn-writer. His verses have a direct, simple style and were intended to be sung. The collection *Geistliche Andachten* (1667) contained 120 hymns. Many have been translated into other languages and are to be found in hymnbooks throughout the Christian world. The first two verses of his *O Haupt voll Blut und Wunden* are used by Bach as chorales in the *Matthäus-Passion*.

Hermann von Gilm zu Rosenegg, 1812–64. Austrian civil servant and poet. His work is remembered by three poems set by Strauss: *Allerseelen*, *Die Nacht* and *Zueignung*.

Johann Wolfgang Goethe, 1749–1832. Goethe was elevated to the nobility in 1782, from which year he was known as von Goethe. During his long life Goethe was poet, dramatist, novelist, theatre director, lawyer, civil servant, philosopher, scientist and painter. His literary works include love lyrics, ballads, philosophical poems, classical plays, comedies, tragedies, novels, scientific articles, travel journals, criticism and autobiography. Goethe's poetry attracted many composers and he was the first writer of importance to contribute to the great tradition of German Lieder. In 1774, after an unhappy love for Charlotte, Goethe wrote *Die Leiden des jungen Werther*, a sensationally successful novel that glorified the emotions of love and turned away from the rationalism of the Enlightenment. In 1775 Goethe went to Weimar, where he lived and worked for most of his life. He travelled in Italy for two years (1786–8) and he came to prefer classical forms to the impulsive style of his earlier poems, which were characteristic of the Sturm und Drang movement. The first volume of the novel *Wilhelm Meisters Lehrjahre*, which contains the 'Mignon Lieder' and the 'Gesänge des Harfners' (songs of the harper), was published in 1795. 1808 saw the publication of the first part of the tragedy *Faust*. In that year he met Napoleon and in 1812 Beethoven, but no significant friendship with the composer developed. Mendelssohn created a more favourable impression when, as a young man, he played to the aged Goethe. In his last years Goethe completed the second part of *Faust*, which had occupied him for almost the whole of his creative life.

Friedrich Halm, 1806–71. Pseudonym of Baron von Münch-Bellinghausen, Austrian poet and dramatist. He lived and worked in Vienna as a senior civil servant, custodian of the court library and manager of the two court theatres. He published two volumes of poetry and his plays were successfully performed at the Burgtheater.

Eduard Hanslick, 1825–1904. Austrian writer and music critic. In 1846 Hanslick settled in Vienna and for the next fifty years contributed articles on music to the *Wiener Zeitung*, *Die Presse* and the *Neue Freie Presse*, and was Vienna's foremost critic. His book on aesthetics, *Vom Musikalisch-Schönen*, was published in 1854. Hanslick was a musical conservative, a champion of the classical tradition and a staunch admirer of Schubert, Schumann and Brahms. As a young man of twenty, he wrote a perceptive article on *Tannhäuser*, recognizing Wagner's greatness, but early admiration changed over the years to condemnation. He opposed Wagner's music and his concept of the 'Gesamtkunstwerk'. Wagner brought the hostilities to a personal level when he parodied Hanslick in the character of Beckmesser in *Die Meistersinger*. Hanslick's music criticism offers a penetrating insight into nineteenth-century musical life.

Heinrich Heine, 1797–1856. German poet, satirist and journalist. A Jew by birth, he was baptized in 1825. As a young man Heine lived in Germany and wrote poetry and prose. *Die Harzreise* (1824) is a prose account of his travels in the Harz mountains. His early poems were published in the *Buch der Lieder* (1827), which became a major source for Romantic composers; six of the poems are used in Schubert's 'Schwanengesang' collection. The song cycle *Dichterliebe* is a setting by Schumann of sixteen of Heine's poems. In 1831 Heine moved to Paris, where he worked as a journalist for both French and German newspapers. He lived in Paris until his death.

Hermann Hesse, 1877–1962. German poet and novelist. His father was a missionary in India and Hesse himself began to study theology; but he soon left the Protestant seminary and worked as a bookseller in Germany until 1899, when he moved to Switzerland to concentrate on writing. His first volume of poetry, *Romantische Lieder* (1899), is firmly in the German Romantic tradition. But it is primarily as a novelist that Hesse is remembered, and the themes of his novels express his interest in the East, music and psychoanalysis. He was awarded the Nobel Prize for Literature in 1946.

Hugo von Hofmannsthal, 1874–1929. Austrian poet, dramatist and essayist. Hofmannsthal came from a wealthy family and was educated in Vienna. His early poems, rooted in the nineteenth-century Romantic tradition, were published under the pseudonym Loris when he was sixteen years old. He was hailed as a poetic genius, but at the turn of the century he became disenchanted with the lyric and rejected it as a form for the new age. He turned instead to writing plays for the theatre and the opera house. He collaborated with Strauss for twenty years and together they produced six operas: *Elektra*, *Der Rosenkavalier*, *Ariadne auf Naxos*, *Die Frau ohne Schatten*, *Die ägyptische Helena* and *Arabella*.

Martin Luther, 1483–1546. German theologian. Of humble birth, Luther became the leading figure of the German Reformation. He studied theology, became an Augustinian monk and was made professor at Wittenberg University. He broke with the Church of Rome over his assertion that the papacy was a historical rather than a divine institution and his belief in communication with God without a priestly mediator. He was excommunicated in 1521. Luther's immense literary output consists mainly of theological works in German. The newly invented printing press made possible the wide dissemination of his writings, and this, combined with his decision to express himself in the language of the common people, gained for him a huge following. He wrote over forty powerfully worded hymns, which became as widely known as folksongs. Luther's greatest literary achievement was his translation of the Bible. This work shows a mastery of the vernacular and of poetry, and it was to influence the German language for generations.

John Henry Mackay, 1864–1933. Scottish poet and novelist, educated in Germany. His only volume of poetry, *Sturm*, was published in 1887; he was principally a writer of novels with anti-authoritarian themes.

Friedrich von Matthisson, 1761–1831. German poet. His first volume of poetry, *Lieder* (1781), was favourably reviewed by Schiller. Although widely read in his lifetime, Matthisson is known today principally for three poems set by Beethoven: *Adelaide*, *Opferlied* and *Andenken*.

Alfred Mombert, 1872–1942. German poet. Mombert was a lawyer but later devoted himself to writing. *Der Glühende* (1896) was the first of several volumes of poetry that he published. His writing has a mystic, spiritual quality. He was a friend of Dehmel. As a Jew, he was sent to a concentration camp in 1940 but was rescued and taken to Switzerland, where he died soon afterwards.

Eduard Mörike, 1804–75. German lyric poet. Mörike was for many years a country curate and pastor. His first collection of 143 poems, *Gedichte*, was published in 1838, and further, extended, editions followed in 1856 and 1867. Mörike's poems are masterpieces of the Romantic lyric, expressing man's emotions in contemplative moments. In 1855 he wrote the Novelle *Mozart auf der Reise nach Prag*, a spirited account of an imaginary episode in the life of Mozart. Fifty-three of his poems were set by Wolf as the *Mörike Lieder* (1888).

Julius Mosen, 1803–67. German poet, dramatist and novelist. Mosen was a lawyer, who was appointed director of the court theatre in Oldenburg in 1844. His poetry, novels and plays were popular in his time, but he is remembered chiefly for the poem *Der Nußbaum*, set to music by Schumann.

Friedrich Rückert, 1788–1866. German poet. Rückert was an academic and his interest in oriental languages led to his appointment as professor in that discipline at Erlangen in 1822. From 1841 to 1848 he was professor in Berlin, after which he devoted himself to writing. His large output of poetry includes love poems (*Liebesfrühling*, 1832) and philosophical poetry (*Die Weisheit des Brahmanen*, 1836–9) based on his knowledge of Oriental literature. Mahler set five of his poems in the collection *Rückert Lieder*, and five more (which had been posthumously published in 1872) in *Kindertotenlieder*.

Hugo Salus, 1866–1929. Austrian poet and dramatist. Salus worked as a doctor in Prague, but he was also a popular writer. He published eleven volumes of poetry, and wrote plays and short stories with erotic and satirical themes.

Emanuel Schikaneder, 1748–1812. German librettist and theatre manager. Schikaneder was an actor and singer before becoming the manager of the Kärntnertortheater and later the Theater an der Wieden in Vienna. He wrote the libretto for *Die Zauberflöte*, persuaded Mozart, a fellow Freemason, to write the music and sang the role of Papageno in the first performance in 1791. Schikaneder also wrote librettos for other composers. In 1800 he was made manager of the new Theater an der Wien.

Arthur Schnitzler, 1862–1931. Austrian dramatist and novelist. Schnitzler was born into a well-to-do Jewish family in Vienna. He studied medicine and practised as a doctor. His plays and stories portrayed the preoccupations of middle-class Viennese society as it was in his day, at the end of an era and on the brink of a new age. In drama and in prose his style was experimental. The themes of honour, love, sex and anti-semitism are presented in a light-hearted way, but underneath lies a penetrating analysis of contemporary society.

Robert Schumann, 1810–56. German composer and music critic. Schumann studied law but soon forsook it for music and literature. Although primarily a composer, Schumann wrote articles on music throughout his life. He was founder and editor of the *Neue Zeitschrift für Musik* from 1834 to 1844. He wrote under two pseudonyms: Florestan was his impetuous self while Eusebius represented the more melancholy and contemplative side of his nature. In 1840 Schumann married the pianist Clara Wieck. He met Brahms in 1853 and, in the article 'Neue Bahnen', hailed the young composer as a genius. In 1854 Schumann became mentally unstable, attempted suicide and spent the last two years of his life in an asylum.

Joseph Sonnleithner, 1776–1835. Austrian theatre director. Sonnleithner was manager of the Burgtheater (1804–14) and the Theater an der Wien (1804–7) in Vienna. A musician and librettist, he is best known for his translation from the French of the libretto for Beethoven's opera *Fidelio*.

Louis [Ludwig] **Spohr**, 1784–1859. German violinist, composer and conductor. Spohr was a child prodigy as a violinist and spent much of his adult life travelling in Europe, playing and conducting. He successfully toured Russia, Italy and England, and spent some years in Vienna where he met Beethoven. Spohr's autobiography gives a lively account of musical life in Europe in the first half of the nineteenth century.

Cosima Wagner, 1837–1930. Cosima was the illegitimate daughter of Marie d'Agoult and Liszt the Hungarian pianist and composer. She was brought up in Paris by her grandmother. In 1857 she married the German pianist and conductor Hans von Bülow, by whom she had two children. At the age of thirty-one she left her husband to live with Richard Wagner and the two daughters she had borne him. They lived at Tribschen, where their third child, Siegfried, was born in 1869. In that year Cosima began to keep a diary, recording the momentous events and the day-to-day details of her life with Wagner until his death in 1883.

Richard Wagner, 1813–83. German composer, poet and essayist. Literature was an abiding interest of Wagner and his own writings fill ten volumes. In his early years as a conductor and composer in Germany and Paris he wrote articles to make a living. By the late 1840s he had become a successful composer, but he was also a controversial political figure because of his support for the revolutionaries in the uprisings of 1848–9. He was forced to leave Germany and settled in Zürich. Here he wrote a series of theoretical essays, including 'Das Kunstwerk der Zukunft' (1850) and 'Oper und Drama' (1851), expounding his concept of the 'Gesamtkunstwerk', in which music and drama unite to create a new art form. He also produced political essays, including the outrageously anti-semitic 'Das Judentum in der Musik' (1850). Wagner wrote the texts for all his operas in pursuance of his idea of the 'Gesamtkunstwerk'. His literary style is laboured and archaic and was, to Hanslick, as unacceptable as his music. Wagner's autobiography *Mein Leben* was written at the request of Ludwig II of Bavaria and covers his life up to 1868.

Stefan Zweig, 1881–1942. Austrian poet, novelist, dramatist and librettist. Zweig's first publications were poetry but he later turned to prose. In World War I he was a pacifist and moved from Vienna to Zürich. He wrote wrote several plays, but is best known for his biographies, which are psychological studies of writers and historical figures. In 1935 he wrote the libretto for an opera by Strauss, *Die schweigsame Frau*; as Zweig was a Jew, this collaboration inevitably came to an end when the Nazis came to power in Germany. In 1938 he emigrated to England, New York and finally to Brazil. Zweig was keenly aware of the part Vienna had played in European cultural traditions and his autobiographical novel *Die Welt von Gestern* is an account of Viennese life before and after its cultural decline.

Summary of Grammar

Declension of articles

	masculine	feminine	neuter	plural
nominative	der	die	das	die
accusative	den	die	das	die
genitive	des	der	des	der
dative	dem	der	dem	den

	masculine	feminine	neuter	plural
nominative	ein	eine	ein	*keine
accusative	einen	eine	ein	keine
genitive	eines	einer	eines	keiner
dative	einem	einer	einem	keinen

*keine is used as there is no plural of ein

Personal pronouns

nominative	accusative	dative
ich	mich	mir
du	dich	dir
er	ihn	ihm
sie	sie	ihr
es	es	ihm
wir	uns	uns
ihr	euch	euch
Sie	Sie	Ihnen
sie	sie	ihnen

Declension of nouns and adjectives

1

	masculine	feminine	neuter	plural
nominative	der alte Mann	die schöne Frau	das kleine Buch	die reichen Leute
accusative	den alten Mann	die schöne Frau	das kleine Buch	die reichen Leute
genitive	des alten Mannes	der schönen Frau	des kleinen Buches	der reichen Leute
dative	dem alten Mann	der schönen Frau	dem kleinen Buch	den reichen Leuten

2

	masculine	feminine	neuter	plural
nominative	ein brauner Tisch	eine neue Stadt	ein hübsches Mädchen	keine guten Männer
accusative	einen braunen Tisch	eine neue Stadt	ein hübsches Mädchen	keine guten Männer
genitive	eines braunen Tisches	einer neuen Stadt	eines hübschen Mädchens	keiner guten Männer
dative	einem braunen Tisch	einer neuen Stadt	einem hübschen Mädchen	keinen guten Männern

3

	masculine	feminine	neuter	plural
nominative	roter Wein	warme Suppe	kaltes Wasser	gute Freunde
accusative	roten Wein	warme Suppe	kaltes Wasser	gute Freunde
genitive	roten Weins	warmer Suppe	kalten Wassers	guter Freunde
dative	rotem Wein	warmer Suppe	kaltem Wasser	guten Freunden

Common prepositions and the cases they govern

With the accusative case

ausgenommen	*except*
bis	*until, as far as*
durch	*through, by*
entlang	*along*
für	*for*
gegen	*against, towards*
ohne	*without*
um	*round, at, for, for the sake of*
wider	*against, contrary to*

With the dative case

aus	*out of*
außer	*except, besides*
bei	*at, at the house of, near, with*
entgegen	*towards*
gegenüber	*opposite*
mit	*with*
nach	*after, to, according to*
seit	*since*
von	*from, by*
zu	*to, at*

With the genitive case

außerhalb	*outside*
infolge	*as a result of*
innerhalb	*inside, within*
statt	*instead of*
trotz	*in spite of*
während	*during*
wegen	*on account of, because of*

With the accusative case for movement and the dative case for state

an	*at, on, to, by*
auf	*on, onto*
hinter	*behind*
in	*in, into*
neben	*next to, near, beside*
über	*over, above*
unter	*under, below, among*
vor	*in front of, before*
zwischen	*between*

255

Strong and irregular verbs

Infinitive	3rd person singular present	3rd person singular imperfect	Imperative familiar singular	3rd person imperfect subjunctive	Past participle[1]
backen	bäckt	backte	back(e)	backte	gebacken
befehlen	befiehlt	befahl	befiehl	beföhle	befohlen
beginnen	beginnt	begann	beginn(e)	begänne	begonnen
beißen	beißt	biß	beiß(e)	bisse	gebissen
bergen	birgt	barg	birg	bürge	geborgen
betrügen	betrügt	betrog	betrüg(e)	betröge	betrogen
biegen	biegt	bog	bieg(e)	böge	gebogen
bieten	bietet	bot	biet(e)	böte	geboten
binden	bindet	band	bind(e)	bände	gebunden
bitten	bittet	bat	bitte	bäte	gebeten
blasen	bläst	blies	blas(e)	bliese	geblasen
bleiben	bleibt	blieb	bleib(e)		*geblieben
brechen	bricht	brach	brich	bräche	gebrochen
brennen	brennt	brannte	brenn(e)	breunte	gebrannt
bringen	bringt	brachte	bring(e)	brächte	gebracht
denken	denkt	dachte	denk(e)	dächte	gedacht
dringen	dringt	drang	dring(e)	drange	gedrungen

[1] Verbs are conjugated with **haben** unless the past participle is preceded by an asterisk, which indicates conjugation with **sein**.

Infinitive	3rd person singular present	3rd person singular imperfect	Imperative familiar singular	3rd person imperfect subjunctive	Past participle[1]
dürfen	darf	durfte	—	dürfte	dürfen gedurft
empfangen	empfängt	empfing	empfang(e)	empfinge	empfangen
empfehlen	empfiehlt	empfahl	empfiehl	empföhle	empfohlen
empfinden	empfindet	empfand	empfind(e)	empfände	empfunden
essen	ißt	aß	iß	äße	gegessen
fahren	fährt	fuhr	fahr(e)	führe	*gefahren
fallen	fällt	fiel	fall(e)	fiele	*gefallen
fangen	fängt	fing	fang(e)	finge	gefangen
finden	findet	fand	find(e)	fände	gefunden
fliegen	fliegt	flog	flieg(e)	flöge	*geflogen
fliehen	flieht	floh	flieh(e)	flöhe	*geflohen
fließen	fließt	floß	fließ(e)	flösse	*geflossen
frieren	friert	fror	frier(e)	fröre	gefroren
gebären	gebiert	gebar	gebier	gebäre	geboren
geben	gibt	gab	gib	gäbe	gegeben
gehen	geht	ging	geh(e)	ginge	*gegangen
gelingen	gelingt	gelang	geling(e)	gelänge	*gelungen
gelten	gilt	galt	—	gölte, gälte	*gegolten
genießen	genießt	genoß	genieß(e)	genösse	genossen
geschehen	geschieht	geschah	—	geschähe	*geschehen

Infinitive	3rd person singular present	3rd person singular imperfect	Imperative familiar singular	3rd person imperfect subjunctive	Past participle[1]
gewinnen	gewinnt	gewann	gewinn(e)	gewänne	gewonnen
gießen	gießt	goß	gieß(e)	gieße	gegossen
gleichen	gleicht	glich	gleich(e)	gliche	geglichen
gleiten	gleitet	glitt	gleite	glitte	geglitten
graben	grabt	grub	grab(e)	grübe	gegraben
greifen	greift	griff	greif(e)	griffe	gegriffen
haben	hat	hatte	hab(e)	hätte	gehabt
hangen	hängt	hing	hang(e)	hinge	gehangen
halten	hält	hielt	halt(e)	hielte	gehalten
heben	hebt	hob	heb(e)	höbe	gehoben
heißen	heißt	hieß	heiß(e)	hieße	geheißen
helfen	hilft	half	hilf	hülfe	geholfen
kennen	kennt	kannte	kenn(e)	kennte	gekannt
klingen	klingt	klang	kling(e)	klänge	geklungen
können	kann	konnte	—	könnte	können
kommen	kommt	kam	komm(e)	käme	*gekommen
					gekonnt
kriechen	kriecht	kroch	kriech(e)	kröche	gelassen
laden	läd	lud	lad(e)	lüde	lassen
lassen	läßt	ließ	laß / lasse	ließe	*gelaufen
					gelitten

Infinitive	3rd person singular present	3rd person singular imperfect	Imperative familiar singular	3rd person imperfect subjunctive	Past participle[1]
laufen	läuft	lief	lauf(e)	liefe	geliehen
leiden	leidet	litt	leid(e)	litte	gelesen
leihen	leiht	lieh	leih(e)	liehe	gelegen
lesen	liest	las	lies	läse	geloschen
liegen	liegt	lag	lieg(e)	läge	gelogen
löschen	lischt	losch	lisch	lösche	gemieden
lügen	lügt	log	lug(e)	löge	mögen
meiden	meidet	mied	meid(e)	miede	gemocht
mögen	mag	mochte	—	möchte	müssen
					gemußt
müssen	muß	mußte	—	müßte	
nehmen	nimmt	nahm	nimm	nähme	genommen
nennen	nennt	nammte	nenn(e)	nennte	genannt
pfeifen	pfeift	pfiff	pfeif(e)	pfiffe	gepfiffen
raien	rät	riet	rate	riete	geraten
reißen	reißt	riß	reiße	risse	gerissen
reiten	reitet	ritt	reit(e)	ritte	*geritten
riechen	riecht	roch	riech(e)	röche	gerochen
rufen	ruft	rief	ruf(e)	riefe	gerufen
schaffen	schafft	schuff	schlaff(e)	schüfe	geschaffen
scheiden	scheidet	schied	scheide	schiede	geschieden

259

Infinitive	3rd person singular present	3rd person singular imperfect	Imperative familiar singular	3rd person imperfect subjunctive	Past participle[1]
scheinen	scheint	schien	schein(e)	schiene	geschienen
schieben	schiebt	schob	schieb(e)	schöbe	geschoben
schießen	schießt	schoß	schieß(e)	schöße	geschossen
schlafen	schläft	schlief	schlaf(e)	schliefe	geschlafen
schlagen	schlägt	schlug	schlag(e)	schlüge	geschlagen
schließen	schließt	schloß	schließ(e)	schlöße	geschlossen
schmelzen	schmilzt	schmolz	schmilz	schmölze	*geschmolzen
schneiden	schneidet	schnitt	schneid(e)	schnitte	geschnitten
schrecken	schreckt	schreckte	shrick	schreckte	geschreckt
		schrak		schräke	geschrocken
schreiben	schreibt	schrieb	schreibe(e)	schriebe	geschrieben
schreien	schreit	schrie	schrei(e)	schriee	geschrie(e)n
schweigen	schweigt	schwieg	schweig(e)	schwiege	geschwiegen
schwimmen	schwimmt	schwamm	schwimm(e)	schwömme	*geschwommen
schwingen	schwingt	schwang	schwing(e)	schwänge	geschwungen
schwören	schwört	schwor	schwör(e)	schwüre	geschworen
		schwur			
sehen	sieht	sah	sieh(e)	sähe	gesehen
sein	ist	war	sei	wäre	*gewesen
senden	sendet	sandte	send(e)	sendete	gesandt
		sandete			gesendet

Infinitive	3rd person singular present	3rd person singular imperfect	Imperative familiar singular	3rd person imperfect subjunctive	Past participle[1]
singen	singt	sang	sing(e)	sänge	gesungen
sinken	sinkt	sank	sink(e)	sänke	*gesunken
sitzen	sitz	sa	sitz(e)	säße	gesessen
sollen	soll	sollte	—	sollte	sollen
					gesollt
sprechen	spricht	sprach	sprich	spräche	gesprochen
springen	springt	sprang	spring(e)	spränge	*gesprungen
stehen	steht	stand	steh(e)	stände	gestanden
				stünde	
stehlen	stiehlt	stahl	stiehl	stähle	gestohlen
				stöhle	
steigen	steigt	stieg	steig(e)	stiegen	*gestiegen
sterben	stirbt	starb	stirb	stürbe	*gestorben
stoßen	stößt	stieß	stoße	stieße	gestoßen
streichen	streicht	strich	streich(e)	striche	gestrichen
streiten	streitet	stritt	streit(e)	stritte	gestritten
tragen	trägt	trug	trag(e)	trüge	getragen
treffen	trifft	traf	triff	träfe	getroffen
treiben	treibt	trieb	treib(e)	triebe	getrieben
treten	tritt	trat	tritt	träte	*getreten
trinken	trinkt	trank	trink(e)	tränke	getrunken

Infinitive	3rd person singular present	3rd person singular imperfect	Imperative familiar singular	3rd person imperfect subjunctive	Past participle[1]
tun	tut	tat	tu(e)	täte	getan
verderben	verdirbt	verdarb	verdirb	verdürbe	verdorben
vergessen	vergißt	vergaß	vergiß	vergäße	vergessen
verlieren	verliert	verlor	verlier(e)	verlöre	verloren
vermeiden	vermeidet	vermied	vermeid(e)	vermiede	vermieden
verschwinden	verschwindet	verschwand	verschwind(e)	verschwände	*verschwunden
wachsen	wächst	wuchs	wachs(e)	wüchse	*gewachsen
waschen	wäscht	wusch	wasch(e)	wüsche	gewaschen
weichen	weicht	wich	weich(e)	wiche	*gewichen
weisen	weist	wies	weis(e)	wiese	gewiesen
wenden	wendet	wandte	wend(e)	wendete	gewandte
		wendete			gewendet
werden	wird	wurde	werd(e)	würde	*geworden
werfen	wirft	warf	wirf	würfe	geworfen
wiegen	wiegt	wog	wieg(e)	wöge	gewogen
winden	windet	wand	wind(e)	wände	gewunden
wissen	weiß	wußte	wiss(e)	wüßte	gewußt
wollen	will	wollte	wolle	wollte	wollen
					gewollt
ziehen	zieht	zog	zieh(e)	zöge	gezogen
zwingen	zwingt	zwang	zwing(e)	zwänge	gezwungen

Answers to Exercises

Chapter 1

1 The student lives in London and is studying at the College of Music.
2 The man likes smoking a pipe.
3 The woman does not like studying.
4 What are you doing?
5 The orchestra is playing a symphony.
6 We are learning German.
7 The child buys the book.
8 The man is very old.
9 You play well.
10 We are listening to the music. It is beautiful.
11 Nein. Der Wagen ist alt.
12 Ja, es ist alt.
13 Ich heiße Richard.
14 Der Student studiert an der Musikhochschule.
   Der Student studiert an der Universität.
15 Danke, es geht mir gut.
16 Ja, wir hören gern Musik.
17 Nein, das Land ist nicht groß, es ist klein.
18 Nein, die Stadt ist nicht klein, sie ist groß.
19 Ja, ich singe gern.
20 Er spielt Klavier.
21 Ich höre gern Musik.
22 Die Frau spielt nicht gut.
23 Wir wohnen in London.
24 Das Kind lernt Deutsch.
25 Sie üben gern.
26 Wie geht es Ihnen?
   Wie geht es Dir?
   Wie geht's?
   Danke, gut.
27 Er kauft das Buch.
28 Das Haus ist groß und alt.
29 Rauchen Sie?
   Rauchst du?
30 Auf Wiedersehen.

Chapter 2

1 Zehn und siebzehn ist siebenundzwanzig.
2 Acht und drei ist elf.
3 Zwei und sechs ist acht.
4 Vierundvierzig und neun ist dreiundfünfzig.
5 Hunderteinundzwanzig und fünfundvierzig ist
   hundertsechsundsechzig.
6 Zwei Geigen spielen in einem Streichquartett.

7 Ich bin zwanzig Jahre alt.
8 Eine Oboe ist ein Holzblasinstrument.
9 Eine Orgel ist ein Tasteninstrument.
10 Eine Trommel ist ein Schlaginstrument.
11 Eine Bratsche ist ein Streichinstrument.
12 Karajan ist Dirigent.
13 Er arbeitet in Berlin.
14 Ich komme aus London.
15 Ich bin Student.
   Ich bin Studentin.
16 Ich wohne in einem Haus.
   Ich wohne in einer Wohnung.
17 Zwei Studenten wohnen mit Anna in der Wohnung.
18 Die Wohnung hat sieben Zimmer.
19 Gabriele hat drei Geschwister.
20 Peter spielt Flöte.
21 Anna kommt aus London.
22 Peter ist zwanzig Jahre alt.
23 Gabriele wohnt bei ihren Eltern in einem alten Haus.
24 Er ist Dirigent.
25 Gabrieles Mutter ist Lehrerin. Sie arbeitet in einem Gymnasium.
26 Ich studiere Gesang.
27 Diese Frau ist Sängerin.
28 Diese Musik ist schön.
29 Anna und Gabriele spielen gern zusammen.
30 Dieses Instrument ist sehr alt.

Chapter 3

1 Nein, ich habe keinen Hund.
2 Nein, ich habe keine Schwester.
3 Nein, ich habe keinen Wagen.
4 Ja, ich höre das Lied.
5 Nein, er spielt kein Instrument.
6 Ja, ich habe diese Stadt gern.
7 Nein, dieser Mann hat keine Kinder.
8 Ja, es gibt ein Opernhaus in dieser Stadt.
   Nein, es gibt kein Opernhaus in dieser Stadt.
9 Nein, ich habe keinen Bruder.
10 Nein, ich fahre diesen Wagen nicht gern.
11 Das Auto fährt langsam durch die Stadt.
12 Der Tourist geht um den Dom.
13 Die Kinder laufen die Bonngasse entlang.
14 Das Buch ist für den Lehrer.
15 Wir haben einen Garten.
16 Sie hat die Kirche gern.
17 Der Bus fährt schnell um den Bahnhof.
18 Der Verkäufer kauft die Autos.
19 Haben Sie einen Bruder?

20 Nein, ich habe keine Geschwister.
21 Köln hat neunhunderttausend Einwohner.
22 Köln liegt am Rhein.
23 Die Geschäfte und Kaufhäuser sind am Neumarkt.
24 Der Kölner Dom ist in der Stadtmitte.
25 Die wichtigen Gebäude sind in der Stadtmitte.
26 Bonn ist die Hauptstadt der Bundesrepublik.
27 Das Beethovenhaus ist in der Bonngasse.
28 Das Beethoven-Denkmal ist am Münsterplatz.
29 Das schöne Rathaus ist am Markt.
30 Das neue Bundeshaus ist am Rheinufer.
31 Entschuldigen Sie bitte! Wie komme ich zum Rathaus?
32 Sie gehen links, dann rechts und dann geradeaus.
33 Vielen Dank.
34 Entschuldigen Sie bitte! Wo ist der Bahnhof?
35 Es tut mir leid, ich weiß es nicht.

Chapter 4

1 Wir sind oft in München.
2 Wer gibt dem Kind einen Apfel?
3 Das Baby schläft jede Nacht zehn Stunden.
4 Nimmt er Zucker?
5 Sprechen Sie Deutsch?
6 Siehst du das alte Rathaus?
7 Ich bin sehr glücklich hier.
8 Fährt dieser Bus zum Bahnhof?
9 Ißt du gern Käse?
10 Mein Vater liest gern Bücher.
11 Lauft schnell durch den Park, Kinder!
12 Trinken Sie den Wein, meine Damen und Herren!
13 Nimm den Apfel, Klaus!
14 Gehen wir heute abend ins Theater.
15 Halt! Da kommt ein Auto.
   Halten Sie! Da kommt ein Auto.
16 Der Film beginnt um halb acht.
17 Wir essen um halb eins zu Mittag.
18 Ich fahre um acht Uhr morgens ins Büro.
19 Der Zug nach Wien fährt um einundzwanzig Uhr fünfzig.
20 Es ist Viertel nach zehn.
   Es ist zehn Uhr fünfzehn.
21 Ich trinke morgens Kaffee.
22 Ich esse Brötchen mit Butter und Marmelade zum Frühstuck.
23 Ich esse Fleisch, Gemüse und Salat zu Mittag.
24 Ja, ich trinke gern Bier.
   Nein, ich trinke Bier nicht gern.
25 Die Deutschen sagen 'Guten Appetit', bevor sie essen.
26 Essen Sie gern Kuchen?
27 Ich trinke abends gern ein Glas Wein.

28 Abendbrot ist um sieben Uhr.
29 Nimm diese Tasse Kaffee.
   Nehmen Sie diese Tasse Kaffee.
30 Das Konzert beginnt um acht Uhr.
   Das Konzert beginnt um zwanzig Uhr.

Chapter 5

1 Man darf im Theater nicht rauchen.
2 Er soll vier Stunden pro Tag üben.
3 Willst du diesen Film sehen?
4 Der Herr kann das Gepäck hier lassen.
5 Ich will meine Familie besuchen.
6 Kann ich mit Reiseschecks bezahlen?
7 Er muß um zehn Uhr am Bahnhof sein.
8 Ihr sollt früh ins Bett gehen, Kinder.
9 Sie dürfen nicht auf der Autobahn halten.
10 Können Sie Deutsch?
11 They are sleeping now so that they are not tired later.
12 The boys run home quickly to see the football match.
13 Many housewives work to earn money.
14 I hope to be there at six o'clock.
15 The children go into the playroom in order to play there.
16 Zwei Kilo Kartoffeln kosten drei Mark fünfzig. (DM 3,50)
17 Der Schreibblock kostet drei Mark vierzig. (DM 3,40)
18 Schallplatten sind auf der zweiten Etage.
19 Die Briefmarken kosten fünf Mark siebzig. (DM 5,70)
20 Das Zimmer kostet sechzig Mark. (DM 60)
21 Ich hätte gern diese Flasche Wein.
22 Ich hätte gern ein Pfund Käse.
23 Was kostet dieses Buch?
24 Haben Sie ein Doppelzimmer für eine Nacht?
25 Kann ich mit Reiseschecks bezahlen?

Chapter 6

1 Im August regnet es oft.
2 Bald ist das Konzert zu Ende.
3 Jeden Sommer fahren wir nach Italien.
4 Um zwölf Uhr kommen die Kinder nach Hause.
5 Im Sommer sind die Tage lang.
6 Es ist schön, warm und sonnig.
7 Im Winter ist es kalt.
8 Im März ist es oft windig.
9 Im November kann es in England neblig sein.
10 Im Juli ist es heiß.
11 Die Blumen blühen im Frühling.
12 Die Blätter fallen im Herbst.
13 Das Obst wird im Herbst reif.
14 Im Winter wird es früh dunkel.

15 Weihnachten ist im Dezember.
16 Sie liebt den Jungen.
17 Das Geld ist für diesen Studenten.
18 Die Bauern arbeiten im Winter.
19 Ich liebe den Frühling.
20 Es wird dunkel.

Chapter 7

1 Herr Schmidt schickt der Dame schöne Blumen.
2 Hilft sie dem Mädchen bei der Arbeit?
3 Der Polizist folgt dem (dative singular) Jungen die Straße entlang.
  Der Polizist folgt den (dative plural) Jungen die Straße entlang.
4 Der Verkäufer zeigt dem Mann die Autos.
5 Sie gibt einer Freundin die Noten.
6 Das Geschäft ist dem Bahnhof gegenüber.
7 Der Vater spielt am Wochenende gern mit den Kindern.
8 Nach dem Konzert wollen wir bei meinem Freund ein Bier trinken.
9 Meiner Meinung nach ist er mit den Schülern zu streng.
10 Fahren Sie mit der Bahn oder mit dem Bus?
11 Er fährt mit dem Auto.
12 Frau Schmidt fährt mit der Straßenbahn.
13 Richard fährt mit dem Fahrrad.
14 Seine Schwester geht zu Fuß.
15 Ich kaufe den Flugschein in einem Reisebüro.
16 Gute Reise!
17 Ich möchte eine Fahrkarte nach Wien.
18 Ich möchte eine Rückfahrkarte nach Köln.
19 Lauf schnell nach Hause!
  Lauft schnell nach Hause!
  Laufen Sie schnell nach Hause!
20 Ich arbeite zu Hause.

Chapter 8

1 Die Katze springt auf das Bett.
2 Die Hausfrau geht in das Geschäft.
3 Die Großeltern gehen jeden Sonntag in die Kirche.
4 Der Kellner stellt die Flasche auf den Tisch.
5 Sie sitzen im Kino und lachen.
6 Die alte Dame sitzt am Fenster und träumt.
7 Er steckt das Geld in die Tasche.
8 Nach dem Essen kocht meine Mutter Kaffee für die Gäste.
9 Der Polizist wartet vor der Tür.
10 Wir wandern in den Bergen.
11 Der Kellner stellt sie darauf.
12 Ich gehe oft mit ihr spazieren.
13 Das Kind spielt damit.
14 Der Polizist folgt ihm die Straße entlang.
15 Ich liebe sie.

16 Die Kinder haben sechs Wochen Schulferien.
17 Sie fährt nach Österreich.
18 Die Familie Schmidt fährt nach England.
19 Sie fahren erst im September.
20 Die Kinder baden und spielen am Strand.
21 Kennen Sie diese Stadt?
22 Wissen Sie, wo ich wohne?
23 Wir verbringen eine Woche auf dem Lande.
24 Ich möchte nach Österreich fahren.
25 Sie wandern gern in den Bergen.

Chapter 9

1 Wegen des Wetters bleiben wir zu Hause.
2 Ich vergesse immer den Namen dieses Mannes.
3 'Sie werden innerhalb einer Woche wieder gesund', sagt der Arzt.
4 Ich fahre das Auto meines Bruders.
5 Während der Sommerferien arbeiten wir nicht.
6 Am Ufer des Rheins sind viele Burgruinen.
7 Ich wohne in der Wohnung meiner Schwester.
8 Wer hat heute Gerburtstag?
9 Wem gibst du das Geld?
10 Wir spielen mit dem Ball. Womit spielst du?
11 Die alte Burg is oben auf dem Berg.
12 Der Weg führt in einen Wald.
13 Sie hören die Vögel zwitschern.
14 Die Familie sitzt draußen und trinkt.
15 Man kann den Fluß, das Tal, das Dorf, den Wald und die ganze Umgebung sehen.
16 Er spielt während des Vormittags.
17 Wir gehen zur Kirche trotz des Wetters.
18 Sie wohnen außerhalb der Stadt.
19 Wir genießen die herrliche Aussicht.
20 Wessen Fahrrad ist im Garten?

Chapter 10

1 Er freut sich, in Italien zu sein.
2 Ich interessiere mich nicht für neue Musik.
3 Treffen wir uns vor dem Bahnhof.
4 Das Kind wäscht sich im Badezimmer.
5 Setzen Sie sich bitte.
6 Er schenkt seiner Freundin einen Ring.
7 Sie gibt ihrer Tante ein Buch.
8 Sie sind mit ihren Geschenken zufrieden.
9 Er kann mein Fahrrad nicht reparieren.
10 Wo sind eure Bücher, Kinder?
11 Die Geschenke liegen um den Weihnachtsbaum.
12 Helga bekommt ein Fahrrad von ihren Eltern.
13 Er bekommt einen Plattenspieler von seinen Eltern.

14 Um Mitternacht geht die Familie in die Kirche.
15 Sie singen Weihnachtslieder.
16 Die Burg befindet sich auf dem Berg.
17 Sie unterhalten sich im Restaurant.
18 Wir freuen uns.
19 Die Kinder mögen den Weihnachtsbaum.
20 Fröhliche Weihnachten und ein glückliches Neues Jahr!

Chapter 11

1 Er steht um acht Uhr morgens auf.
2 Ich kaufe immer auf dem Markt ein.
3 Wann fährt der Zug ab?
4 Es hört zu regnen auf.
   Es hört auf zu regnen.
5 Die Hochzeit findet im Dom statt.
6 Wir verreisen jedes Jahr im August.
7 Sie hofft nächstes Jahr ihr Studium in Berlin anzufangen.
8 Die Kinder dürfen wegen des Wetters nicht spazierengehen.
9 Du mußt hier aussteigen.
10 Wann sollen wir in Köln ankommen?
11 The student receives a grant from the government.
12 We can recommend this hotel to your parents.
13 What is happening in the town?
14 The castle is situated on the top of the mountain.
15 She runs quickly down the stairs.
16 Come up here! The view is wonderful.
17 This building looks like a school.
18 He hopes to be able to take part in the competition.
19 The brass support the theme in the strings.
20 The woodwind and strings take part in the main theme.

Chapter 12

1 Was wirst du machen?
2 Wird die Reise viel Geld kosten?
3 Wir werden erst am Montag zurückfahren.
4 Ich werde es dir noch einmal sagen.
5 Wirst du vielleicht mit uns spielen können?
6 Meine Schwester ist älter als ich.
7 Im Winter ist das Wetter kälter als im Sommer.
8 Gehen Sie abends lieber ins Kino oder ins Theater?
9 Der Montblanc ist höher als der Snowdon aber nicht so hoch wie der
   Everest.
10 Ich trinke Tee lieber als Wasser aber nicht so gern wie Wein.
11 Auf den Autobahnen passieren weniger Unfälle als auf den
   Landstraßen.
12 Sie spielt das erste Stück gut aber das zweite spielt sie besser.
13 Ein Arzt verdient mehr als ein Lehrer.
14 Dieser Rotwein schmeckt süßer als der Weißwein.

15 New York ist größer als Paris aber nicht so groß wie London.
16 The workers are demanding more and more money.
17 The blond girl plays the best.
18 This is the most beautiful valley in the region.
19 Run as quickly as possible and give the man this letter.
20 The sound gets louder and louder.

Chapter 13

1 Mendelssohn schrieb sehr interessante Briefe.
2 Sie grüßte ihre Nachbarin.
3 Ich wußte den Namen des Mädchens nicht.
4 Sie spielte den ganzen Vormittag.
5 Was sagtest du?
6 Der Professor sprach mit dem Amerikaner.
7 Die Vorstellung begann pünktlich.
8 Die Kellnerin brachte das Bier.
9 Wann fuhr der Zug ab?
10 Sie gingen durch den Park.
11 Der Student arbeitete in seinem Zimmer.
12 Der Bischof gab dem Bettler einige Münzen.
13 Er kam sehr spät an.
14 Der Ton wurde allmählich stärker.
15 Sie war krank und konnte nicht aufstehen.
16 Ich mußte das ganz Wochenende arbeiten.
17 Sie wollte ihm ein Geschenk kaufen.
18 Es wurde dunkel im Wald, denn es kam ein Gewitter.
19 Sie hatte eine sehr wertvolle Geige.
20 Wir mußten nach Wien fahren.
21 Wir durften spät nach Hause kommen.
22 Er nahm an dem Wettbewerb teil.
23 Ich kannte die Stadt nicht.
24 Wo warst du?

Chapter 14

1 Nicht er, sondern seine Frau spielt Bratsche.
2 Seit der Reformation ist Deutschland teils lutherisch und teils katholisch.
3 Sie trinkt keinen Alkohol, weder Wein noch Bier.
4 Ich verstehe ihn gut, denn ich kann etwas Französisch.
5 Der Doktor besitzt sowohl ein Haus in der Stadt, als auch ein Ferienhaus auf dem Lande.
6 Das Baby weint, wenn es Hunger hat.
7 Ich fahre lieber mit dem Zug, weil es am schnellsten geht.
8 Er spielt seine Schallplatten, während ich zu lesen versuche.
9 Wir warten hier, falls er noch kommt.
10 Ich muß nach Hause gehen, obwohl ich länger bleiben möchte.
11 Sind Sie sicher, daß der Zug bald abfährt?
12 Wenn wir abends nichts zu tun haben, gehen wir ins Kino.

13 Während er sprach, klingelte das Telefon.
14 Sobald er aus dem Haus ging, fing es zu regnen an.
15 Du machst ihm eine Freude, indem du ihn besucht.
16 Als sie ihn sah, lächelte sie freundlich.
17 Ich kaufte mir einen Stadtplan, da ich die Stadt nicht kannte.
18 Er besuchte die Universität, wo er studiert hat.
19 Er spricht deutlich, damit die Ausländer ihn verstehen können.
20 Wir werden den Gipfel erreichen, bevor es dunkel wird.

Chapter 15

1 Der Polizist, der im Wagen wartet, trägt eine Pistole.
2 Der Film, den wir gestern sahen, war uninteressant.
3 Alles, was wir essen, ist ganz frisch.
4 Der Baum, den wir dort sehen, ist eine Linde.
5 Das Opernhaus, in dem wir *Fidelio* sahen, ist sehr modern.
6 Die Terrasse, auf der wir sitzen, ist schön sonnig.
7 Ich möchte etwas erzählen, was dich amüsieren wird.
8 Die Dame, deren Kinder Deutsch sprechen, ist Engländerin.
9 Die Soldaten, denen der König dankt, blieben treu.
10 Das Buch, das er kaufte, kostete dreißig Mark. (DM 30)
11 I am sorry I cannot go with you.
12 Do you like it here in Germany?
13 How are you?
14 Are you too cold?
15 We like this music.

Chapter 16

1 Die Sängerin hat drei Lieder gesungen.
2 Der Tourist ist aus Schweden gekommen.
3 Was hast du hier in England gemacht?
4 Der Fremde hat den Film nicht ganz verstanden.
5 Es ist kalt geworden.
6 Wir haben schlechtes Wetter gehabt.
7 Mozart hat die ersten Jahre seines Lebens in Salzburg verbracht.
8 Es ist kühl geworden, weil die Sonne untergegangen ist.
9 Wo bist du gewesen?
10 Er hat seine Schallplatten gespielt, während ich ein Buch gelesen habe.
11 Sie hat Angst gehabt, sobald sie ihn gesehen hat.
12 Die Vorstellung hat uns gut gefallen.
13 Sie haben uns nicht helfen können.
14 Was haben Sie von ihm gewollt?
15 Das Orchester hat unter der Leitung von Bruno Walter gespielt.

Chapter 17

1 Er hatte mir einen Brief geschrieben.
2 Was hatte er gesagt?
3 Wir waren sehr weit gegangen.

4 Ich hatte ihn nicht verstanden.
5 Die erste Aufführung hatte in der Thomaskirche stattgefunden.
6 Ich hatte am Wochenende verreisen wollen.
7 Wir werden ihn am Samstag gesehen haben.
8 Er wird das Gespräch vergessen haben.
9 Sie werden schon weggefahren sein.
10 Die Aufführung wird außerordentlich gut gewesen sein.
11 Lieber Richard!
12 Liebe Helga!
13 Sehr geehrter Herr Professor Schmidt.
14 Sehr geehrter Herr.
15 Mit freundlichen Grüßen.
16 Mit herzlichen Grüßen.

Chapter 18

1 We run through the green wood.
2 One of the girls has blond hair.
3 We live at the end of a long street.
4 Cool apple juice tastes good.
5 In hot weather I like to go swimming.
6 The taste of red wine is delicious.
7 He eats a boiled egg for breakfast.
8 She greeted the laughing child.
9 They have seen me crying.
10 We heard the birds twittering in the wood.
11 Die italienischen Touristen stehen vor dem berühmten Dom.
12 Wir steigen bis zur alten Burg hinauf.
13 Ihr Freund hat ihr einen goldenen Ring geschenkt.
14 Der Wirt hat uns einen ausgezeichneten Wein angeboten.
15 Der Briefträger hat ein gelbes Fahrrad.
16 Wir leben im zwanzigsten Jahrhundert.
17 Der Wettbewerb findet am ersten Juni in unserem kleinen Dorf statt.
18 Sie hängt das frisch gewaschene Hemd in den Kleiderschrank.
19 Sie stand weinend vor dem brennenden Haus.
20 Trotz strömenden Regens gingen Hunderte von Arbeitern auf die Straßen.

Chapter 19

1 When was this building built?
2 Ludwig van Beethoven was born in Bonn.
3 Many composers are not recognized by their contemporaries.
4 In Germany the presents are unwrapped on Christmas eve.
5 At carnival time there was much dancing and singing.
6 Because of his illness, he has been forbidden to smoke.
7 Unfortunately this beautiful house is not for sale.
8 Bach's *St Matthew Passion* was not heard for a hundred years.
9 Men and women should be paid the same for the same work.
10 I am having my hair cut.

Chapter 20

1 Where would you like to study?
2 He lay on the earth as if he were dead.
3 He thought he would receive a grant.
4 If only we were alone!
5 What would you like to drink?
6 I should like information on a flight to Paris.
7 I thought you were ill.
8 He said he would not play.
9 He should have told me that yesterday.
10 If I had time I should visit the castle.
11 If I had had time I should have visited the castle.
12 We must drive home although we should like to stay longer.
13 Would it be better if students were independent from their parents?
14 What would you do if you were unemployed?
15 Would you continue to work if you had children?

Bibliography

Recommended Books

Dictionaries

Collins German Dictionary (London and Glasgow: Collins, 1980)
Der Große Duden, vol. 6: *Aussprachewörterbuch* (Mannheim: Dudenverlag, 1974)
H. Leuchtmann, ed., *Wörterbuch Musik/Dictionary of Musical Terms* (Munich: Verlag Dokumentation, 1977)

Grammars

J. E. Clapham, *Basic German Grammar* (London: John Murray, 1971)
A. E. Hammer, *German Grammar and Usage* (London: Edward Arnold, 1971)

Lieder texts and commentaries

The three sources listed below contain most of the song texts that appear in this book, and provide useful English translations.

D. Fischer-Dieskau, *The Fischer-Dieskau Book of Lieder* (London: Gollancz, 1976)
L. Phillips, *Lieder Line by Line* (London: Duckworth, 1979)
S. S. Prawer, ed., *The Penguin Book of Lieder* (Harmondsworth: Penguin Books, 1977)

Reference works

H. and M. Garland, *The Oxford Companion to German Literature* (London: Oxford University Press, 1976)
M. Kennedy, ed., *The Concise Oxford Dictionary of Music* (London: Oxford University Press, 1980)
R. Kloiber, *Handbuch der Oper* (8th edn, Munich: Deutscher Taschenbuch Verlag, 1973)
A. Thorlby, ed., *The Penguin Companion to Literature*, vol. 2: *European Literature* (Harmondsworth: Penguin Books, 1969)

Sources of Texts

The texts in this book have sometimes been simplified and abbreviated.

p. 74   K. Vogelsang, *Dokumentation zur Oper Wozzeck von Alban Berg* (Laaber: Laaber-Verlag, 1977), p. 14
p. 78   N. Lloyd, *Großes Lexikon der Musik* (Gütersloh: Bertelsmann Lexikon-Verlag, 1974), p. 307
p. 82   R. Wolf, sleeve note to *Stille Nacht, heilige Nacht*, Schwann AMS 3522
p. 87   A. Mahler, ed., *Gustav Mahler Briefe 1879–1911* (Berlin: Paul Zsolnay Verlag, 1924), p. 157–8

p. 93   R. Schumann, *Gesammelte Schriften über Musik und Musiker*, vol. 1, ed. M. Kreisig (Leipzig: Breitkopf und Härtel, 1914), p. 1

p. 111   C. Czerny, 'Über den richtigen Vortrag der sämtlichen Beethoven'schen Klavierwerke', *Erinnerungen an Beethoven* ed. P. Badura-Skoda (Vienna: Universal Edition, 1963), p. 10

p. 117   W. Reich, ed., *Mozarts Briefe*, (Zürich: Manesse Verlag, 1948), p. 273

p. 148   H. D. Bruger, ed., *J. S. Bach, Kompositionen für die Laute* (Zürich: Möseler Verlag, 1921), p. 51

p. 150   S. Hensel, *Die Familie Mendelssohn 1729–1847* (Freiburg: Karl Alber Verlag, 1959), pp. 400–402

p. 155   C. P. E. Bach, *Versuch über die wahre Art das Clavier zu spielen*, ed. W. Niemann (7th edn, Leipzig: Kahnt, 1965), p. 7

p. 156   D. Drew, ed., *Über Kurt Weill* (Frankfurt: Suhrkamp Taschenbuch Verlag, 1975), p. 77

p. 161   H. Hesse, *Gertrud* (Hamburg: Rowohlt Taschenbuch Verlag, 1973), pp. 8–9

p. 164   R. Schumann, *Gesammelte Schriften über Musik und Musiker*, vol. 2, ed. M. Kreisig (Leipzig: Breitkopf und Härtel, 1914), p. 287

p. 168   M. Gregor-Dellin and D. Mack, eds., *Cosima Wagner, Die Tagebücher*, vol. 1: *1869–1877* (Munich: Piper Verlag, 1976), pp. 329–30

p. 171   L. Spohr, *Lebenserinnerungen*, ed. F. Göthel, vol. 1 (Tutzing: Hans Schneider, 1968), pp. 176–8

p. 178   A. Schnitzler, *Leutnant Gustl*, ed. J. P. Stern (Cambridge: Cambridge University Press, 1966), p. 109

p. 181   S. Zweig, *Die Welt von Gestern* (Frankfurt: Fischer Taschenbuch Verlag, 1977), pp. 27–8

p. 183   W. Schuh, ed., *Richard Strauss und Hugo von Hofmannsthal, Briefwechsel* (4th edn, Zürich: Atlantis Verlag, 1970), p. 91

p. 184   E. Hanslick, *Geschichte des Concertwesens in Wien*, vol. 2 (Vienna: W. Braumüller, 1870), p. 350

p. 186   H. Steinhauer, *Deutsche Kultur* (New York: Oxford University Press, 1962), p. 149

p. 188   J. W. Goethe, *Wilhelm Meisters Lehrjahre* (Munich: Goldmann Klassiker Verlag, 1979), pp. 149–50, 250, 375, 539–40

p. 193   W. Schuh, ed., *Richard Strauss und Hugo von Hofmannsthal, Briefwechsel* (4th edn, Zürich: Atlantis Verlag, 1970), pp. 576–7

p. 195   'Schriften zur Literatur', ed. H. J. Schrimpf, *Goethes Werke*, vol. 12, ed. W. Weber and H. J. Schrimpf (6th edn, Hamburg: Christian Wegner Verlag, 1967), p. 270

Index of Grammar